The Complete Book of YIQUAN

by the same author

The Mysterious Power of Xingyi Quan
A Complete Guide to History, Weapons and Fighting Skills
Master C S Tang
ISBN 978 1 84819 140 2
eISBN 978 0 85701 115 2

of related interest

The Essence of Taijiquan Push-Hands and Fighting Technique
Wang Fengming
ISBN 978 1 84819 245 4
eISBN 978 0 85701 190 9

XinYi WuDao
Heart-Mind—The Dao of Martial Arts
Master Zhongxian Wu
Foreword by Grandmaster Zhao ShouRong
ISBN 978 1 84819 206 5
eISBN 978 0 85701 156 5

The Four Dragons
Clearing the Meridians and Awakening the Spine in Nei Gong
Damo Mitchell
Foreword by Dr Ole Saether
ISBN 978 1 84819 226 3
eISBN 978 0 85701 173 2

The Complete Book of YIQUAN

Master C S Tang

SINGING DRAGON
LONDON AND PHILADELPHIA

First published in 2015
by Singing Dragon
an imprint of Jessica Kingsley Publishers
73 Collier Street
London N1 9BE, UK
and
400 Market Street, Suite 400
Philadelphia, PA 19106, USA

www.singingdragon.com

Library of Congress Cataloging in Publication Data
A CIP catalog record for this book is available from the Library of Congress

British Library Cataloguing in Publication Data
A CIP catalogue record for this book is available from the British Library

ISBN 978 1 84819 225 6
eISBN 978 0 85701 172 5

Printed and bound in Great Britain

FSC www.fsc.org MIX Paper from responsible sources FSC® C013604

The Thinker (French: *Le Penseur*)
A bronze and marble sculpture by Auguste Rodin held in the Musée Rodin in Paris. It depicts a man in sober meditation battling with a powerful internal struggle.

CONTENTS

PART II SYSTEM OF YIQUAN TRAINING

PART IV SPECIAL FEATURES

FOREWORD

In Chinese martial arts, the "concepts" and ideas have always prevailed over the "techniques." Many styles have a number of forms of linking movements with weapons and void-hand, but in the end, the point is to develop a skill or quality which is described as "kung fu."

Every artistic expression, such as painting, calligraphy, poetry, and seal engraving, for example, can show this level through its realization or kung fu. Thus, when we look at an artist while doing a masterpiece, we can say that "his kung fu is really good" or "he has that thing we don't know how to describe but that reveals a high level of execution."

Kung fu means "time and effort," and it has two aspects. On the one hand, it requires a technique which can be learned; and on the other hand, a skill which cannot be learned. This skillfulness can only be developed through time and practice, and it is tied to the spirit of the person.

The difference between a "masterpiece" made by an artist and a good copy of a specialist lies in how much time and effort the artist has devoted to refining his spirit. In martial arts, the difference would be this refinement together with technique, as a result of the experiences, training, and apprenticeship under a qualified master.

Master C S Tang is an "artist" and a master of internal martial arts; master of Bagua Zhang, Yiquan, Taiji Quan, and Xing Yi Quan; and an artist in seal engraving and calligraphy. Through this book, you can read about and learn this technique in a very detailed way. You will also be imbued with the spirit of the artist that expresses emotions and ideas.

This book is unlike most books of today. It is not one of those books with the air of having been written in a single day, out of several books that were read the night before. But just the opposite—there are many stories, anecdotes, teachings, and instructions about Yiquan, which have been recollected over many years of learning and experience by the teaching of this master.

Master C S Tang has been gathering all this knowledge and experience from the authentic Yiquan masters, distilling with time his own art and way to shape Yiquan; and, at the same time, representing a faithful development of the original style, but without losing the individual form of an artist who knows how to create his personal way.

Yiquan is a system developed by the famous martial artist Wang Xiang Zhai (王薌齋) on the basis of three internal martial arts: Xing Yi Quan, Bagua Zhang, and Taiji Quan. From painstaking investigation and innovation throughout his life, he developed a "unique and direct" system which increases health and martial aspects in a quicker and more efficient way.

In China there are many kung fu systems which go from the branches to the trunk. That is to say, they build up the martial artist in many indirect aspects, to finally reach the most important target: to economize movements and make them effective. Yiquan directly trains this aspect without getting lost among the branches. It goes direct to the trunk or root of internal martial arts and is considered as the "heart of internal styles."

The essence of Yiquan is the practice of "static stances," so is worthy for both our health and martial arts. To discover that the origin of any movement lies in quietness is a unique experience. It can only be understood when experienced through practice. But the most important thing that one will discover is the value of the "intention" (Yi) training which, applied to martial arts, turns the mind of the fighter into a powerful tool and the mind of the common practitioner into a strong mind, ready for action and with a positive and happy attitude towards life.

Master C S Tang, with his wide experience and idiosyncrasy, shows in a very clear way many aspects of the system, not yet revealed to the occidental world, that make this book a very valuable work which cannot be left aside hastily, but is to be read and re-read conscientiously.

Since I began learning martial arts, over 30 years ago, I have always heard Master saying that the external styles process is to evolve to the internal, developing aspects which are more characteristic of internal styles such as relaxation, economy of movement, adherent force, concentration, intention, and spirit.

You can directly find all these points in Yiquan, and what is valuable is that you can use it to improve your own martial art system or your health. Yiquan emphasizes all those aspects which have been lost in many kung fu styles or which are only trained in advanced levels.

To have participated in this book has been a great responsibility and tremendous luck for me. As the Spanish publisher, I have been able to transmit to the occidental world a knowledge that springs up from the very Chinese traditional culture, so that the dream of the great martial artist Wang Xiang Zhai through his students and through Master C S Tang, third direct generation of the founder of the system, may spread all over the occidental world, as "food" for the following generations.

J. Sebastián González R. of Centre Jing
Publisher of original Western edition, in Spanish
Spain, November 2007

Master J. Sebastián González R. and Master C S Tang

Yiquan logo (designed by Blanca Oriol, Barcelona, Spain)

DISCLAIMER

Please note that the author and the publisher of this book are not to be held liable in any manner whatsoever for any injuries that may result to any person from his or her reading or following the instructions contained herein.

Since the physical activities described may at times be strenuous and sophisticated for some individuals, it is essential that, before following any of the activities physically or otherwise herein described, the reader should consult his or her physician for advice on whether to embark on such activity.

The author, Master C S Tang

ACKNOWLEDGMENTS

The author wishes to thank the following friends and students who offered their invaluable advice in the writing, translating, and publishing of this book: Bernard Kwan, Osmond Lam, and Eric Poling.

Special thanks are due to J. Sebastián González R. for his patience in translating the Chinese edition into Spanish and invaluable technical support, without which this English edition could not have been produced. Miss Blanca Oriol designed the logo of Yiquan for me and also assisted me in improving many photographs.

Special thanks are also due to Edward Khong, James Carss, and Gordon G. Tso for their excellent job on proofreading and assistance, and to Allen Lui, Samuel Cheng, Anthony Liu, Kelvin Yu, Vincent Ng, and many other friends and supporters both local and from abroad for their valuable encouragement and suggestions.

Performers in the illustrations are: J. Sebastián González R., Annabel Cheng, Anthony So, Anthony Liu, Erica Liu, Joyce Wong, Kelvin Yu, Ngai Wah, Nelson Ho, Y.P. Li, Celene Cheng, James Carss, Stephen Lam, and C S Tang.

INTRODUCTION

Yiquan is a Chinese martial art, which is a part of Chinese culture. It identifies with the characteristics of Chinese culture and tradition as a unity. There are no definite rules of learning and definitions. There are no definite yardsticks to judge the rightness and levels of accomplished masters.

All Chinese culture emphasizes using "heart" (intention, passion, and concentration) to perform. It has to be cherished and digested gradually. It is difficult to simulate, and needs time to build up slowly.

Like other Chinese cultural activities, such as painting, calligraphy, and seal engraving, the techniques grow year by year with your passion and interest. As your in-depth knowledge on history, books, poems, and experience grows, your real "kung fu" is shown through your work in the art. There are no short cuts.

Art is life. Even if you learn and try to emulate very closely, the kung fu, or the accumulated in-depth knowledge, cannot be simulated. When a master writes calligraphy and you try to write the same, the power and "skeleton" (間架) of the master cannot be simulated and your artwork will look childish in comparison.

Those who learn from me live,
Whilst others who only assimilate will lose it.

Qi Bai Shi (齊白石) (1864–1957)

The lifelong aim of an artist is to establish his own style. In order to achieve this, the artist must explore. He must have passion, belief, industriousness, intelligence, inwardness, spirituality, high moral conduct, and intuitive ability to know right or wrong. Therefore, the mere ability to imitate is a dead skill.

Famous Chinese painter and calligrapher Qi Bai Shi

A martial artist does not learn and practice in order to kill people. He has to explore humanity, nature, and the world. It is shameful and meaningless to learn just for money. He should absorb and cherish the power of the sky and earth, and develop his own face and style. Artists should be flexible. The famous Chinese painter Shi Tao said, "As the situation changes, your techniques should also change" (石濤石濤 (1641–1718) 語：筆墨當隨時代). Do not be annoyed and impatient; always be quiet, tranquil, and peaceful. One should not be eager for quick success and instant benefit.

Yiquan is a modern martial art. The founder tried to combine traditional and modern training methods to form a new and straightforward training system. However, new sports techniques and theories have emerged since then. Practitioners should absorb and adopt new knowledge and theories into Yiquan to perfect the core system.

BE AWKWARD

Nowadays, the various arts have been tailored to be like merchandise for sale. Techniques are turned into "merchandise." People like the blossoms of the flowers, instead of their fruits. This means they chase external appearance instead of the internal content. Practitioners are happy with window-dressing postures, accompanied by music and dancing. They have deserted and forgotten the original ideals of martial arts power and speed.

Chang Zhi Lang (常志朗先生) always gave this advice to practitioners: "Better to be clumsy than to be over-refined" (寧拙無巧).

THE THEORY OF STAGES OF FIVE ELEMENTS

I have been practicing Yiquan since 1967. I have met different ranks and lineages of Yiquan masters. I have studied other internal and external Chinese martial arts. Therefore I have been able to study and look at this art objectively.

I found that there are certain basic approaches for studying and learning the arts of Yiquan. This is the Way of Yiquan, and includes the theory of stages of Five Elements which Master Wang expounded in his first book, *The Right Path of Yiquan.*

1. Wood stage

The core of Yiquan is the *Static Stance.*

The first stage in building up a Static Stance is to establish a skeleton. If you are using wood as a beam to support the floor and the roof of a building, you need strong and sufficiently straight vertical poles and horizontal beams to stretch and prop up the building. Pole-driving deeply into the ground is important as it will make the foundation stronger.

In the same way, an artist knows how to adjust the alignment of posture of arms and legs. If a person stands higher, the width of steps can be smaller. If he sinks lower, his Mabu, or the width of steps, should be wider in order to support the weight of the body. Sinking the body lower improves the endurance and strength of muscle of the thigh. During combat one has to stand higher in order to move efficiently and quickly.

During standing, if you hold the circle of the arms too wide, you will lose the tension and power by being too relaxed. Stretching both elbows sideways will send out your spirits. Pushing your head upwards and imagining that you are standing 20 floors above and looking downwards, you seem to be taller than others. This will add to your confidence. The more power of wood you have, then the more you can support yourself at the front, back, left, right, top, and down directions, and the stronger your physical frame will be. And this frame becomes a castle—a safeguarded, invincible castle.

Your body is embedded in a sphere; the whole surface is round and full. Your power should not extract and extend outside of your protected sphere.

After your structure has become protective, you have to convert the parts of your body, the wood, into attacking weapons. You have to sharpen your fingers, fists, palms, elbows, and knees for attack.

As an artist, you must not be ambiguous; you must strengthen and sharpen every part of your body as a weapon. You must practice with patience to achieve this from feeling and thinking in a static stance to applying them through test and release of power. Practice from beginner level to advanced level.

2. Water stage

Yiquan is an art of intent. Intent is imagery combined with simulations. Apply resistant force throughout intent movements. The first intent is Water, and its characteristic is to change shape when poured into different shapes of vessels. It can be soft or it can be very strong. "There is nothing in the world softer than water, yet there is nothing better for attacking the adamant and strong" (*Lao Tzu*, Ch. 78) (老子說: "天下莫柔於水，而攻堅強者莫之能先也，以其無以易之也。水之勝剛也，弱之勝強也，天下莫弗知也，而莫之能行也").

Starting from the Static Stance, Stance 1, imagine your hands are holding two pots of water, which become heavier and heavier. In Stance 2, you imagine your hands on a wooden plank on the surface of the water and feel the rising up and falling. The lower part of your body is dipped into water as in a swimming pool. You try to feel the water gushing towards your body and you have to keep your balance (如空中旗、浪中魚).

When testing power, you feel water flowing through your fingers. You feel water gushing towards your chest and back. You walk in the mud, you walk in deep water, and feel the walking is difficult. When releasing power, you generate and release your power like a strong wave.

When you dip into the cold water, your skin feels cold and the hair on your arms is erect. Your skin becomes very sensitive to touch and incoming power. You will react very quickly (毛髮如戟).

3. Fire stage

When you have saved enough energy, you have to release it. You contract and twist so as to generate a six-direction explosive power. The moment you release your power, you imagine your skin has accidentally caught fire. Your body reacts immediately and stretches strongly (發勁猶如火燒身). This reflection power is practiced through countless repetitions. There are no exceptions but expectations of luck.

4. Gold stage

The body must be hard and heavy enough to resist attack from others or to attack others (體整如鑄, 身如鉛灌).

Your skeleton is like melted copper and irrigated with lead. Melted means your enemy cannot split away any part of your body skeleton. Even when you have been pushed away, you retrieve your whole body and your frame is still stable without collapse. When you attack, you go with full force and power, with the whole power of your body united like a tank.

Your body is heavy when you are relaxed, so let the weight of your body sink entirely. Your opponent cannot push or pull you away because your center of gravity is low and heavy, like a plant rooted deeply into three feet of ground. However, when you attack, your whole body is like a mountain, huge and heavy. One strike at your opponent, and he will be thrown away. Even if your body is heavy, you move fast, because you can enlighten your upper body with practice of the steps of Mocha Bu (靜如處子, 動若山飛). You move fast like a strong wind, sweeping away all the leaves on the ground and striking down the trees that are in its way (去勢好似捲地風).

5. Earth stage

The last stage of your practice is calm.

The first stage is to train up a strong resistance (穩固); the last stage is to train up an alert spirit. Practitioners must keep calm, standing like a tree, very stable and upright, and be quiet and firm. Do not show your alertness, happiness, anger, fright, or readiness to fight (不露形).

Your posture simulates a big tree planted into the earth. You should keep your body relaxed, skin alert, hairs erect, skeleton melted, weight sunk, toes clawed, and eyes gazing steadily. Your body is full of energy like a rhinoceros or a balloon full of air. Whatever directions your opponent may come from, you can face him and attack him fiercely.

"USE 'YI' TO DO IT!"
C S Tang's seal artwork
in a special "Bird and Worm" character

REFERENCES FOR CHINESE SENTENCES AND QUOTES

神猶霧豹 氣若靈犀
靜如山岳 動若山飛
中定神凝 鬆固凝
論四形之四如境界： 體整如鑄 身如鉛灌 肌肉如一 毛髮如戟

Spirit like a leopard, breath like a rhinoceros,
Quiet like a mountain, movement like a flying mountain,

Stay centred, relaxed and stable; concentrate.

Four levels: whole body as though it's melted, body as though it's filled with lead, muscle becomes united and hair like a sword.

Part I

ORIGINS AND DEVELOPMENT OF YIQUAN

Chapter 1

THE HISTORY OF YIQUAN

ORIGIN

Yiquan is also known as Dachengquan. The meaning of Yiquan is to emphasize the use of mind. Dachengquan means the successful achievement of martial arts. Dacheng is also a term of Buddhism, meaning the upper level. Yiquan is based on the foundation of Xing Yi Quan, absorbing the steps and flexibility of Bagua Zhang, relaxation of Taiji Quan, and the throwing techniques of Chinese wrestling and other modern martial arts of the twentieth century. This is in line with the concept of bees gathering honey from different flowers. The system aims at providing a short cut to martial arts without wasting time on irrelevant movements and forms.

The origin of Yiquan can be traced back to Xing Yi Quan, one of three famous internal martial arts in China. Legend has it that the founder of Xing Yi Quan was Yue Fei (岳飛), a general of the Song dynasty.

However, the founder was not really Yue Fei. This is a traditional Chinese custom, whereby attributing a theory on sports to famous historical persons would give it a halo of reverence. Examples are that scholars studying Chinese literature worship Confucius, carpenters worship Lu Ban (魯班), decorators worship Wa Guang (華光), chefs worship Zao Jun (灶君), Taiji Quan practitioners worship Zhang San Feng (張三丰), police force and triad members worship Guang Gong (關公), and the Hong Sheng festival (洪聖誕) and Tian Hou festival (天后娘娘) are for fishermen.

Zhang San Feng (張三丰)

Guang Gong (關公)

Xing Yi Quan practitioners worship Yue Fei (岳飛) because he represents justice and is a famous warrior with the spear. The fighting concept of Xing Yi Quan applies spear techniques. However, during the ceremony of my accepting disciples, the first master shown in my lineage is Bodhidharma. Then Yue Fei is the second master.

Yue Fei (岳飛)

Bodhidharma (菩提達摩達摩) was the Buddhist monk traditionally credited as the founder of Chán (Zen) Buddhism in China. He was a South Indian monk who journeyed to southern China. He traveled to the northern Chinese kingdom of Wei, to a cave near Shaolin Monastery, in which he faced a wall for nine years, not speaking for the entire period. He developed a system of martial art practice and taught the monks there, and so was claimed to be the founder of Shaolin martial arts.

BODHIDHARMA (菩提達摩達摩)

The original name of this school was Xing I Lue Hei Quan. This includes the Ten Animal Forms and several other techniques. Later it was developed into Dai Shi Xing Yi Quan, which incorporated the Taoist concept of slow and explosive power and added the Five Elements Fist. When Li Lo Lun (李老農, 李洛能) learnt this art and began teaching in Hebei, he modified the Five Elements Fist into creation and destruction according to the theories of the five elements. He taught Guo Yun Shen (郭雲深) and Ju Yi Zhai (車毅齋). Guo Yun Shen taught Li Cun Yi (李存義), who approached Ju Yi Zhai to complete the system and later enhanced the forms to include the twelve animals. Ju also taught Song's family and Bu Xue Kuan (布學寬).

Xing Yi Quan was developed into three main branches:

- the Conservative Hebei branch—represented by Li Cun Yi
- the Shan Xi branch—represented by Ju Yi Zhai
- the Song branch—represented by Song's family.

THE FOUNDER, WANG XIANG ZHAI (王薌齋) (1886–1963)

Wang Xiang Zhai, alias Nibao, Zhenghe, or Yuseng, was born on November 24, 1886 (also said to be October 9, 1885, Lunar month) in Wei Jia Lin village (魏家杯村) of Hebei province of China. His ancestors originated from Zhejiang province (浙江省莫干山).

Wang studied Xing Yi Quan under Guo Yun Shen (郭雲深), a famous master of the art. Guo was famous for his "Peng Fist at Half Step," which was unrivaled in the whole of China. Wang, aged 8, became a student of Guo when the latter was quite old. When Wang was young, his body was weak. His brother-in-law, Li Bao, invited Guo to stay at his home in his old age, and learnt from him. Li taught Wang martial arts so that the latter could become stronger.

Guo could not walk in his old age, and he would just sit on the bed. Some said that Wang learnt movements from Guo's son and performed in front of Guo, who corrected the forms. Guo instructed him then to practice static stances.

In 1907, aged 22, Wang left his homeland. He came to Beijing city to meet Guo's senior students. He joined the army as a martial arts instructor there. A general, Wu Feng Jun (吳封君), being a Wu Zhuang Yuan (Number One Scholar of Warrior in the imperial examination), liked Wang's hard-working and good martial arts foundation, and let Wang marry his daughter Wu Su Zhen (吳素貞). General Wu was the son of a famous historical general of the Qing dynasty, Wu San Gui (吳三桂), who led the Qing army to invade China. Wang began to study Chinese culture.

In 1913 Wang defeated Li Rui Dong (李瑞東), founder of Li-style Taiji Quan, who was instructor of the President's guards. Subsequently Wang became chief of the Department of Combat of Land Forces. He was familiar with many other instructors such as Sun Lutang, Shang Yunxiang, and Liu Wenhua.

Starting in 1915, Wang defeated Zhou Zi Yan (周子炎) three times in three different years. Zhou was a master of the Praying Mantis style. He then became Wang's student.

Wang's adventures

In 1918, because of political changes, the Department of Combat stopped operating, so Wang traveled to the southern part of China to research martial arts. He came to Shaolin Monastery at Henan, where he shared his knowledge of Xing I Ba with the monk Henglin. In Hubei province, Wang learned from the eccentric master Jie Tiefu. In Fujian province, he was appointed as martial arts instructor of the army. He met masters of the White Crane style, Fang Qia Zhuang and Jin Shao Feng. Coming back north, he met the famous master of Xinyi, Huang Muqiao, from whom he learned the "Health Dance." In Xi'an, he met a master famous for his quick kicks, Liu Peixian. He also learned Bagua

Zhang from Liu Fengchun, and met Taiji Quan masters Yang Shaohou and Yang Chengfu. These were only some of the masters with whom Wang exchanged experiences.

Initial stage and the named art

In 1925, Wang started teaching Zhan Zhuang and placed less emphasis on practice of forms. He called this system Yiquan, discarding the element xing (form). The first student of Yiquan in Beijing was Qi Zhidu. In Tianjin, another student was Zhao Enqing, also called Zhao Daoxin, winner of the free fighting tournament at the Third China Sports Competition; he was also famous for defeating the Norwegian boxer Andersen, having uncomfortable slippers on his feet, and being the founder of Xinhui Zhang. Others were Gu Xiaochi, Ma Qichang, Deng Zhisong, Miao Chunyu, Zhang Zonghui, Zhang Entong (later, in the 1950s, Zhang Entong defeated the Chinese heavyweight wrestling champion Zhang Kuiyuan, who after this started studying Yiquan), Qiu Zhihe, Zhao Fengyao, and Zhao Zuoyao.

In Tianjin, Wang met Xue Dian (薛顛), a master of Xing Yi Quan, who was teaching there. Wang showed his great prowess and earned the admiration of Xue.

In 1928, together with his student Zhao Enqing and a Xing Yi Quan master from Tianjin, Zhang Zhankui, Wang went to Hangzhou, where he was the referee at a Free Sparring tournament at the Third China Sports Competition and also demonstrated the training methods of Yiquan. His student Zhao Daoxin won the tournament. Then Wang was invited to Shanghai, where he founded the Yiquan Society. Wang fought with the Hungarian Inge, the boxing world champion, after which Yiquan became quite well known. Those who became Wang's students during this period were: You Pengxi, Gao Zhendong, Zhu Guolu, Zhu Guozhen, Bu Enfu (Chinese champion of boxing and shuai-jiao wrestling), Zhang Changxin (winner of a boxing tournament in Shanghai), Zhang Changyi, brothers Han Xingqiao and Han Xingyuan, Wang Shuhe, Ma Jianzhao, and Ning Dachun.

Han Xingqiao, Zhao Daoxin, Zhang Changxin, and Gao Zhendong became famous in Shanghai as the "Four Warriors" (四大金剛). At this time, Wang wrote his first Yiquan treatise, *Right Path of Yiquan* (意拳正軌), though Wang Xiang Zhai's Yiquan was already quite different from what was being taught by other Xing Yi Quan masters.

During his stay in Shanghai, Wang met Wu Yihui (吳翼翬), master of Liuhebafa (LHBF), whom Wang described as one of the three greatest masters he met during his travels all over China.

In 1935, aged 50, Wang Xiang Zhai, together with his students Bu Enfu, Zhang Entong, Zhang Changxin, and Han Xingqiao, moved to Wang's home village in Shen county. They concentrated on training and studies on martial arts theory. Most training methods used currently in Yiquan were developed and perfected at that time.

In 1937 Wang moved to Beijing. He taught Yiquan and worked further on the theories of the system. Hong Lian Shun (洪連順), master of Xing Yi Quan and Tan Tui, was quite famous in Beijing at that time. When Hong heard about Wang's incredible skill, he came to challenge Wang. Hong was defeated and became Wang's student, after which he passed his students to Wang, including Yao Zongxun. Other students during the Beijing period were: Dou Shiming (who once with one punch defeated Gao Yanwang, bodyguard of general Fu Shuangying), Dou Shicheng, Li Yongzong, Yang Demao, Zhang Zhong, Zhang Fu, Wang Binkui, Yang Shaoqing, Li Wentao, Li Jianyu, Wang Shichuan, Jiao Jingang, Ao Shuopeng, Ao Shuohong, and Tong Guocao.

In 1939, Wang published in the *Shibao* newspaper a text in which he invited all masters of martial arts to exchange experiences and ideas. The new challengers usually wanted to compare their skills with Wang. Wang, however, chose four of his students to fight instead of him: Han Xingqiao, Hong Lianshun, Yao Zongxun, and Zhou Ziyan. Only after defeating one of them could the challengers fight with Wang, but no one succeeded.

In 1940, a big martial arts festival was held in Tokyo in which the Chinese team also participated. Some Chinese masters who collaborated with the Japanese went there. The chief of the team tried to persuade Wang Xiang Zhai to participate, but Wang refused to go. Afterwards many Japanese started coming to Beijing to visit Wang. Many of them challenged Wang, and were defeated. They included Watanabe (渡邊), Yada (八田), Usami (宇作美), and Hino (日野). Some of them wanted to become Wang's students, but only one was accepted—Kenichi Sawai (澤井健一), who later created his new version of Yiquan in Japan, known as Taiki-ken (太氣拳).

Establishment and mature stage

In Shanghai, Wang combined the best elements of internal martial arts and simplified them into a direct and effective system that was straightforward in developing one's internal power without wasting time on other irrelevant movements. He omitted Xing from Xing Yi Quan and called it Yiquan.

In 1941 Wang bestowed honorary names on his six best students. In this way he was expressing his high opinion of their skills and abilities. Zhao Enqing received his given name Daoxin, Han Xingqiao became Daokuan, Bu Enfu became Daokui, Zhang Entong became Daode, Zhao Fengyao became Daohong, and Yao Zongxun became Jixiang.

Yiquan was already a system completely separate from Xing Yi Quan. People suggested a new name, Dachengquan, meaning boxing of great success. But most of Wang's students still used the name Yiquan.

In 1944, with the help of his students, Wang revised the book on his theories from *Central Pivot of the Way of Fist* to *Theory of Dachengquan*. Training methods were based on different concepts. In using these new methods, one could achieve easily the same or better results in a shorter time.

From 1945 onwards, after the Japanese war, Wang started putting more attention on the health aspect of Yiquan exercises. He taught personally the "health" group. Some of the students of this group were: Chen Haiting, Qin Zhongsan, Yu Yongnian, Bu Yukun, Mi Jingke, Sun Wenqing, Zhang Yuheng, Qi Zhenglin, and Wang Xiang Zhai's daughter Wang Yufang. In 1947, this group, who practiced in the Ancestors Temple, which currently is the Labor Cultural Center, had about 100 members. Many of them were able to cure some illnesses that could not be cured in any other way. Therapeutic efficiency and lack of side-effects of these exercises were later proved scientifically.

Yiquan for health

In 1949, when Wang was 64, China became liberated. Wang started teaching in the parks.

In 1950, Wang was appointed as Vice-President of the Wushu section of the Whole-China Physical Culture Committee. For the next few years he taught almost entirely the health version. The health group moved to Zhong Shan Park where they could practice freely. Yu Yong Nian presented to the authorities a report about the therapeutic values of Zhan Zhuang exercises, which resulted in introducing this method in many hospitals all over China. Wang was also asked to teach in the hospitals.

In 1960, Wang stopped teaching in Zhong Shan Park and stayed at home. Later he was invited to teach stances for curing at Beijing Chinese Medicine Research Institute. Wang invited Li Jiang Yu to assist him to teach.

In the spring of 1961, the Institute invited Wang to pose for 24 photographs of stances, after which he retired, leaving Li Jiang Yu to teach.

From November 1961, he moved to the Hebei Chinese Medicine Research Hospital in Bao Ding, Hebei province, to teach stances.

In 1962, Wang participated in a Qigong conference, where he performed some exercises, which were met with great interest.

In the spring of 1963, Wang had a stroke. He recovered, but became half paralyzed with speaking difficulties. He was sent back home to Beijing and later moved to Tianjin. He lived at the home of his third daughter Wang Yu Bai. He had family problems and passed away on July 12, 1963 in Tianjin, at the age of 78.

Wang was the father of three daughters, Wang Yu Zhen, Wang Yu Fang, and Wang Yu Bai; and two sons, Wang Dao Zhuang and Wang Dao Nan.

Collections of Wang's writings

Wang and his students wrote several books on Yiquan. They are:

Right Path of Yiquan	(意拳正軌)
Talks on Health Stance	(養生椿漫談)
Zhan Zhuang	(站椿功)
Answers to a Journalist	(答記者問)
Central Pivot of the Way of Fist	(拳道中樞)
Theories of Dachengquan	(大成拳論)
Theories of Yiquan, Zhuang, and Four Forms	(意拳論—椿功與四形)
Essence of Combat	(斷手述要)
Yiquan Manuscript	(意拳拳譜)
Learn and Gain from Fist	(習拳一得) 李見宇, 孫聞青錄
Essence of Yiquan	(意拳要點) 何鏡平錄

ANECDOTES ABOUT WANG XIANG ZHAI

Western clothes

We have found in one of the photographs that Master Wang was wearing Western clothes with a necktie. Was he a modernized man or a rich man? Actually Master Wang was quite traditional. He had deep knowledge of Chinese culture, and he always wore the traditional Chinese long gown. The photograph was taken in Shanghai when he stayed there, and it is the only one showing Wang in Western clothes.

Stance learnt from Master Guo

Master Wang placed much emphasis on the Static Stance, so what posture of stance did he learn from his teacher Guo Yun Shen? Madam Wang Yu Fang said there was only one posture he had learnt, and it was the push-up combat stance.

Water sticking to his hand

Master Wang Yu Fang told us that once Wang demonstrated Test Power by putting his hand on the surface of some water. He then moved his hand up and down above the water and, using his intent, caused the water to stick to his palm and leave the surface.

Ching Ting Wah's fireball

Who did Wang really admire? Master Li Jiang Yu recalled that it was the Bagua Zhang master Ching Ting Wah he admired most. Master Wang said he saw Ching practicing Bagua, moving powerfully, and he felt Ching looked like a fireball striking at him. He felt Ching's pressure and could never forget the experience.

Later years of the master

Wang adopted a very low profile in his older years. During the 1960s, he lived at Bu En Fu (卜恩富)'s Chinese wrestling center for half a year. Bu's student, Tian, recalled that they always saw an old man standing there watching them practice but without giving any comment. He just walked around, relaxing, and did not practice anything.

Chinese calligraphy

His last student, Chang Zhi Lang, recalled that Wang loved Chinese calligraphy and painting. His near neighbors were famous painters: Qi Bai Shi (齊白石) and Pan Tian Shou (潘天壽). He would go to their studio and chat till sunset. He would also spend the whole day in the antique streets of Beijing. He liked to do Chinese calligraphy and painting self-portraits. We can see that from some of his artwork, for example the short message to Lee Ying Ngor, and the ink title for Li Jiang Yu's book. Also there is a Chinese flower painting now used on the cover of the Yiquan book, with Ian Fok keeping the original copy of the painting.

Antiques and hobbies

Wang liked Chinese seals quite a lot and had deep knowledge of the seal culture. His collection was rich. However, these all vanished during the Chinese cultural revolution when the Red Guards came to his house. His daughter Wang Yu Fang tried to protect his collection and fought against them. A soldier came behind her and used the wooden handle of a rifle to strike at the back of her knee. She was beaten until unconscious. All of Wang's collection was taken out in front of his home and burnt.

More anecdotes

These further anecdotes were told by Dou Shi Cheng (竇世誠) to the author. Master Dou Shi Cheng was born in Beijing and was 71 when I interviewed him in September 1995. He went to Taiwan in 1949 where he changed his name to Dou Zhi Jiang (竇志江).

Master Dou told me how he learnt Yiquan. First, he started to stand with Pi Quan Zhuang (劈拳樁) for over six months. He started learning Yiquan while he was of school age. Grandmaster Wang told him to start learning from Shi Xiong (elder brother) Hong Lian Shun (洪連順) first. Hong was a bodyguard at that time; his nickname was "Man of Smashed Steel" (開碑手), and he was also known as "Comparable Overlord" (賽天霸). He carried with him 12 darts (飛鏢) and never missed a target. Master Dou, his brother Dou Shi Ming (竇世明), Yao Zong Xun (姚宗勳), Li Yong Zong (李永宗), and Zhang Zhong (張中) were the last ones who had officially kowtowed as disciples to Master Hong. That was in 1937, and this style became known as Daicheng Quan (大成拳).

"Grandmaster Wang's skills were so great that one could hardly imagine them," Master Dou sighed. When Grandmaster Wang saw them training in another style of martial arts, he often remarked, "What is the use of training in that martial art?"

Master Dou also related a few very precious anecdotes that he witnessed personally, which are given here.

1. Taming of Kenichi Sawai (澤井健一) (1903–1988)

The fight between Master Wang and Kenichi Sawai is widely known about. However, since Master Dou personally witnessed the fight, it can be told with a great deal of realism.

It happened at a martial arts meeting provided by Zhang Bi (張璧), where many grandmasters of different styles of martial arts were present. Japanese Army Major Kenichi Sawai, who had achieved Kendo fifth Dan and Judo fourth Dan, was proficient in Mandarin. At the meeting, he sneered at Chinese Kung Fu that it was only acrobat training. As a result, everybody present urged Grandmaster Wang to teach him a lesson. Sawai used a rope to tie around Wang's waist in order to throw him, but twice was sent tumbling away. Sawai asked to try weapons, but Wang said, "Ordinarily if I do not use weapons, I have only 30 percent power. But if I pick up anything, I have 70 percent power and it won't be a simple friendly trial."

Sawai used a bamboo sword. Wang stood with his own walking staff. Sawai walked in a circle and suddenly struck from the top. However, he was thrown tumbling away upon touch. He asked to try again. He struck from the front. Wang only lifted his staff, and the same thing happened as before—Sawai was thrown badly. Sawai was totally subdued and asked to follow Wang. Wang asked Yao Zong Xun to train him. Thus Sawai and his Japanese friend Hino (日野) and Yu Zuo Mei (余作梅) went to live in Yao's apartment to learn. Master Dou also learnt Sawai's Judo and Kendo skills. All Sawai's techniques were taught by Yao, and Wang never taught him.

Sawai returned to Japan after World War II and named his teaching Taiki-ken (太氣拳).

2. Grandmaster Wang's suspension in the air

Master Dou's father, Dou Zong Han (竇宗漢), once invited Shang Dong governor Zhang Ji Xin (張繼新) for dinner. Zhang was 84 and Wang was 56. Zhang lamented that he was too old to train. Wang asked him to do a stance, pulled up his right hand and pointed it to the roof eaves. Then Wang pressed on his right arm. Wang suspended himself one foot off the floor by using his arm. Everybody present was amazed and would never have believed it except by seeing with their own eyes.

3. Finger knock

Once, Wang asked Master Dou to show what he had learnt by asking Dou to attack him. Dou gave a hard, straight punch. Wang used his index finger to knock on his right arm. Dou shouted in pain and kneeled down, sweating. His right arm was swollen and bruised. Wang's strike was done unintentionally.

4. House break

Dou Shi Ming (竇世明) had a trial with Grandmaster Wang. Upon contact, Wang slapped both Dou's arms. Dou's whole body jumped upward and broke the ceiling of the room, and then he dropped down with his face full of dust. All the participants laughed.

5. Fight in Western Arcade

In 1943, in Western Arcade, 11 of Wang's students fought with their bare hands against 300 armed triad members. The students included:

Yao Zong Xun	姚宗勳
Dou Shi Ming	竇世明
Dou Shi Cheng	竇世誠
Li Yong Zong	李永宗
Zheng Chao Xiang	鄭朝項
Zhao Zhong Yuan	趙中原
Kong Qing Hai	孔慶海
Ao Shuo Peng	敖碩鵬

Some of the triad members were wounded and they had to be retained in hospital. On the students' side, Li Yong Zong had one eye blinded, while Ao Shuo Peng hurt his neck. This fight became well known and was a glorious episode for Yiquan.

DEVELOPMENT OF YIQUAN

Yiquan branches

Yiquan has now spread all over the world and is famous for enabling practitioners to gain power and practice meditation quickly.

In Beijing, Yu Yongnian, Wang Yu Fang, and Sun Chang You (Yao Zongxun's student) are teaching Yiquan. Yao Zongxun's sons, Yao Chengguang and Yao Chengrong, are teaching there also.

Yao Zongxun's students Bo Jiacong and Cui Ruibin (Vice-President and Secretary of the Yiquan Association) are teaching in England and Sweden; Liu Pulei (board member of the Chinese Wushu Association and Vice-Secretary of the Yiquan Association) has students in Malaysia.

Li Jiangyu, Dou Shiming, Zhang Zhong, Wang Anping, and Han Xingqiao's sons, Han Jingyu and Han Jingsheng, are teaching in Zhuhai.

You Peng Xi's Kong Jin (Empty Force) has influence in America. Wang Xuanjie's students are teaching Dachengquan.

Wang Bin Kui (王斌魁) taught his sons and many good fighters. Wang An Ping (王安平) is teaching the health aspect of Yiquan and gaining good results.

Master Moy Lin-shin is the founder of the Taoist Tai Chi Association in Canada, having studied Liuhebafa from Suen Zhi in Hong Kong. His main school is in Toronto but he has satellite branches in Nova Scotia, New Brunswick, Newfoundland, Quebec, Ontario, Manitoba, Saskatchewan, Alberta, British Columbia, and the Northwest Territories. He teaches Liuhebafa and Taiji Quan.

Kenichi Sawai was a student of Wang Xiang Zhai, and created his own version of Yiquan called Taiki-ken, which is now widespread in Japan.

Yiquan in Hong Kong

Liang Zi Peng, a student of You Pengxi, first introduced Yiquan to Hong Kong in 1950 and had many students. Liang was also a teacher of Bruce Lee. His student Suen Zhi (孫秩) taught at the Silver and Gold Exchange Society after Liang passed away.

Han Xing Yuan also later taught a version of Yiquan named Xing Yi Dachengquan.

The Hong Kong Yiquan Society was formed on July 17, 1987. Ian Fok (霍震寰) is the President and he promotes Yiquan. The society invites masters of Yiquan from China every year to give speeches and organize seminars. The society has also published a collection of Wang's articles, called *Yiquan Collection.*

Now in Hong Kong, the author teaches a systematic way of Yiquan; others, such as Master Chan Ching Chung, Tu Hing Kin, Huen Siu Chan, Lee Tin Tak, Ho Ka Hing, Chan Tak Chuen, Siu Cheuk Hung, Chung Lai Man, and Si Kin On, are teaching in different places and classes.

THE THOUGHTS OF WANG XIANG ZHAI ON MARTIAL ARTS

Wang Xiang Zhai carried on the orthodox practice of Xing Yi Quan. However, during his stay in Shanghai during the 1930s, he saw how foreign culture had invaded China. Russian strong men, European boxers, and Japanese Judokas all invaded the circles of Chinese culture and martial arts. The new concept of sports and the new theories of the physics of Western science influenced the traditional culture.

Wang lived in that turbulent age. He recognized that practicing martial arts in the old way could not reach worldwide acceptance. That was why he sought a simple and direct training method, whose objective was to increase power and speed. Each attack or punch has to be powerful, non-defensible, and effective. The power it uses is explosive power. This can be developed through Static Stance. Thus Static Stance became his core training.

Warm-up exercises and cool-down exercises were usually ignored by the Chinese and so they suffered from knee pain and rheumatism. Scientific conditioning and body-building methods were outdated in China. Therefore he tried to select his students and brought them back to his village to train. His purpose was to establish a team that could travel the world to fight all other martial artists and to recover the glory of Chinese martial arts.

In his training, he did not object to hitting sand bags or wrestling. He knew that one could use whatever techniques in order to win. Although he himself did not hit sand bags, he let Yao Zongxun teach his students boxing and body-building. He also let his students learn the Japanese sword from Kenichi Sawai. When Bu Enfu used wrestling to fight with his classmates, Wang did not object. But he insisted that students had to practice Static Stance to get the explosive power.

He tried to train in such a scientific way that he eliminated all Chinese superstition and never talked about Qi. He built his system by incorporating the training method of wrestling into the advanced stance. The Taming Tiger and the Yielding Dragon are movements in Chinese wrestling. He added the Bagua Zhang stepping method into Yiquan's footwork. He added the vocalization as Shi Sheng from the Thunder Sound of Xing I Lui Ho Quan. His students trained with wooden swords as in Japanese Kendo, and in the pole-rubbing technique from the traditional tremble pole. He also tried to develop the stance shapes into 24 models in his earlier initial stage.

All his life, he sought the truth of martial arts and never hesitated to absorb anything that was effective in health and combat. He was a highly creative and powerful master, and he encouraged his students to be creative too.

PHOTOS SHOWING THE HISTORY OF YIQUAN

Xing Yi Quan

Practitioners performing Xing Yi Quan in a park in Beijing in the 1930s, showing Crushing Fist with whole-body united strength

Two famous Xing Yi Quan masters in Shangxi province in the Qing dynasty: Ju Yi Zhai (車毅齋—middle left in black) and Guo Yun Shen (郭雲深—right)

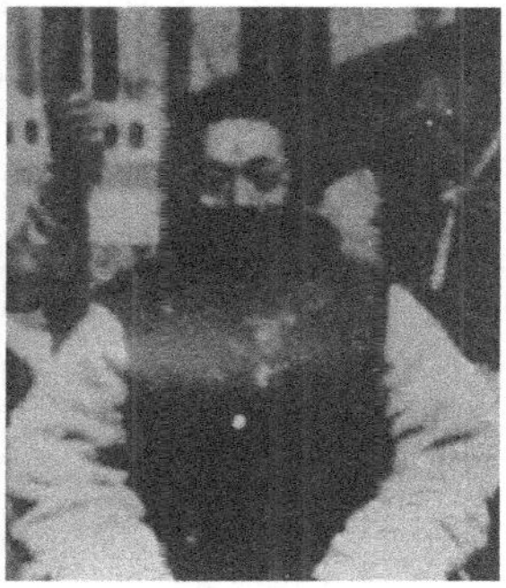

Master Guo Yun Shen, teacher of Wang Xiang Zhai

Master Wang Xiang Zhai

Master Wang Xiang Zhai, a photo from his daughter's home

Wang Xiang Zhai in the 1940s and 1950s

Wang Xiang Zhai's kick stance

Relaxing at the hill

New photos of Master Wang discovered recently

With Li Jiang Yu in Beijing, 1958

Master Wang with martial artists

First disciples celebration in 1946

Second group of disciples celebration

Master C S Tang standing in front of the entrance of the "Grand Temple" in 2002

Master Wang Xiang Zhai taught Yiquan Static Stance here.
It is now named "Beijing Labor People's Cultural Center"

THE ARTWORK OF MASTER WANG XIANG ZHAI

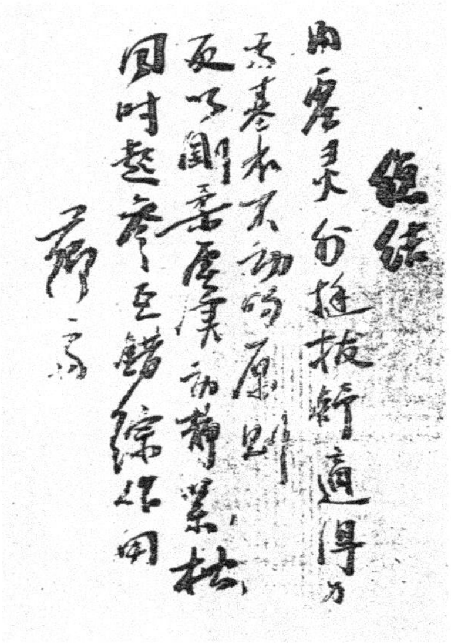

1.

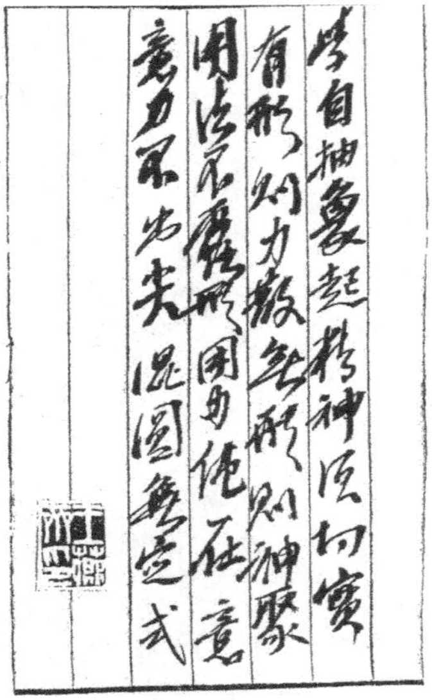

2.

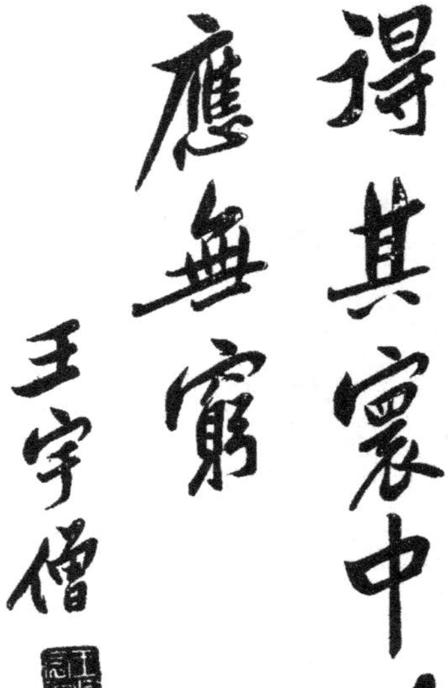

3.

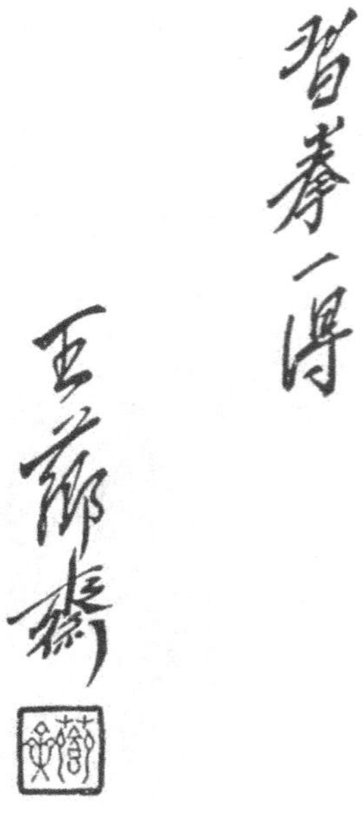

4.

Calligraphies by Wang Xiang Zhai

Calligraphies 1 and 2 were kept by Lee Ying Arng

A Wang Xiang Zhai painting that was kept by Ian Fok

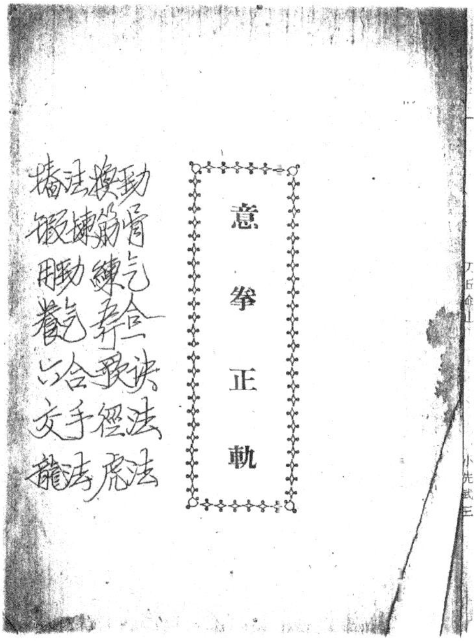

意拳正軌

First book written by Wang Xiang Zhai

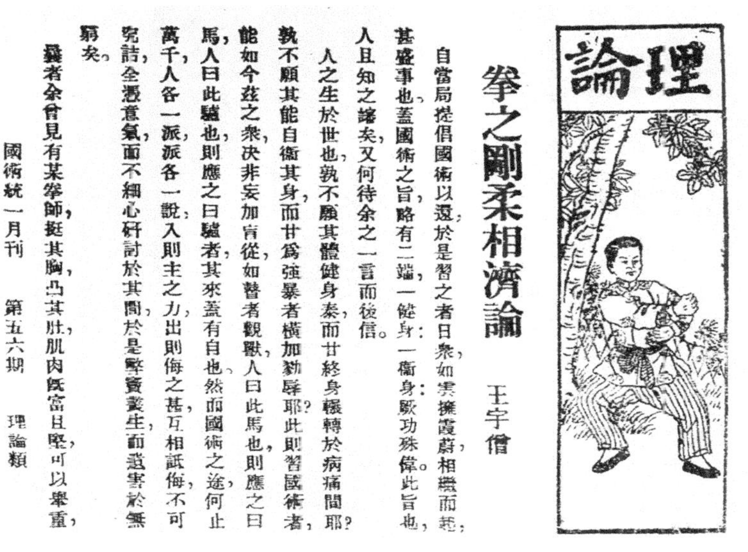

理論

拳之剛柔相濟論

王宇僧

自當局提倡國術以還，於是習之者日衆，如雲擁霞蔚，相繼而起，甚盛事也。蓋國術之旨，路有二端，一健身，一衞身：厥功殊偉。此旨也，人且知之諗矣，又何待余之一言而後信。

人之生於世也，孰不願其體健身泰，而甘終身輾轉於病痛間耶？孰不願其能自衞其身，而甘爲強暴者橫加勠辱耶？此則習國術者，能如今玆之衆，決非妄加盲從，如瞽者觀獸，人曰此馬也，則應之曰馬，人曰此驢也，則應之曰驢者，其來蓋有自也。然而國術之途，何止萬千，人各一派，派各一說；入則主之，出則侮之，甚互相詆侮，不可究詰，全憑意氣，而不細心硏討於其間，於是擊實囊生，而遺害於無窮矣。

曩者余曾見有某拳師，挺其胸，凸其肚，肌肉既富且堅，可以舉重，

國術統一月刊　第五六期　理論類

An article written by Wang Xiang Zhai

Chapter 2

YIQUAN MASTER LIANG ZI PENG

THE LEGEND

Liang Zi Peng, Hong Kong, 1968

INTRODUCTION

On the fortieth anniversary of Bruce Lee's death in 1973, there were a large number of commemorative events and exhibitions across Hong Kong. When Bruce Lee talked of his experience in learning the martial arts, he mentioned that he had had ten teachers: he studied Taiji Quan from his father Lee Hoi Chuen, he studied Hung Kuen under Choy Lai Fut, studied Judo under Oohyoue, studied Western boxing under his middle school teacher, studied Northern Jing Wu boxing under Xiao Hansheng, and studied internal arts under Liang Zi Peng. When he was in America he studied Philippine Escrima and studied Taekwondo under Rhee Jun Goo.

His internal arts teacher was Liang Zi Peng, who is not widely known despite being one of the foremost people in transmitting Yiquan and Liuhebafa to the South. Who was Liang Zi Peng? What did he teach Bruce Lee, and for how long and how much did he study? And what impact did Yiquan have on Jeet Kune Do, the martial art system and philosophy of life founded by Bruce Lee? This chapter seeks to answer the first question; Chapter 3 addresses the rest.

FROM LEFT: MRS. LI, LI YING ANG, MRS. YOU, AND YOU PENG XI

BIOGRAPHY

Liang Zi Peng was born in Canton province, Nanhai county. He studied Eagle Claw under Master Chen Zi Zheng, Bagua Zhang under Jiang Xin Shan, Yiquan under You Peng Xi, and Liuhebafa under Wu Yi Hui. He was the first person to transmit Yiquan and Liuhebafa to Hong Kong.

Master Liang grew up learning to fight. The Liang name was historically transmitted from father to single son, and his father hoped that the martial arts could strengthen his body and spirit as a foundation to success, so he hired many martial arts teachers to teach him, and he grew up loving the martial arts.

When he was young he moved to Shanghai and worked as an office clerk in a Western company. He enrolled in the Jing Wu Athletic Association, and first started to learn Tan Tui. Liang learned five sets of Tan Tui in a single night! For a young man who had never studied the northern arts before, one could see how clever and dedicated he was.

He studied the 18 weapons at the Jing Wu Association. At this time the Jing Wu Association was flourishing, and invited masters from many arts to teach. Whether it was Cha Quan, Shaolin, Taiji Quan, Eagle Claw, or Mantis, they were all taught by a renowned master of that art. At that time the Saint of Eagle Claw, Chen Zi Zheng, was in charge of teaching the art. When Liang saw the intricacy of the art, he made a special effort to learn Eagle Claw. Chen Zi Zheng was the face of Jing Wu and was very well known for a time. He had a hat made of iron, and he carried it with him everywhere; he used it to train his fingers, and hence his fingers became extremely strong. Chen was also the referee for many Guoshu competitions, and when the loser did not accept the outcome, he would himself go onto the stage and at that point the loser would happily admit defeat; thus he also had the sobriquet

"King of Eagle Claw." Liang Zi Peng, Li Pei Xuan, and Zhang Jun Ting all studied boxing at the same time, and were the key disciples of Chen Zi Zheng.

After joining the Eagle Claw school, he studied extremely hard, and spent a lot of effort on the sets and sparring. In order to train in Eagle Claw, one could not avoid studying iron fingers. As part of this, Liang was extremely dedicated to sticking his fingers in the sand, and every time his fingers broke during practice, he resumed as soon as he recovered. Liang's third finger on his left hand became permanently crooked, due to having been injured so many times. Master Chen doted on his disciple, and often sparred with him without holding back, and sometimes dislocated Liang's wrist upon contact. Chen would immediately put the joint back into place and continue sparring. One time, when they were both sparring with the staff, Master Liang was a little slow and Master Chen's staff hit him on the little finger, which left a lifelong scar.

Liang was skilled in a hundred arts, and had tried studying Five Elements Tongbei Quan, and studied 30 types of hard boxing. He studied the whip, flying darts, lightness skills, staff, and spade, weapons belonging to the Shaolin external styles, all to an extremely high level. When he went out to fight he won, and due to his knowledge, he could understand each art once he saw it. He was called "The Lark" (百靈鳥). He often wore metal shoes to train his lightness skills. From a standing position, he could bend his knees and jump a foot higher than his own height. His high kicks were three inches higher than his head. The hollows in his palms were extremely large, like geese eggs, so one could see how strong his wrists were. His palms were also especially big, which was the fruit of Eagle Claw training.

When he was at Jing Wu, he was called one of the four heavenly protectors. One day when he was eating with relatives, there was a famous martial artist from another school on the next table. He did not know that Liang was a student of Eagle Claw, and in a drunken state loudly criticized the Eagle Claw school as impractical. Upon hearing this Liang was not happy, and wanted to demonstrate his skills. Just using the power from his backside, Liang's opponent was unable to keep his balance and fell to the ground, knocking his own table over. Having suffered a grave humiliation, he asked Liang what style he studied. Liang laughingly replied that he studied Eagle Claw, and his opponent knew that he had put his foot in it, and was deeply ashamed.

One of the stories that people liked to share about Liang Zi Peng's kung fu was related to when he was living in Shanghai, when the building he was living in caught fire, which started to spread from the top downwards. Fleeing using the stairs was impossible. Realizing the situation was dire, and that his mother and wife were not strong, Liang was momentarily scared witless. Necessity being the mother of invention, he took a long rope and tied it around his waist, and then carrying his mother he abseiled down the building using the rope. After his mother was safe he went back for his wife and elder daughter, but also had a younger daughter who was still a toddler and had been sleeping on the mat in the middle of the room.

Due to his agitated mental state he had forgotten about her, and only after the rest of the family had reached the street level safely did he realize and went back up the rope; but the fire was burning fiercely now, and he was unable go back in. Eventually he had to sacrifice this valuable life, which was something he regretted for the rest of his life. Afterwards, the newspapers published details of this incident and mentioned that he was a disciple of Chen, and this greatly increased his fame.

He was also associated with Ma Cheng Xin, who was a disciple of the Mantis Grandmaster Luo Guang Yu, and they were both hot-blooded youths. Ma Cheng Xin became famous in Shanghai because he placed first in the National Sports Guoshu Competition. So when Master Luo Guang Yu later went south to Canton and Hong Kong to spread Mantis, he passed all his teaching responsibilities to Ma, who became head of the Mantis school without intending to do so. However, when Chen went south, he had originally planned to hand over his position at Jing Wu to Liang, but due to Liang's flourishing business, and that to him martial arts was an extra-curricular activity, he did not want to advance himself in the world of Guoshu and humbly declined. He would help out at the Association from time to time, out of duty, and would spar with some of the students there. At this time the number of masters at Jing Wu were as numerous as the clouds, and as a member, Liang was very interested in further researching the internal arts—he was very good friends with Wu Jian Quan and Tian Jiao Lin. He had already begun to study Taiji Quan and also studied Bagua Zhang under Jiang Xin Shan and continued doing so until the Japanese invaded and destroyed the Jing Wu Association in Shanghai.

Ma Cheng Xin would first test applications before studying the art

MA CHENG XIN

Ma Cheng Xin was a dentist by profession, tall of stature and immensely strong. Having taken Luo Guang Yu as his teacher, he studied hard and made his name. He went to fight in the ring numerous times, and took the championship each time, earning many honors for the Mantis school. He later heard that Grandmaster Wang Xiang Zhai was teaching Yiquan, using the Yi to lead the Jin, not discussing any fancy movements, and using Zhan

Zhuang as the main training method. His technique was akin to those of the gods. At one time Grandmaster Wang had an article in the paper mentioning that he welcomed any challengers. Upon reading this Ma paid him a visit.

Before taking a person as a teacher, one would first test his skills; this was common practice in the martial world in those days. As soon as Ma saw Master Wang, he attacked him, and using his Jin Master Wang pushed him away. As he did not admit defeat, Master Wang then asked him, "What did you eat before coming?" Ma replied, "Noodles." They engaged again, and this time Wang used the move Half-Step Breaking Fist (半步崩捶), drilling directly into Ma's stomach; Ma immediately threw up all the noodles he had previously eaten. Wang laughed, "At least you are honest." Ma admitted defeat and took him as his teacher.

Ma was extremely diligent, rising early to practice the arts. Returning to his clinic, he would draw the curtain and practice Zhan Zhuang. Unfortunately he came from a poor family, and was unable to look after Master Wang to the extent that You Peng Xi did, and thus did not receive the key instructions in the art.

Han Xing Huan stated that Ma Cheng Xin was the strongest of them all: in push hand with one easy lifting movement he could make the opponent step back. When the Jing Wu Association opened a Taiji class, Ma's reputation was such that no one wanted to teach the class. Eventually Wu Jian Quan oversaw the class with Li Xu Dan and Wu Gong Yi assisting. Ma arrogantly entered the class to issue a challenge but no one dared to take it up. His fellow student Zhao Dao Xin was so angry that he took down the sign for the class and took it away with him.

Ma received the most teachings from You Peng Xi, and changed his status from fellow student to study under him. As You was from a rich family, he did not care about money and taught Ma for free.

You Peng Xi (尤彭熙) (1902–1983)

Liang Zi Peng (in Cantonese pronounced as Leung Chi Pang) learnt Yiquan from Master You Peng Xi in Shanghai.

You was a medical professor, born in Wu Xin, Jiangsu province. He graduated from Shanghai Medical Academy, becoming Medical Professor at Heidelberg University, Germany, and a famous dermatology doctor.

He practiced Six Harmony-style and Wuji-style martial arts. In 1928 he practiced Yiquan under Wang Xiang Zhai. He accepted Wang into his home, treated him as a father, and gave him blank check books so that he could use money easily.

He was friendly with Zhang Zhang Xin (張長信). He was also close to mesmerist Le Huan Zhi (樂幻智). He believed in Tantra, and invested secret theories from Shamanism and developed the Soar power, Ling Kong Jin, now commonly called Empty Force.

In 1981, Stanford University Research Institute in America invited him to come to California for research. He left China with his wife, Madam Ou Yang Min (歐陽敏). He died in 1983. Madam Ou Yang died at the age of 100 on July 29, 2009.

Farewell ceremony for Master You on leaving for the USA, Shanghai, 1981

Madam Ou Yang Min and Master You Peng Xi

Zhang Zhang Xin

Mesmerist Le Huan Zhi

LIANG ZI PENG TESTS YOU PENG XI

Master You Peng Xi

At the time of this story, Wang Xiang Zhai's disciple You Peng Xi was teaching in Shanghai, and Liang knew that You was a man famous for the internal arts, with a profound knowledge in Xinyi, Bagua, and Taiji. Especially with respect to Wang's Zhan Zhuang method, he had reached a level of mastery. Liang was very interested in Xinyi's Zhan Zhuang and wanted to study under You.

Liang and Ma were not only famous fighters at Jing Wu but also good friends, and shared their training secrets with each other. Liang had heard of You's prowess and had hoped for an audience with him, although after Ma demurred Liang eventually went to visit him on his own initiative. You was wearing white linen with long sleeves, cloth shoes, and was fanning himself; he was the image of a Confucian scholar, totally unlike a warrior. Liang doubted his ability. Entering You's home arrogantly, Liang saw a hundred or more people standing in Zhan Zhuang, for it was a holiday and the number of students was larger than usual.

Upon sitting down, Liang stated, "Master You, I have come because I wish to test myself against you." You agreed, and as he knew Liang was a strong proponent of Eagle Claw, he rolled up his sleeve and said, "You may use Eagle Claw to grab my wrist." The favored move of Eagle Claw is to attack the opponent's wrist, so Liang attacked and immediately found that he lost his grip. Attacking again, he could not lock on to his target. Each time he tried, the result was the same. Even using his well-honed techniques, he could not grab the opponent's hand, and he admitted defeat.

When Liang first started studying Zhan Zhuang he found it boring and uninspiring, and began to hate doing it and often fooled around with the other disciples, always using Eagle Claw, thinking that the external arts were the most useful. Upon seeing this, Master You explained, "With your level of kung fu you have not been able to understand the path of our art, and you are winning due to your greater experience; this is an ineffective method for the future." As Liang had studied many years of Shaolin and hard skills, You ordered him to relax as much as possible, to change to a new form of power, and slowly his skills began to appear.

OTHER INCIDENTS INVOLVING LIANG

After studying Yiquan with You, Liang was involved in a number of incidents of interest.

When he was young, Liang would go hiking with his seniors. After climbing hundreds of steps he was not out of breath, and upon returning he was still able to run through two fighting sequences without any change of facial color.

When he was a certain age, both he and Ma were fond of soccer. Once while watching a match he turned while tracking the trajectory of the ball and bumped into a lady. The lady started crying that Liang had intended to molest her. As Liang did not understand Shanghainese, he could not reason with her. More than a hundred Shanghainese answered her call and the two fellow students had no choice but to fight back-to-back against more than ten people. After fighting for a while both sides realized that it was a misunderstanding and stood down.

There was one time when a strong man insulted Guoshu, and Ma, getting angry, kicked him out of the hall, knocking down the two screen doors at the same time. Master You reprimanded him for being too quick to anger.

There was another time when Liang's house was being renovated, and through a misunderstanding he started arguing with the carpenter. Due to the argument, the carpenter resorted to violence and took up an ax and attacked Liang. With a twist of his hand Liang disarmed the opponent, and the carpenter admitted defeat.

When Liang was young and the Japanese had invaded China, he hired a laborer to carry his luggage, with the intention of leaving the city. That man's strength was astonishing, and he picked up several metal trunks and carried them down the stairs as though they were nothing. Liang greatly admired his strength, but when the laborer completed his job he asked for a very high fee. Liang asked him, "We had already decided on a price, why are you renegotiating?" The strong man replied, "If you do not pay the full price, why don't you carry the trunks back upstairs?" Liang did not argue with him and paid, but angrily jumped on the lorry. The lorry was five feet high, and Liang had leapt on without any effort, impressing the strong man. Liang later visited Master You and inquired after the man, describing his appearance and mannerisms in great detail. You replied that this man was a famous external martial artist whose body was trained as though it were forged from metal, and had Liang fought with him, he would have surely lost.

Master You was skilled at Yiquan and could attack an opponent with his back as well as his front. After Liang received the key teachings from You, he could use his presence to intimidate his opponent; it was like hypnosis. With a shout, he could stun his opponent—what a great ability to have when fighting!

Liang was from Nanhai and was older than You by a year. At that time he was working at the Asia Company as an accountant, and was addicted to Zhan Zhuang. After coming back from work, he would go to his room and close the door and windows and take off his shirt and practice shirtless, stating that he was testing the reactions of his body.

After coming to Hong Kong, he would often practice Zhan Zhuang at the Botanical Gardens. One time it was raining and, placing the books that he was carrying on his head, he continued to practice until the thunder startled him. Zhan Zhuang is the secret training for Xing Yi Quan, and for a beginner it is not advisable to practice in the rain, as one's pores are open when training and it is easy for the damp and cold to enter the body. However, after one has mastered the art, it is necessary to train in the rain and wind to see if one is able to resist it.

Liang once sparred with Tian Jiao Lin's disciple Ye Da Mi, and they later became good friends. Liang felt that Tian Jiao Lin's Taiji had the true transmission. He also praised Yang Chen Pu's student Zhang Manqing, saying that he was sufficiently loose and he had good kung fu.

LIUHEBAFA (LHBF)

Guoshu had a period of popularity after the Jing Wu Association started promoting it. The Liuhebafa master Wu Yi Hui had just arrived in Shanghai, and was on friendly terms with Wang Xiang Zhai. With the help of Wang, he improved his method of boxing, adding in Xinyi methods. As there were many similarities with his boxing, Liang was interested in Wu's style, and thus began to study under him. From the time that Liang started studying with You, he placed extreme importance on studying the body methods, and learned a set of Liuhebafa.

Liang was tall and thin, and was very nimble. He had an affinity with the martial arts and was gifted with intelligence. When studying Eagle Claw and Shaolin, he was able to pick them up right away and he had more than 30 years of training. Under the tutelage of You in Xinyi Zhan Zhuang, he was able to become an inner disciple in three years. It was Wu who called Liang "The Lark," and he was able to learn Liuhebafa in just a few months.

When Liang was training in Shaolin, he especially looked down on Taiji, as he had doubts about its practicality due to its softness. After studying Yiquan with You, he began to see Taiji in a different light, and appreciate its intricacies. As few people really understood the secrets of Taiji, so few people could actually put it into practice. From looking down on it to earnestly studying Taiji, this change had a lot to do with his relationship with Tian Jiao Lin, his acquaintance with Wu Jian Quan, and the fact that he highly praised Xu Zhiyi's cultivation and ability to explain. Due to the fact that could understand a form by just looking at it, and his study of books, he was able to become proficient in Taiji without having had any teacher. He liked to teach Yang Taiji and disliked Wu Taiji.

LEAVING HIS TEACHERS TO COME SOUTH TO HONG KONG

As Liang Zi Peng had garnered a deep understanding of boxing methods, he wanted to promote Yiquan Zhan Zhuang and Liuhebafa. Due to the nature of the times, as control of the mainland changed hands to the Communists, he bid farewell to You Peng Xi. As Master You was a famous doctor, the mainland did not allow him to leave the country. You gave Liang 600 silver dollars to subsidize his journey, but Liang refused his money, saying he could pay for everything himself. As Liang was not rich, You had helped him many times in the past. You stated, "Once you arrive in Hong Kong, you have to make my Yiquan famous." Upon this Liang took his leave of You.

Liang relied on trading as his profession; his wife was originally the daughter of a millionaire. Upon reaching Hong Kong, he did not openly try to attract students. He took a job as a clerk in the Oriental Cloth Company with a salary of 6000 Hong Kong dollars. However, Liang did not forget You's instruction and intended to demonstrate the power of Yiquan. At that time the Lingnam Group and Taiji Group were the most prominent, and Yiquan Zhan Zhuang and Liuhebafa had not yet made an appearance. Assessing the situation, Liang made a special effort to seek out masters and make friends, to promote his own reputation.

Once Liang had arrived in Hong Kong he treated every martial arts visitor as a VIP. Every time he sparred he would immediately throw the opponent backwards, and rarely would he injure them.

Although he had been one of the four heavenly protectors of the Shanghai Jing Wu Association, once he had come to Hong Kong he did not enter the Hong Kong Jing Wu at all. Even when official invitations came in the mail, he respectfully declined.

Even though he had studied martial arts for many years, his hands remained soft and white as a baby's hands, and even during the depths of winter they gave off warmth, and his eyes were like electricity. The pupils and whites of his eyes were clearly delineated without any muddy mixing, and the pupils were small but the eyeballs were clear and brilliant. His body moved like a snake and his feet moved like tornados. When moving and twisting his waist, his stomach was as though it was full of water, emitting a gurgling sound.

LIANG SPREADS YIQUAN TO THE SOUTH

Liang came to Hong Kong in 1946, and was a manager at the Chunyuen Import–Export Company and the Oriental Cloth Company. Zhang Jun Ting, with whom he had studied Eagle Claw in Shanghai, and Wu Jian Quan's disciple, Zheng Rong Guang, were especially close to him, and knowing that he taught Liuhebafa went to study with him as friends and received his true transmission.

Zhang Jun Ting was a bureaucrat in the Department of Social Services, and held a high position in the Jing Wu Association. So when he was free he studied Liuhebafa diligently with good results.

After Zheng Rong Guang had been introduced to Liang, he once bumped into him on the tram. Liang mentioned that he would like to try his technique, so they went home together to practice. With one push, the curtains fell down, and one foot of the bed was broken, so for the rest of his life Zheng followed Liang in studying Yiquan. After Zheng Rong Guang had studied Yiquan and combined this with Wu Taiji, he learned the skill of being able to take any punch to the stomach, and was able to use his Qi to heal people.

From this point on the people who especially admired Liuhebafa included Sun Dit, Tang Hong Hoi, and Li Ying Arng. Both Sun Dit and Lee Ying Arng were inheritors of the true transmission in Taiji Quan, having studied under Chen Weiming and Dong Ying Jie. Lee Ying Arng was a disciple of the Wudang Sword Grandmaster Guo Qifeng, so both of them had a very profound basis in the internal arts. They both went to study with Liang at the same time, and asked him to transmit the teachings of Liuhebafa. Unfortunately, due to work commitments, Liang could not teach during the day, so he invited them to learn in the evenings at his house. They were very dedicated and came up to his house every day.

In 1953, Chen Chufan, another disciple of Wu Yi Hui, also known as Yiren, came to Hong Kong with the intention to go on to Singapore, but remained in Hong Kong for a period of time. He also wanted to learn Liuhebafa and studied under Liang, and other students of Liang would also ask for his advice.

Tang Hong Hoi originally studied under the tutelage of Yang Shou Chung and Dong Ying Jie, and later changed his allegiance to Liang to study Yiquan and Liuhebafa. Liang lived in a building on Hennessy Road in Wanchai, which was very spacious and suitable for martial arts, so he would teach Liuhebafa and Yiquan there. Lee Ying Arng, after learning from Liang, also taught many students.

Later, Liang's classmate, Chan Yick Yan (陳亦人), came and taught LHBF in Hong Kong. He had a gimp leg and could never assume a low stance and larger movements. He had a monk classmate who also came to Hong Kong. He learnt at the same time with Chan Yik Yan, Liang Zi Peng, Yin Tien-Hsiung (尹天雄), and Leung Qi Zhong (梁啟忠). The monk was Peng Xue Qiu, also called Guang Zhi (彭雪秋－釋名廣智). He stopped practicing martial arts and concentrated on Buddhism. He died at the temple on Lantau Island.

Wu Yihui (吳翼翬) was a Manchu, tiny in stature. Some said he was very strong. Once at a dinner party in Shanghai, he threw Leung Zi Pang head over heels while both were sitting down.

Master Lee Ying Arng talking about Yiquan on September 15, 1968

A RECORD OF LIANG ZI PENG'S ORAL STORIES

After Wang Xiang Zhai, only You Peng Xi had the true transmission. He would arrange to be attacked by three people in a triangular formation, with one attacking his back. Master You would be able to throw the person off just by using the power of shaking his back.

Every time there was a request to enter into a Western boxing competition, it would be Liang or Ma who would take part. Liang would train Zhan Zhuang diligently, and during the winter he would stand in his room and when he had finished the floor would be covered with sweat stains.

One time in Shanghai, Wu Jian Quan was pushing hands with You Peng Xi and You marginally had the upper hand. However, Wu declared that he had won. Ma was so angry that he announced that if Wu ever entered Jing Wu again he would personally beat him. At that point, Wu decided to make a trip to the south.

Liang once made a trip to Taiwan and the 300-pound Zhang Zhi Fan was teaching Taiji in the park. Dragging Liang over to demonstrate, he was easily lifted up in one movement by Liang. The next day he waited with his disciples at the gate of Liang's residence, seemingly wanting revenge, but actually he and his disciples wanted Liang to take them as his students. Liang hurriedly stated that he was not staying long; he was happy to give pointers but would be unable to take them as his disciples.

Han Xing Huan was a fervent Christian, but this was a problem on the mainland, so he moved to Hong Kong. He contacted Lee Ying Arng, who took him to see Liang. It was Han's first visit to Hong Kong and he had hoped to promote Dachengquan, but was unable to advertise. Liang and Lee conferred about this and put together some money for him to open a studio. It was Lee's student Jiang Qiu who took two pieces of scrap wood and whittled them into two long poles and, after ferrying these poles to Han's studio, enabled him to teach the long staff.

Liang said that Han had one vertebra that had contracted TB and was very weak. If anyone pushed hands with him they had to be very careful so as not to harm his body.

Lau Kum, who was resident in Hong Kong, once said that Liang's hands were very thin and easy to snap. Liang gave him his hand and, with one twist, caused Lau Kum so much pain that he collapsed to the ground.

LIANG'S THREE TREASURES

The kung fu taught by Liang was called "Southern Yiquan," and his Zhan Zhuang, Dun Yao, and Tuo Yao were called the "Three Treasures." When he taught, both principles and applications were taught at the same time: when students asked questions, he would first demonstrate using his power, so that they could feel the energy, and then he would follow with an explanation. When he had free time he also liked to go to the park to watch others practicing kung fu. If there were any aspects that were wrong he would enthusiastically go forth to correct them.

When teaching, he did not ask for fees. When he taught in Shanghai's Xiang Yang Park, his students included Li Run, Rong Li Quan, and Fang Bo Cheng, and many followed him to Hong Kong to study. His disciples included: Lee Ying Arng, Li Pei Xuan, Xiang Tun Mao, Deng Xiang Hai, Chen Zhen Yi, Zhang Jun Ting, Cheng Rong Guang, Liu Jing Zhi, Sun Dit, Liu Tui, Cheng Jiao Ji, Hu Yuan Huan, Hu Guang Chi, Lu Xiu Dong, Chen Yi Rong, Wei Hua, Zhi Sheng, C S Tang, Cheng Jin Pei, Zhang Jin Zhi, and Wong Ming, among others.

Grandmaster Liang Zi Peng died on May 1, 1974, in Grantham Hospital, at the age of 78.

Yiquan practitioners: Lee Yuen, unknown, Master Liang Zi Peng, Chan Yuet Sun, Lam Zhi Sang and Ngai Wah

SPECIAL FEATURES OF LIANG ZI PENG'S MOVING STANCE

1. One's eyes must give off electricity like a leopard.
2. The whole body must express peng jin, strong balloon power. If there are other pedestrians they will be pushed off the side of the road.
3. The chin should be tucked in; the throat must not be exposed.
4. When moving quickly there also has to be power, combined with the fierce emission of sound.
5. Fingers are all curved because of Eagle Claw iron finger practice.

LIANG IN HONG KONG

Liang Zi Peng learnt Yiquan from You Peng Xi. He brought his classmate Ma Cheng Xin (馬成鑫) to learn under You. He also learnt from LHBF master Wu Yi Hui (吳翼翬). He learnt only for a short time and introduced Liang Qi Zhong (梁啟忠) to learn from Wu.

During his stay with You, they practiced in the courtyard of You's clinic. Liang said Madam You Ou Yang Min was a very strong and powerful woman. She always practiced push hand with them.

Every Saturday night, You would lead them to the temple to attend the gathering of Tantra teaching, a form of Tibetan Buddhism. Here, You developed his technique of "Empty Force." They also practiced the Prostration—the antidote to pride (叩大頭, 即大禮拜). Liang brought this exercise to Hong Kong students as a conditioning training.

According to Chan Yuet Sun, Liang Zi Peng talked about the Ling Kong Jin practice of You: he would hold a roll of newspaper, and if he swiped you with it you would lose balance and fall down. If you tried to follow him, he would just turn the side of his clothing a little bit, and you would fall on the ground immediately.

Tantra 密宗

Tantra is that Asian body of beliefs and practices which, working from the principle that the universe we experience is nothing other than the concrete manifestation of the divine energy of the Godhead that creates and maintains that universe, seeks to ritually appropriate and channel that energy, within the human microcosm, in creative and emancipatory ways.

There are three main schools of Tantra in India: Mishra Tantra, Kaula Tantra, and Samaja Tantra.

GATHERING OF YIQUAN MASTERS IN HONG KONG

LIANG ZI PENG'S TEACHING

Liang had to travel for his work between Nan Jing and Shanghai. He taught Bagua Zhang at Xiang Yang Park (上海襄陽公園), Shanghai. Liang came to Hong Kong in 1946 because his company, Oriental Yarn Factory, started a branch there.

Liang taught in Jordan Path on Kowloon side. He taught students free of charge because he had a top post in a factory and did not need the money. He corrected the postures of Taiji Quan and taught the students how to use power. He asked his students to call him Mr. Liang instead of teacher or Sifu; he said this was a more polite and modern title for a teacher. There were no rankings of his students. Also, the students of his students could come directly to him for lessons.

Liang taught many famous students, including, among others:

Lee Ying Ngor	李英昂
Lee Yun	李潤
Lee Pui Yuen	李佩弦

Yung Lai Chuen	容禮泉
Heng Tim Mui	香添茂
Tang Heng Hoi	鄧香海
Chan Chun Yee	陳震儀
Cheung Chun Ting	張俊庭
Cheng Wing Kwong	鄭榮光
Suen Zhi	孫秩
Liu Dui	劉堆
Hu Yun Zhui	胡雲焯
Hu Guang Chi	胡廣池
Lo Sau Tung	盧秀東
Fong Pak Sing	方伯誠
Chan Yuet Sun	陳乙燊
Ngai Wah	魏華
Tang Cheong Shing	鄧昌成
Lam Jit Sang	林植生
Ko Man Yuen	高文遠
Cheng Kam Pui	鄭錦培
Zhang Jin Chi	張錦熾
Huang Ming	黃明

The teaching of Liang in Yiquan is simple. People called it Liang's Three Treasures:

1. The three stances of Zhan Zhuang: the Huan Yuan Stance, the Health Stance, and the Santi Stance
2. Dun Yao
3. The two techniques of Tuo Yao: Tuo Yao and Cuo Yao
    a. Moving steps and Test Sounds
    b. Push hand.

His emphasis was on real contact, and this resulted in his students being upgraded and becoming famous in fighting very quickly.

In a lesson with Liang, I said to him, "The Taiji Quan practitioners nowadays are so weak, it seems that nobody is a real fighter." Liang replied, "No! At least, what I saw and realized is that Tian Zhao Lin (田兆麟) is an existing high-ranking real Taiji fighter."

Group photo with Master Liang on January 27, 1970

Group photo with Master Liang on November 14, 1972

Master Liang
Zi Peng

Master Jiang Xin Shan, Liang's
Bagua Zhang teacher

Master Chen Zi Zheng, Liang's Eagle Claw teacher

Master Chen Zi Zheng, fist posture

Master Wu Yi Hui, LHBF

Master Wu Yi Hui's fist posture

Photograph given to C S Tang by Lee Ying Arng

Yao Zong Xun and Chan Yick Yan in Shanghai

Liang Zi Peng and Chan Yick Yan in Hong Kong

Wu's student, Peng Xue Qiu, on Lantau Island

Wu's student, Liang Qi Zhong, and C S Tang in Shanghai, 2007

Chapter 3

BRUCE LEE AND YIQUAN

INTRODUCTION

Bruce Lee was born in November 1940 in San Francisco, the son of Lee Hoi Chuen (李海泉), a singer and movie actor of Cantonese Opera. His family name was Lee Juan Fan, meaning "Shaking Foreign Country." One year later, the family returned to Kowloon in Hong Kong. At the age of five, young Bruce appeared in children's roles in minor films including *The Birth of Mankind* and *Fu Gui Fu Yun*. At the age of 12, Bruce attended La Salle College, and was later beaten up by a street gang, which inspired him to take up martial arts training. Bruce also did Cha-Cha dancing, and at the age of 18 won a major dance championship in Hong Kong.

When Bruce was in Hong Kong he studied Choy Li Fut with Chen Nian Bo, the Jing Wu sets and Tan Tui with Xiao Han Sheng, Wing Chun with Yip Man, and last of all Yiquan with Liang Zi Peng.

At that time Liang would teach in King's Park in Ho Man Tin. Walking along the path and stopping at each student, he would correct them in sequence.

Bruce's father was also practicing in the park and studying Taiji under Liang and was on friendly terms with Liang. He knew Liang was good at fighting and one day said to Liang, "My son has just come back from overseas and loves kung fu, please instruct him." Later he took Bruce to the park to see Liang, and Liang saw that this young man was eager to learn, so asked him to stand in Zhan Zhuang while Liang was discussing boxing and fajin with the other students and throwing them into the air. Thus Bruce was able to appreciate the power of Yiquan.

Bruce's father knew that Liang had a powerful internal martial art, so he urged his son to learn from him. Bruce was also interested and eager to learn from this powerful man.

One day, Lee brought Bruce to visit at Liang's house. At that time, Liang was lecturing on the secrets of internal and external martial arts. In this lecture, Bruce heard many things which he had never heard before. Liang talked about the many different techniques and stories of martial arts that he had seen and knew in Shanghai. Bruce became more and more interested in his speech. However, Liang insisted that Bruce must first throw away all that he had learnt before, and change his strength from external to internal. Of course, Bruce was not willing to do so. But he always remembered Liang's philosophy. Bruce often attended Liang's student gatherings and he assimilated many principles concerning the secrets of internal and external martial arts.

When Liang taught, he did not care about the forms, but was intent on imparting the principles. First one had to have the frame and then have explosive power. He encouraged his students to study the manuals, to understand the principles and improve their cultivation. He told them to avoid the streets, the brawls, and fighting, and stressed that boxing was one of the arts of China. Liang taught all sorts of people: whether they studied Taiji or southern styles, he used the principles of Yiquan to correct them, while explaining the applications at the same time, and used their own movements to throw them backwards. He was very different from many teachers at the time, who only taught the forms and not how to apply the movements.

This enlightened method, which encapsulated all forms of boxing—and was able to knock people down like "breaking mountains" and "pouring out the sea," and throw people back several feet—greatly impressed Bruce and expanded his horizons.

Bruce later returned to San Francisco. He studied at the University of Washington in Seattle. He investigated Karate, boxing, Jujits, and Nunchaku. He sought out his own fighting theory and style. He finally developed a fighting system of Jeet Kune Do, meaning the way of Intercepting Fist.

On July 20, 1973, on waking and getting ready to go to the office, I heard on the radio that Bruce had been rushed to hospital and had passed away. This news shocked me, as it also shocked most citizens of Hong Kong. People could not accept this news. Bruce was a great star and felt close to me because we had learnt from the same master. I can just say, "To treasure the person and things beside you" (珍惜你身邊的人及事).

THE YIQUAN ABSORBED BY BRUCE LEE

Although the time Bruce spent learning Yiquan was short, the philosophy of Yiquan deeply influenced the framework and principles of his Jeet Kune Do.

1. There is no taolu; any sequence or movement can be used

The core of Yiquan is not to use any set methods, and to overcome the opponent in an instant. Thus the body has to be trained and prepared to a high level of fighting technique, with the ability to utilize explosive power at any time. One can react and counter-attack at any time, and one does not waste time on extraneous, flowery movements.

2. Search out one's own strengths, train appropriately, and set up one's own system

According to Liuhebafa, one has to be like a bee collecting pollen from a hundred flowers, taking the best of other schools and digesting them to become one's own.

3. Wu De (morality)

Do not waste your time being a rascal on the streets; one must have culture and refinement, one must study the ancients, and one must become a person with manners and dignity, be humble, self-controlled, and forgiving, and a master who enthusiastically helps others.

4. Search out one's identity

One must constantly reflect, stand, and experience the flow of Qi in the body, and understand the smallest changes in the muscles of the body, the impact of the external weather and environment on one's thoughts and emotions, seek movement in stillness, and calmly react to change.

5. Softness can overcome hardness

Only when the muscles are relaxed can one's movements be fast and react with explosive energy.

6. Throw the opponent several feet away

When Bruce studied martial arts in the past, it was to beat people. Yiquan uses the whole frame of the body to throw the opponent flying. This led Bruce to later try to make the opponent fly in both his movies and his teaching.

7. Utilize the whole body strength

In the past, Bruce would use his attack to cause the opponent pain, but began to understand the importance of full-body power through Yiquan. With the whole body framework, even if the opponent resists, the full-body power will rise up to break the opponent, leaving him with no way to block or deflect.

8. Jeet Kune

The principle of Yiquan is that if the opponent moves slightly, you will reach first and catch the opponent's movement, rendering him unable to use his strength, covering his entire body. Bruce later developed Jeet Kune Do which incorporated this principle.

9. Extend your hand

Extend your hands and do not retract; extend the hands fully to your opponent, and use your frame to block him. If you retract, you will lose your ability to defend.

10. Issue sound

Master Liang liked to issue sound when practicing fajin. Whether he was practicing Tuo Yao or Walking Step he would also issue sounds, and he would use different kinds of sequenced sounds to throw the opponent away. He would use his sound to augment his presence and intimidate. His disciple Sun Dit was very good at this. Bruce Lee also used his teaching in his movies.

11. Solid and real and not empty

Every time you attack, it needs to be accurate, brutal, and effective; it has to be a real attack and not a fake, flowery movement. Every movement has its use, and has to maintain balance and frame, using full power; it is practical and useful.

BRUCE'S SOURCE OF MARTIAL ARTS

Yip Man is commonly recognized as the teacher of Bruce Lee, but actually Bruce learnt from several teachers in Hong Kong. Written down in his biography, there were ten teachers from whom he learnt. In Hong Kong, the known teachers were his father, Shao Han Sheng (邵漢生) of Shaolin, Chen Nian Bo (陳年柏) of Choy Li Fut, and Liang Zi Peng (梁子鵬) of Yiquan.

His father, Lee Hoi Chuen (李海泉)

In Bruce's younger days, he often saw his father practicing a kind of slow-motion exercise in the garden. His father was a student of a famous master, Liang Zi Peng. His father liked to discuss books about the effectiveness of Taiji Quan with Bruce. When he had free time, Bruce simulated the Taiji Quan of his father. He always followed his father to the park to practice Taiji Quan. He was impressed by the theories of how slowness can win over quickness and how Taiji Quan can cope with everything under the universe, Yin and Yang, the five elements, and the eight diagrams. Also, the idea that Taiji Quan can cure many diseases, and grant you a long life.

Yip Man (葉問) and Wing Chun (詠春拳)

During his stay in Hong Kong, Bruce was introduced by his friend William Cheung (Zhang Zhuo Qing, 張卓慶) to Yip Man in order to practice Wing Chun. He always went out with Huang Chun Liang (黃淳樑) to engage in street fights and roof fights. He gained many real fight experiences at that time.

Bruce believed firmly that, to win in a fight, one must make use of the shortest distance in attack.

He later learnt Choy Li Fut from Chen Nian Bo (陳年柏) in Wong Tai Sin Park. One day, Bruce went to visit friends in Wong Tai Sin. When passing a grassy field Bruce saw an old man teaching people. Bruce challenged him and was knocked down. He then practiced with him.

Shao Han Sheng (邵漢生) and Cang Zhou Shaolin (滄州少林)

Shao Han Sheng was an old member of Guangzhou Jing Wu Association (Ching Woo Association). In 1920, he entered the Association, learning Cang Zhou Shaolin (稔手拳) from the founder's son Huo Dong Ge (霍東閣, son of Huo Yuen Jia 霍元甲), learning Eagle Claw (鷹爪) from Chen Zi Zheng (陳子正), and Luo Han Quan (羅漢拳) from Sun Yu Feng, "King of Broadsword of Five Provinces" (五省万王孫玉峰). Shao also learnt Hung Gar (洪家) from Feng Rong Biao (馮榮標), alias Fisher Can (賣魚燦), and Choy Li Fut (蔡李佛) from Kong Chang (孔昌). His styles were different from existing popular lineages. In his Hung Gar, apart from the usual forms such as Gong Zi Fu Hu and Fu He Shuang Xing (工字伏虎拳, 虎鶴雙形拳), he had special forms including Xiao Luo Han, Yun Tian Xing, and Chuan Xin Zhang (小羅漢, 運天星, 穿心掌).

In 1950, Shao was employed by a movie company in Hong Kong. He acted as producer and fighting instructor and also participated as kung fu actor in many famous Chinese movies of the Huang Fei Hong series. Guan De Xing (關德興), Shi Jian (石堅), and Shao became a famous triangle in the 99 movies of that series. His movies included:

> *Wong Fei-hung at a Boxing Match* 黃飛鴻擂臺比武
>
> *Wong Fei-hung's Fight in Foshan* 黃飛鴻大鬧佛山
>
> *Wong Fei-hung and the Courtesan's Boat Argument* 黃飛鴻花艇風雲
>
> *Wong Fei-hung's Battle at Shuangmendi* 黃飛鴻大戰雙門底.

In 1959, before Bruce left for America, Bruce's father was an actor and familiar with Shao, and Bruce addressed Shao as "uncle." Bruce knew that Shao was a graduate from Jing Wu Association, so he insisted on learning Jing Wu forms from him.

One day, Bruce brought Shao to a coffee shop and asked to exchange skills with him. He said he had no money to pay for the lessons; the condition was that Bruce would teach him Cha-Cha and he would teach Bruce kung fu. Bruce had won a Cha-Cha championship in Hong Kong. Shao agreed, feeling that this would be easy; they then started to exchange techniques in the park at Kowloon side. Bruce took only three nights to learn the whole form of Jie Quan (節拳) and the 12 series of Tan Tui (譚腿). Bruce built a good foundation of Northern leg kicking techniques at this time. He also demonstrated several movements of Jie Quan in his movie *The Return of the Dragon* (猛龍過江). However, Shao, at the age of 70, was still confused and had not even learnt the simple steps of Cha-Cha!

In 1972, Shao taught in the students club of Hong Kong University and trained many good students. Apart from teaching kung fu during his later age, in 1980 he created a combination form of six different styles, including Jing Wu forms, Northern Mantis, Eagle Claw, Hung Gar, Choy Li Fut, and Luo Han Quan. The form was called the "Eighteen Postures of Jin Gang."

Bruce pushing hands with his father

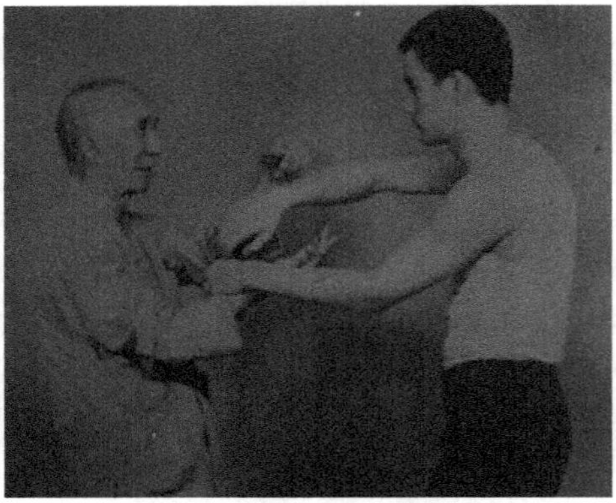

Bruce with Yip Man practicing Wing Chun

Shao Han Sheng

Shao Han Sheng, Bruce, and Shi Jian

Hu Feng, Bruce, Sheng Jun Mian, and Shao Han Sheng

Guan De Xing, Shao Han Sheng, and martial artists

Master Shac Han Sheng performing Eagle Claw style

Master Shao Han Sheng performing Hung Gar at age 81

Master Shao Han Sheng presenting a prize to C S Tang after the Wushu competition of 1992

Liang Zi Peng

Liang did not teach openly and did not operate a studio. He taught his followers in the park on Sundays. Liang always wore formal dress properly. Even when he came to the park to push hand with his students, he still wore a tie and pure white shirt. He was tall and slim and wore eyeglasses. This was for Bruce a world away from the lower-class teachers dressed in their singlets, who were always swearing and never far away from alcohol and cigarettes. His appearance made him into a "kung fu idol" that Bruce was deeply impressed with.

When Liang taught students in the park, he explained clearly and he continuously showed applications. This kind of teaching is quite distinct from other Taiji Quan teachers, who only emphasize the health aspects. Once Liang made contact with the learners, they could not resist his force, and were all thrown far away. The news spread, and many people came to learn from him. They had never seen a teacher as powerful as him.

Students came from every part of Hong Kong to listen to his teaching. After the lesson, they would go to a nearby Chinese restaurant to have lunch—"Yumcha." Then they would go to Liang's house to continue the lesson.

Bruce also often went with other students to Liang's house, which was number 18 Austin Road in Jordan. Liang loved to move, and before they could make themselves comfortable, Liang would ask them to get up and do Zhan Zhuang. As soon as he touched them, he pushed them onto the sofa. Lee was intoxicated by the speed at which his hands shot out; without being able to settle, he was already flying backwards and seeing stars.

Liang told Lee that he had been taught by You in the same way. First he had to give up each movement of the external styles, and begin again from Zhan Zhuang, converting the muscular resistance into true jin, before he could reach the next level of martial arts. Just like a glass which is full, if you pour more water into it, it will overflow. If the water is muddy and unclear, it is imperative to pour out the polluted water before one can pour in the clear water. In order to understand the philosophy, one has to study the classics, of which *Zhuang Zi* and *Lao Zi* were the best.

When Liang came to Hong Kong, he brought along many martial arts books; he loved to read them, and would correct them using a red pen. He gave two books, *Orthodox Zimen Style* (子門真宗) and Chen Naizhou's *Boxing Manual* (萇乃周拳譜), to Bruce, telling him to study them diligently. Eventually Bruce went back to the United States and never returned the books.

Liang Zi Peng performing Liuhebafa in Hong Kong, 1968

Jordan Path, where Bruce learnt Yiquan from Liang

Sun Zhi performing burst sound and free movements

Chapter 4

MY WAY OF YIQUAN

THE INFLUENCE OF MY FATHER

I started learning martial arts when I was young. My father, who had learned martial arts in the Qing Wu Association (精武體育會) in Hong Kong, influenced me quite a lot. He also learned Dong Ying Jie's Taiji Quan from Wong Huen (黃煊). He started teaching me Yi Jin Jing (易筋經). This strengthened my tendons and bones at a young age. These exercises were single movements and stretches. We trained those postures with power for a minute, then changed to the following movements. He also taught me the 12 series of Tan Tui (譚腿).

One particular Qigong he taught me was the Sun Qigong. He led me to an open area before sunrise, to then gaze at the sun without blinking as it rose in the sky. He said he had been looking at the sun for so many years that now, during the cold afternoons, he could still look at the sun and see its middle circle, whereas normal people will only see a bright light.

He also taught me an eyesight training technique. Every morning, he took out a basin of water and put his head into it. He breathed deeply with his nose audibly. His eyes were not allowed to close, and they had to stare at the bubbles without blinking. By adopting this method, I could train the staring power of my eyesight and also strong exhalations.

He had met Shaolin teachers and practiced different weapons and Dim Mak. He did not practice a lot, but whenever he did practice he showed strong power and gaze. So far in all my encounters I have only seen two persons with such sharp eyesight: they were Master Liang Zi Peng and Madam Wang Yu Fang.

When I was 12, there were many American naval ships coming to Hong Kong for the protection of Taiwan. When the battleships came, the naval officers, wearing uniform, came to Wanchai for drinks. They always created trouble when they were drunk. One night, after dinner, we were resting outside our house, and along came three American naval officers. They were holding bottles of beer and shouting, and were grasping a girl and laughing. Many neighbors gathered and were very angry. They asked the officers to release the girl. But the officers laughed loudly. Then my father stepped forward and grasped a hand of one of the officers, which made him release the girl. Then another of the officers came forward and tried to strike my father's face with a right-handed punch. My father just moved a step aside to avoid the punch, bent and held the man's body, and threw him over his back. The man fell on the ground, his whole face bleeding. The other two officers were so shocked that they just stood there and dared not move. All the neighbors clapped. This scene has remained in my mind since then.

My father left to me several secret handwritten manuscripts. They are *72 Q&A of Ophthalmology* (眼科七十二問答), manuscripts on Dim Mak (江湖一點穴), old martial arts books of Wu-Style Taiji Quan (吳家太極拳, 吳公藻), and *Application of Yang-Style Taiji Quan* (楊式太極拳使用法, 董虎嶺). These encouraged me to collect martial arts books when I grew up.

THE INFLUENCE OF NOVELS AND COMIC BOOKS

At that time, there were several famous martial arts novels by Jin Yung and Louis Cha (金庸). How Cheung Mu Ji (張無忌), who learnt from Zhang San Feng (張三丰), the originator of Taiji Quan, was very interesting. He hid and watched Master Zhang practicing the Taiji Sword, and when asked to demonstrate what he could remember, he forgot it all. Cheung said that he finally understood it because he did not aim at the forms but concentrated on the concept and techniques.

Another novel is by Ling Wu Chung (令狐沖), showing all the important techniques from the drawings of Dok Koo Kau Bai (獨孤求敗). But then his previous master would just practice Qi and could put the Qi into any technique or attack without forms. This became a separation into the Qi and Jin branches of those who emphasized Qi versus those who emphasized technique.

THE INFLUENCE OF ROOF STREET FIGHTING

I was born and raised in Wanchai district. The place where I grew up had a flat roof and was shared with many refugees from mainland China. After school, we always went to the roof to watch people practice martial arts there. There were two styles of martial arts taught in the district. One was the Seven Star Praying Mantis (七星螳螂) and the other was Hung Fat Pai (洪佛派). Of course, with two different martial arts taught in the same area, there was a lot of fighting then. I saw a lot of street fighting when I was young.

Li Zheng Po (黎正甫), a Choy Li Fut master, rented a room from our house. He was quite friendly with us. He showed me his fingers, all of which were of the same length. He practiced striking sand when he was young and all his fingers became the same length. When he struck his enemy, his palm looked like a shovel. He learnt this Dim Mak from his teacher, Tan San (譚三). During his whole life he used this technique only twice as he felt it was too harmful to the human body.

THE INFLUENCE OF BAGUA ZHANG

I learnt Bagua Zhang from Master Ho Ho Choy (何可才) in Hong Kong. He never asked what you had learnt before. He liked clever students who only needed to be taught once and did not need to come back for the same lesson again. However, he disliked those students who had learned Taiji Quan or Yiquan earlier. He felt that they came with weakness from Taiji and over-aggressiveness from Yiquan. He liked other internal martial arts. On every Saturday afternoon, when we practiced Bagua weapons, we discussed quite a lot. He was always glad to show us Yang Taiji and Hebei Xing Yi that he had learned in Tianjin. He taught us the essential requirements of Five Elements Fists and the Twelve Animals of Xing Yi, which we followed and practiced.

Our relationship was like father and son. Every Chinese New Year, we went to his home to celebrate (拜年).

THE INFLUENCE OF SOUTHERN-STYLE YIQUAN

Yiquan was my first martial arts training, which I started in 1968. I was very much steeped in the books of martial arts and hoped one day to be able to practice Chinese martial arts, especially internal martial arts. I learnt from Ngai Wah and Chan Yuet Sun. Chan was a herbalist and he operated a clinic where he taught Taiji, Liuhebafa (LHBF), Xing Yi Quan, and Yiquan in the evening. At that time, we practiced what was called Zhan Zhuang (站樁). This included two main front stances and two side stances. Then we started some footwork called "moving step," followed by two kinds of Test Power, that is, up and down Dun Yie and front and backward Tou Yie, accompanied by a two-man exercise called Jai Yie. We also practiced a conditioning exercise on the ground, called Kau Dai Tou. After that, we used our skeleton to fit into push hand. Our push hand was fierce, always breaking things such as the sofa, mirror, glass, and shoes. Apart from stances, we practiced Yang Taiji Quan to relax our joints and muscles. We practiced LHBF in order to improve flexibility, fighting techniques, and power.

Chan had a deep passion for martial arts. He worked very hard, and took every opportunity to train. He treated me as his son, took me to watch movies, Australian wrestling, and boxing matches, and enabled me to meet martial arts masters. However, he ate quite a lot and slept very little. Every time when we went to the cinema, he fell asleep just after the preview and then woke up when the movie had nearly finished. He fell asleep when he sat on the bus. At this time he contracted a disease which required the removal of one of his kidneys. After recuperation, he moved to Portland, USA. However, he worked so hard in America that a few years later he had apoplexy and became bed-ridden. He wrote to me, and lamented that he had too much good food, too little rest, and not enough relaxation.

Later I was introduced to Master Liang Zi Peng (梁子鵬), the man who introduced Yiquan to Hong Kong. Master Liang was a successful businessman, holding a high position in the Nam Yang Cotton Mill Factory. Being quite well off, he taught students for free. He was a Cantonese and had worked in Shanghai. He was very famous for Eagle's Claw Fist which he had learnt from Great Master Chen Zi Zheng (陳子正). He later discovered to his dismay that his external martial arts skills were no match for Yiquan Master You Pang Hei, so both he and his kung fu brother, Ma Cheng Xin (馬成鑫), learnt from Master You to improve their skills. Later he practiced LHBF under Master Ng Wei Fai. Liang was a very open-minded person. He did not allow his students to call him "Sifu." He said his Yiquan teacher Mr. Yau had insisted that students call him "Mr. Yau," so in the same way all his students addressed him as "Mr. Liang."

Not long after, I started my journey of learning martial arts widely. I learnt Southern Praying Mantis in the Botanic Gardens, where I met many kung fu friends. They practiced different kinds of martial arts and we always exchanged ideas and knowledge. We formed our first club, which was called the "Chinese Martial Arts Research Club." Then I practiced Gao-style Bagua Zhang under Master Ho Ho Choy. I also practiced Ching Wu forms in the Southern Sports Society and Wu-style Taiji Quan in recreation centers. Several Yiquan books were published at that time, and the publisher invited me to write testimonials for the books.

When Ian Fok invited Yao's brother to Hong Kong, Yiquan began to flourish here. Fok formed the Hong Kong Yiquan Society and invited more masters to come to Hong Kong. We therefore had the chance to attend classes and seminars, where I met Yu Yung Lian and Wang Yuk Fang (Wang Xiang Zhai's daughter). During the welcome party, I met Suen Tit, Master Liang's student, again. He had retired and had much free time. He called me up and asked if he could teach me. So I practiced together with Miss Luk Wai Sum, a doctor who had a deep passion for Chinese martial arts, under Suen. He taught us Yiquan and LHBF. When Master Wang Yuk Fang came to Hong Kong again, I practiced under her and was awarded a Certificate in Yiquan coaching. At that time, I felt I had a duty to promote Yiquan.

Another guest teacher was Han Si Huang (韓嗣煌). He came several times to Hong Kong to teach us. He was very knowledgeable in theories and techniques. We trained hard under him. We suffered much from holding the Double Ball Stance for at least 45 minutes; this was the only stance taught to us and then practiced by us. He said that, if we could not pass this test, it would be meaningless for us to continue the practice, because our power could not come out and our skeleton would not be fixed and strong.

Then Li Jiang Yu came. Master Li was a Muslim; he practiced Yiquan with the founder of Yiquan for 40 years. His system was simple and solid: he required his students to do hard and real work instead of talking about empty theories. He taught a class in Hong Kong which I attended. One night, when he corrected my simple initial holding posture and touched my arms and elbows, I felt hot Qi flowing from my elbows to my hands. That shocked me. Then I realized my Yiquan had reached a certain level and everything became clear to me. I knew I had met an extraordinary master of Yiquan. Li is also a Taoist master of Jok Yau For (祝由科), and believed in fate (緣份). So he accepted me as his disciple and we had a ceremony with one of my Yiquan brothers, Tang Sin Ping, a herbalist. I traveled a lot to Beijing and Tianjin to improve my Yiquan and Bagua Zhang. I listened to, tested, and practiced with this honorable master.

Timeline of Master Charles Li Jiang Yu

1924	Born in Beijing, China.
1930	Studied Xing Yi Quan and Chinese painting, and was educated in kindergarten for two years.
1933	Attended primary school for six years.
1939	Studied English in Beijing American School for six years.
1942	Worked in Dai Chung Bank for eight years (beginning while still at school).
1943	Studied Yiquan Stance from Master Wang Xiang Zhai for 20 years.
1946	Introduced by Master Wang to study "Tao Style—Joe Yu School Medical Qigong" under Tin Jin Bo.
1950	Joined the Chinese Calligraphy and Painting Association as a member.
1954	Attended the Chinese Factory of Painting for six years.
1960	Joined the Chinese Medicine Research Institute—Qigong branch.
1985	Retired and taught Yiquan Stance, Chinese calligraphy, and painting in Europe, America, and Hong Kong.
2014	Passed away in Beijing.

Liang Zi Peng's system was simple and could easily develop power. It explained how to make use of the energy generated from static stances. Then we progressed immediately to push hand and fist dance.

Among the visits and teaching of masters from Beijing, I could see that the Yao brothers had an aggressive attacking style and emphasis on punches.

Madam Wang Yu Fang was known for her complete and well-organized system, including massage at the end and her tenacious (韌) and powerful Test Power. Her strong push hand controlled opponents easily.

Yu Yong Nian discovered that power came from both legs. Once you generate the power from the legs, you have succeeded half-way already.

Han Si Huang was another master who had thought carefully about the development of Yiquan. He was good in endurance and the fixing of postures. He knew the importance of correctness against the stances, how to achieve explosive Yiquan punches, calculating distance, and attack tactics.

Li Jiang Yu brought to me the importance of strong stretches, thunder sounds, and the techniques of push hand.

All masters have their own principles and special techniques. I have tried to absorb and integrate and consolidate them into a core system. I have collected facts, evidence, and stories of legends and ancient masters. These have helped me to know the correctness and path of learning and practice. I still want to carry forward the principles of the founder—simple and effective training.

C S Tang practicing the Santi Stance of Yiquan at the famous Big Cannon site where most Yiquan practitioners have stayed, 1968

C S Tang practicing spear at the roof of Wang Hon Fan's studio, 1969

Yiquan practitioners under the guidance of Liang Zi Peng, September 1968

Gao-style Bagua Zhang practitioners under Ho Ho Choy, 1969

With Madam Wang Yu Fang and Chang Zhi Lang in Hong Kong

With Yao Cheng Guang and Yao Cheng Rong in Hong Kong, 1988

With Yu Yong Nian at the latter's home in Beijing, April 5, 2001

With Han Si Huang and Suen Zhi, 1993

With Li Jiang Yu and Ian Fok

With Wang An Ping in Hong Kong

Yiquan conference in Beijing, 2000

Acting as Referee course instructor in HKCMAA

Sanda Referee course with Doctor Luk Wai Sum

Interviewed by CNN television about development of martial arts

Meeting overseas martial artists Dan Miller, Tim Cartmell, and Edward Hines, 1992

Teaching American students in Victoria Park, Hong Kong, 2004 and 2012

Teaching morning Taiji Quan and Yiquan classes in Hong Kong

YIQUAN, BAGUA ZHANG, AND TAIJI QUAN SEMINARS IN BARCELONA, SPAIN, 2006

YIQUAN, BAGUA ZHANG, AND TAIJI QUAN SEMINARS IN BARCELONA, SPAIN, 2007

YIQUAN FOR HEALTH AND COMBAT SEMINARS IN BARCELONA, SPAIN, 2008

LEADING STANDING MEDITATION IN SPAIN, 2008

HUN YUAN QIGONG AND WUDANG SWORD FIGHT SEMINAR IN BARCELONA, SPAIN, DECEMBER 2012

Disciples gathering in Hong Kong, 2006

Students gathering in Hong Kong, 2007

Acting as Judge in Yiquan push hand gathering, December 2005

A visit to Yao Cheng Rong's Beijing Yiquan Academy, 2008

Committee members of Hong Kong Yiquan Association, 2007

Yiquan party, 2012

Committee members of HK Yiquan Society, 2014

Yang Xin Studio members at Yiquan party, 2014

Teaching Yiquan Stance at Sitges, Spain, and seminars in Barcelona, April 2014

Teaching Yiquan and Taiji Quan with Eric
and Grace in Florida, USA, December 2013

Chapter 5

WANG'S VALUABLE WORDS

"INHERIT THE PAST AND PAVE FOR THE FUTURE"

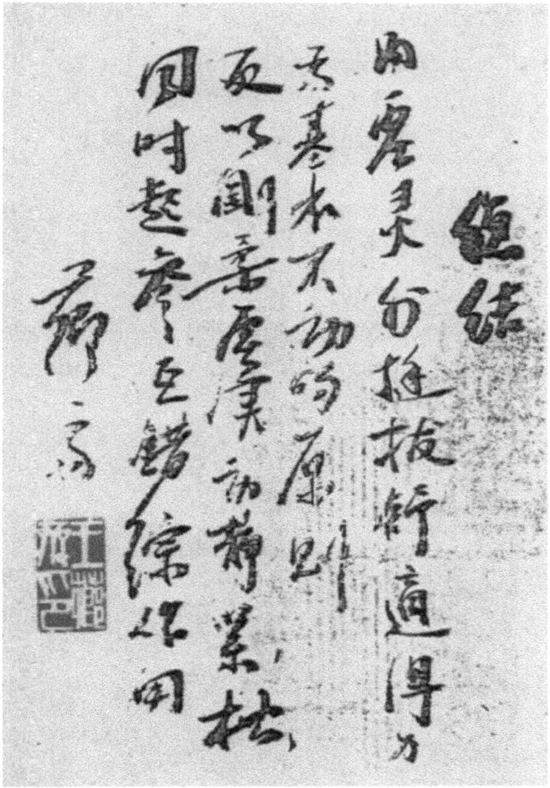

總結：
內虛靈，外挺拔，舒適得力為基本不動的原則。
更以剛柔，虛實，動靜，鬆緊，
同時起參互錯綜作用。
薌齋

SUMMARY OF PRINCIPLES OF PRACTICE

Internally empty and heightened spirit, externally upright and magnificent, comfort and derived strength, are the principles of an immovable foundation. Accompanied with firmness and yielding, emptiness and fullness, movement and stillness, tension and relaxation, concurrently intermingled and indistinguishable throughout the body.

人法地，地法天，天地道，道法自然。
老子　第25章

Man takes Earth as his model,

Earth takes Heaven as its model,

Heaven takes Tao as its model,

Tao takes what is natural as its model.

Many follow the way of Earth, Earth follows the way of Heaven, Heaven follows the way of the Tao, and the Tao follows the way of itself.

SECRET OF FIGHTING

王玉芳老師謂王老晚年總結技擊為六字：
長 忍 狠 謹 穩 準

In March 1992, I asked Madam Wang Yu Fang about the secret of fighting in Yiquan. Wang said that her father, in his later years, decided on six words and passed them to her:

Persistence

Endurance

Ruthless

Cautious

Stable

Accurate.

Chapter 6

YIQUAN SYSTEM OVERVIEW

PREPARATION

Warm up 熱身:

- Five relaxation exercises, circling, stretches, pressing legs
- 鬆身五法, 打圈擰手, 拉筋伸展, 壓腿

Cool down:

- Patting exercises
- 拍打收功

A. STANCES—STATIC EXERCISES 樁法 - 靜功

See Chapter 12 for posture descriptions.

1. Zhan Zhuang (Static Stance) 站樁

a. Front Stance 正樁 (平樁、文樁、三才樁)

Yang Sheng Zhuang (Health Stance) 養生樁, 健身樁

1. Fu Bao Zhuang (Float Hug) 浮抱樁 (手抱乾坤)
2. Fu An Zhuang (Float Press) 浮按樁 (頂天立地)
3. Cheng Bao Zhuang (Prop Hug) 撐抱樁 (懷抱嬰兒) (養心樁)
4. Tui Tuo Zhuang (Push Prop) 推托樁 (掌托天門)
5. Fun Shui Zhuang (Split Water) 分水樁 (白鶴展翅)
6. Ti Cha Zhuang (Lift Jab) 提插樁 (入地三尺)
7. Ti Bao Zhuang (Lift Hug) 提抱樁 (提抱日月)
8. Yang Shen Zhuang (Cultivating Spirit) 養神樁

b. Side Stance 側樁 (戰樁、武樁、混元樁)

Ji Ji Zhuang (Combat Stance) 技擊樁

1. Hun Yuan Zhuang (Sphere) 混元樁 – 側浮抱樁
2. Mao Dun Zhuang (Spear and Shield) 矛盾樁 – 小步樁
3. Fu Yun Zhuang (Float Cloud) 浮雲樁
4. Gou Gua Zhuang (Hook Hang) 勾掛樁
5. Ping Bao Zhuang (Even Hug) 平抱樁 – 扶按樁
6. Dun Bao Bei Zhuang (Hold Treasure) 墩寶貝樁
7. Tui Tuo Zhuang (Push Prop) 推托樁 (托天樁)

c. Power Stance 功力樁

Gong Li Zhuang (Power Stance) 功力大樁

1. Xiang Long Zhuang (Descending Dragon) 降龍樁
2. Fu Hu Zhuang (Taming Tiger) 伏虎樁
3. Du Li Zhuang (Chicken) 子午樁(又名金雞獨立)
4. Ying Zhuang (Eagle) 大步鷹樁 (大式樁)
5. Cheng Tui Zhuang (Stretch Leg) 撐腿樁 (蛟龍出海)

d. Dai Bu Zhuang (Big Step Stance) 大樁

1. Bao Zhuang (Hug) 正抱 – 三平混元樁
2. Cheng Zhuang (Prop) 側撐 – 大式樁

e. Zuo Zhuang (Sitting Postures) 坐式樁

1. Fu Bao Zhuang (Float Hug) 浮抱樁
2. Fu An Zhuang (Float Press) 浮按樁
3. Cheng Bao Zhuang (Prop Hug) 撐抱樁
4. Tui Tuo Zhuang (Push Prop) 推托樁
5. Gou Gua Zhuang (Hook Hang) 勾掛樁

f. Wo Zhuang (Lying Postures) 臥式樁

1. Fu Bao Zhuang (Float Hug) 浮抱樁
2. Fu An Zhuang (Float Press) 浮按樁
3. Cheng Bao Zhuang (Prop Hug) 撐抱樁
4. Tui Tuo Zhuang (Push Prop) 推托樁
5. Gou Gua Zhuang (Hook Hang) 勾掛樁

B. CONDITIONING—MOVING EXERCISES 功法 – 動功

1. Shi Li (Test Strength) 試力

See Chapter 15 for posture descriptions.

a. Front Stance Shi Li 正面

Basic Test

1. Pin Yi Test 平移
2. Li Yao Test (Vertical Wave) 立搖
    a. Cheng Ba–Tui Tuo Stance Test 神龍布雨
3. Ping Xuan Test (Horizontal Rotate) 平旋
    a. Fu An–Ti Cha Stance Test 烏龍攪海/風擺荷葉

Main Test

1. Up and Down 上下
    a. Fu An Shi Li (Float Press) 浮按
    提按試力 (搖轆轤) (吞浪捲浪/波浪試力)
2. Forward and Backward 前後
    a. Ping Tui Shi Li (Level Push) 平推
    推拉試力 – 勾掛 (插糖膠)
3. Left and Right 左右
    a. Ba Shui Shi Li (Pushing Water) 撥水
    分水試力 (風帆試力/搖船試力)
    b. Shun Shui Tui Shou (Push Boat) 順水推舟
    單手推前拉後

b. Advanced Side Stance Shi Li 側面

Special Directions

1. Qing Ting Dian Shui (Dragonfly Skims Water) 蜻蜓點水
2. Shen Gui Chu Shui (Holy Turtle Comes from Water) 神龜出水
3. Ling Xi Pi Shui (Clever Rhinoceros Splits Water) 靈犀劈水
4. Xuan Shou Shi Li (Rotate Slash) 旋手試力
5. Fu Pu Shi Li (Tiger Throw) 虎撲試力

Vertical Movements 立圓試力

1. Shen Long Bai Wei (Dragon Swings Tail) 神龍擺尾
2. Ling He Tong Tian (Clever Crane Reaches Sky) 靈鶴通天

c. Ten Special Movements of Combat Test Strength 專項技擊試力十節功

See Chapter 16 for posture descriptions.

1. Pull Up Tree 拔樹試力 (插糖稀試力)
2. Filter Air 空中濾氣試力
3. Press Spring 按彈簧試力
4. Split Water 分水試力
5. Dragon Turns Arms 回龍轉臂試力 (烏龍捲臂)
6. Hook and File 鉤銼試力
7. Rub Ball 揉球試力
8. Open and Close 開合試力
9. Elbow Filing 銼力試力
10. Bird Can't Fly 鳥難飛試力

d. Waist Techniques 腰法

See Chapter 8 for technique descriptions.

1. Dun Yao (Squat Waist) 蹲腰 (上下) = 正面神龜出水
    a. Move Hands 手動試力
    b. Turn Hands 手翻試力
    c. Hands Stop 手定試力
        i. High Posture
        ii. Middle Posture
        iii. Low Posture
2. Tuo Yao (Drag Waist) 拖腰 – 搖船 (左右) = 撥水試力
    a. Fixed Step Drag 定步拖
        i. Both Hands Drag 雙拖
        ii. Single Hand Drag 單拖
        iii. Left and Right Drag 左拖右拖
    b. Move Step Drag 動步拖
        i. Forward Drag 進步拖|
        ii. Backward Drag 退步拖|雙拖、單拖、左拖右拖
        iii. Triangle Drag 三角步拖|
        iv. Free Step Drag 活步拖|
3. Cuo Yao (Rub Waist) 搓腰 (雙人拖腰)
    a. Fixed Step Rub 定步搓腰
    b. Move Step Rub 動步搓腰

2. Mo Ca Bu (Footwork/Stroll) 走步

1. Basic Practice: Ding Bu (Fixed Steps) 定步
    a. Up and Down Pressing 原地上下踩步
    b. Four Directions Sliding 原地四面趟步
    c. Cheng Bao Zhuang (Prop Hug) 撐抱樁
2. Don Bu (Moving Steps) 動步
    a. Mo Ca Bu (Friction Steps—Rubbing and Sliding Step) 摩擦步
        i. Cheng Bao Zhuang Step 撐抱樁走步
        ii. Hands at Sideways Step 分撐手上下按走
        iii. Hands at Split Water Step 提趟扒縮步 – 分水
        iv. Hands at Skim Water Step 提趟扒縮步 – 點水
    b. Driving Boat Step 陸地行舟
        i. Gou Gua (Push Drag and Hook Hang) 推拉勾掛手, 雙點步走
        ii. Forward and Backward Free Stepping 進退活步走
3. Footwork together with Shi Li 走步試力
    Up and Down 上下
    Pull In 內撥
    Split Water 分水
    Rotate Hands 旋手
    Flying Bird 飛鳥
    Big Eagle Spreads Wings 大鵬展翅
4. Repeat step 2 (Don Bu) again.

3. Fali (Emit Strength) 發力

1. Fixed Steps Fali 定步
    a. Structure Fali 間架發力 – 正側撐抱, 定樁被按發力
    b. Forward Fali 前發力
    c. Upward Fali 上發力
    d. Downward Fali 下挫發力
    e. Slant Fali 斜砍發力
    f. Down Chop Fali 下劈發力 (鬼斬手)
    g. Rooting Strength Fali 落地生根接發力
    h. Crash Fali 對撞發力

2. Moving Steps Fali 動步發力
3. Free Steps Combination Fali 活步自由組合發力

4. Fa Sheng (Emit Sound) 發聲

1. Fixed Steps Emit Sound 定步發聲
2. Tiger Roars Sound 虎嘯
3. Dragon Roars Sound 蒼海龍吟 (神龜出水+發聲)
4. Moving Steps Emit Sound 動步發聲

C. TECHNIQUES 技法

1. Tui Shou (Push Hand) 揉手

See Chapter 20 for posture descriptions.

a. Circling

1. Dan Tui Shou (Single Push Hand) 單推手
2. Shuang Tui Shou (Double Push Hand) 雙推手
   a. Both up
   b. Both down
   c. Up and down
3. Moving Steps Push 2 and 2 活步雙推 (進2退2)
4. Moving Steps Push 3 and 3 活步雙推 (進3退3)

b. Techniques for attack and defense

1. Dan Tui Shou 單推手
   a. Cheng Bao—Fu An Fali 撐抱—扶按發力
   b. Gou Gua—Ping Tui Fali 勾掛—平推發力
   c. Bo Lang Fali (Wave Shock Emit) 波浪剎車發力
   d. Jie Fa Training (Hand-out Push) 接發力
2. Shuang Tui Shou 雙推手
   a. Si Fang Fali (Practice Emit) 練習發力 (前撞、上發、下發、側發)
   b. Fu An Fali (Floating Press Emit) 扶按發力 (下按上推)
   c. Xuan Fali (Rotate Emit) 橫旋發力 (偏掛/旋法轉圈)
   d. Gou Gua Fali (Hook Hang Emit) 勾掛發力 (勾掛前撞)
   e. Fen Gua Fali (Open Hook Emit) 分掛發力 (左右分掛前打)
   f. Xia Gou Fali (Down Hook Emit) 下勾發力 (槓桿)

g. Xia Cuo Fali (Down File Emit) 下挫發力 (滑車)
h. Pian Gua Fali (Spin Side Hang Emit) (偏掛返中 – 左鑽右橫旋打)
i. Xia Cuo Fali (Side Slant Plant Emit) (左右斜栽發力)
j. Hung Fali (Chest Emit) 胸接力/胸發力

2. Dan Cao (Punch Fight) 發拳 – 單操

See Chapter 21 for posture descriptions.

1. Chong Quan (Straight Punch) 沖拳 (豹拳)
2. Zuan Quan (Drilling Punch) 連環勾鑽拳
3. Beng Quan (Breaking Punch) 連環崩拳
4. Pao Quan (Cannon Punch) 鑽炮拳
5. Heng Quan (Cross Punch) 扯橫拳
6. Zai Quan (Planting Punch) 下栽拳
7. Guan Quan (Hook Punch) 貫拳 (馬形拳)
   Single Hand Contact Attack 單搭手打法
   a. Direct Punch 橫旋指中沖拳
   b. Upper Cut 上鑽拳下膶
   c. Press and Attack Heart 下壓直崩心
   d. Hook Back and Attack the Face with Palm 勾旋塌面
   e. Press and Attack Rips 下壓橫崩肋
   f. Upper Turn and Downward Punch 上旋下栽胸

3. Duan Shou (Combat Free Sparring) 斷手

Actual Practice 實作

1. Palm Strikes
   a. Gui Zhan Shou (Ghost Chop) 鬼斬手 (鬼劈手/鬼手斷)
   b. Xue Zhang (Cutting Palm) 削掌
   c. Ta Zhang (Collapse Palm) 塌掌
2. Kicks
   a. Cai Tui (Step/Straight Kick) 踩腿
   b. Ding/Dian Tui (Nail/Straight Kick) 釘腿/點腿
   c. Heng Duo Tui (Slant Stamp Kick) 橫跺腿/截腿 (攔門腿)
   d. Ce Chuai (Side Kick) 側踹腿
   e. Deng Tui (Stomping Kick) 蹬腿
   f. Po Ma Tui (Breaking Steps) 破馬腿

4. Quan Zhuang (Fist Stances) 拳樁

See Chapter 25.

5. Jian Wu (Fist Dance) 拳舞, 健舞, 武舞

See Chapter 26 for posture descriptions.

1. Bailing Waves 揮浪
2. Swimming Dragon 游龍
3. Crane Plays 鶴戲
4. Startling Snake 驚蛇

6. Weapons 器械

See Chapter 27.

1. Pi Jian 劈劍

1. Fixed Step Downward Pi	1. 定步直劈
2. Fixed Step Reverse Pi	2. 定步上崩
3. Forward Step Pi	3. 進步劈
4. Backward Step Pi	4. 退步劈
5. Pad Step Pi	5. 墊步劈
6. Left Cross Pi	6. 左橫劈攔腰
7. Right Cross Pi	7. 右橫劈攔腰
8. Left Slant Pi	8. 左斜劈
9. Right Slant Pi	9. 右斜劈
10. Left Upward Pi	10. 左斜上劈
11. Right Upward Pi	11. 右斜上劈
12. Turn Back Pi	12. 轉身劈

2. Pi Gun 劈棍

1. Pierce and Downward Shake Pole	1. 下抖杆
2. Cross Shake Pole	2. 橫抖杆
3. Upper Shake Pole	3. 上抖杆
4. Slant Shake Pole	4. 斜抖杆
5. Chop Pole	5. 劈杆
6. Rub Pole	6. 磨杆

Part II

SYSTEM OF YIQUAN TRAINING

Chapter 7

OVERVIEW OF TRAINING

The main areas for training are briefly described here. In subsequent chapters these and other aspects are described in more detail.

The basic training of Yiquan consists of two separate but interrelated parts: the health preservation aspect and the martial art aspect.

Yiquan's distinctive approach emphasizes the training of the Yi (consciousness) and the harmonious relaxation of the body. Yiquan employs static postural stance training to develop coordinated body movements. The training ultimately results in mastering the total harmony of the mind and the body in terms of:

- Xing (form) 形
- Yi (intent) 意
- Li (power) 力
- Qi (energy) 氣
- Shen (mental and spiritual presence) 神.

Martial art training in Yiquan consists of practicing Static Stance, Test Strength (sensing dynamic movement), footwork, Test Sound (augmenting with vocalization), Emit Strength (delivering dynamic power), pushing hands, and free sparring.

The health preservation aspect in Yiquan aims to promote proper neuromuscular coordination, cardiovascular stimulation, and body metabolism. This consists mainly of the Static Stance training that has been proven to be beneficial in alleviating some chronic health problems such as arthritis, neurasthenia, hypertension, and gastroenteric and respiratory disorders.

The direct approach in this book will offer individuals who are interested in health, functional kinematics, or martial arts a core view of Yiquan. The training will help in exploring the full potential of the interrelationship between the mind and the body.

CONTENTS

Static Stance (Zhan Zhuang) 站樁

This is a commonly employed training technique in many martial art systems. The uniqueness of Yiquan Static Stance (Yiquan Zhan Zhuang) 意拳站樁 is in the emphasis on the activities of the mental aspect.

Intent (Yi) 意 is the basis of all training. Specific stances are taught to enhance the efficient transfer of energy (Qi) 氣 and to stabilize different postural forms. By using different static stances, the training of intent (Yi) 意 is gradually incorporated into the form (Xing) 形. This unique training will bring the body into the state of "interconnected wholeness"—a "totality" or a "harmonious wholeness" both internally and externally. This solid foundation must be achieved before one embarks on further training in Yiquan.

According to the different aims, Static Stance includes the health preservation stances (using parallel steps) and combat stances (using oblique T-steps). Actually, the health preservation stance is a base for martial arts practice. If one grasps the skills and uses them freely, there are no differences for both types of stance.

The essential points are the following:

- Focus attention.
- Relax the whole body.
- Breathe naturally.

Test Strength (Shi Li) 試力

After acquiring the basic skills in Static Stance, the next step is to verify these skills using slow movements. Specific slow movements involving the head, neck, body, and extremities are practiced.

During these movements different aspects of body coordination are verified. The emphasis of intent (Yi) 意 forms the basis of Shi Li. It is in this stage that the feeling of "interconnected wholeness" within the different body parts during movement and of "interconnected wholeness" of the body to the external environment is further developed.

The aim of Shi Li is to activate the force you obtained in static exercises and to use it freely. The basic idea is that slowness is better than quickness. While practicing, you seem to feel the force of the air with your hands, like swimming, until you can move your hands like snakes. The Static Stance exercise is relatively still, and the key to Shi Li is being fluid and in movement.

Footwork (Mo Ca Bu) 摩擦步

Footwork training is a vital aspect of Yiquan. This involves slow movements of the foot in different directions. Specific techniques of footwork are used in Shi

Li. The different aspects of Fali, when incorporated with the use of footwork, are of primary importance in Yiquan.

Test Sound (Shi Sheng) 試聲

This is the right way of using one's voice to augment Fali. The voice is generated from the Dantian through the throat and bursts out. The spirit of the practitioner will be highly elaborate.

Emit Strength (Fali) 發力

It is in this stage that a practitioner of Yiquan learns how to concentrate and release dynamic strength. The total harmony of the mind and the body in terms of Form (Xing) 形, Intent (Yi) 意, Power (Li) 力, Energy (Qi) 氣, and mental and spiritual presence (Shen) 神 would manifest as an inherent characteristic in all body movements.

Applying force is the effective motive power. Without learning these pragmatic skills, one will never learn how to apply one's striking force well. The general requirements of this force are the sudden explosions and abrupt stops of movement.

Individual Practice (Shan Cao Shou) 單操手

The individual repetitive exercises are essential for developing combat effectiveness. It can improve your skill and is especially helpful for grasping the key requirements and techniques for fighting. The fighting techniques include strikes and kicks.

Push Hand (Tui Shou) 推手

Free sparring in Yiquan is divided into sticking hand (push hand—Tui Shou) and disconnected fight (Duan Shou). Push hand is the training of conditional reflexes of the hands and feet while engaged in different hand-to-hand contact situations. The reflexes are trained in accordance with the movements in Yiquan.

Push hand is a kind of actual combat exercise, embodying the skills of Shi Li and footwork. It can make up for the deficiency of San Shou. Push hand is a unique method of fight training in China. The principle of push hand is that it has laws but no shape; it is within feeling but beyond seeking.

Combat Free Sparring (Duan Shou) 斷手

Free sparring of Yiquan is called disconnected hand fight, San Shou 散手, or actual combat. It is the final target, total achievement, and comprehensive manifestation of combat essential skills. The combat principles of Yiquan are the following:

1. It is able to improve inner energy.
2. Whole body unity power is the general rule.
3. Attack and defense can be executed at any time.
4. Guard the center line and use it to attack and defend.
5. Practice and use it whenever and wherever.

TRAINING STAGES OF YIQUAN

Stage 1: Static Stance—Front Stance

1. Gather and become full of Qi 收集氣份飽滿灌透.
2. Be balanced and symmetrical 平衡對稱力.
3. Fix the shape of the structure, eight balls, and triangles 間架定型, 全身三角八球.
4. Consolidate prop and hold strength 鞏固撐抱力. (Enhance the supporting power of the armpits to enable hanging up for a long time during push hand and punching, without dropping arms.)
5. Pick up all big tendons 挑大筋.
6. Enhance the strength of the legs and thighs after a long period of being in stance.
7. Endurance training.
8. Four phenomena appear as feelings on the hands: hot, numb, swollen, and heavy 四象.
9. Link up the limbs, body, and joints of the whole body 關節連通.

Main format: Cheng Bao Da Zhuang 三才樁.

Supplements:

1. Fu Bao Zhuang (Float Hug) 浮抱樁
2. Fu An Zhuang (Float Press) 浮按樁
3. Cheng Bao Zhuang (Prop Hug) 撐抱樁
4. Tui Tuo Zhuang (Push Prop) 推托樁
5. Fun Shui Zhuang (Split Water) 分水樁
6. Ti Cha Zhuang (Lift Jab) 提插樁
7. Ti Bao Zhuang (Lift Hug) 提抱樁
8. Yang Shen Zhuang (Cultivating Spirit) 養神樁

Target setting: Generate Hun Yuan strength.

Factors: Angles, degree of curves of knee, and timing.

Stage 2: Static Stance—Side Stance

After long-term front stance training, the body is used to endurance and maintaining the requirements at any moment. When the body, hand, and leg structures are stable and strong, and the hands have feelings, then start this side stance. This training is with the intent of the following:

1. Correct errors.
2. Test four appearances/likes 出四如/四形四相 – "一鉛鐵戟."
3. Develop Global Spring force 全身彈簧力.
4. Develop six directions Hun Yuan strength.

Main format: Mao Dun Zhuang (Spear and Shield) 矛盾樁 – 小步樁.

Supplements:

1. Hun Yuan Zhuang (Sphere) 混元樁 – 側浮抱樁
2. Fu An Zhuang (Float Press) 浮雲樁 – 扶按樁
3. Dun Bao Bei Zhuang (Hold Treasure) 墩寶貝樁
4. Tui Tuo Zhuang (Push Prop) 推托樁 (托天樁)

Stage 3: Static Stance—Power Stance

Main format:

1. Dragon Stance—twisting.
2. Tiger Stance—lower posture, rear leg strength, spine straight.
3. Chicken Stance—endurance and stability.
4. Eagle Stance—propping and stretching.

Stage 4: Shi Li—Test Strength

1. Every stance links up a Test Strength movement.
2. Every Test Strength movement must maintain the structure of the stance. Apply the intent of the stance, self, and beyond-body feeling to the test movements of body and arms.

Main format:

1. Up and Down Fu An 搖轆轤
2. Forward and Backward Ping Tui 前後推拉
3. Left and Right Ba Shui 撥水
4. Shen Gui Chu Shui 神龜出水

Target setting: Develop 韌力.

The way: Resistance power 阻力感.

Stage 5: Footwork

1. Every movement must maintain the structure of the stance. Even when you are moving, your upper body and arms are so strong that there must be no collapse, no breaking down, and no flattening; angles must be unchanged.
2. Feel the opposite power derived from Static Stance.
3. Use footwork movement to lead the unity of the body.

Target setting: Stable moving with a force like a tank.

The way: Simulate horse cart, cow pull.

Stage 6: Fali

This is the integrated training of all the practiced items, divided into "Emit" and "Strike." Shi Sheng is also coordinated in Fali.

Factors:

1. Prop strength of rear leg.
2. Spring power.
3. Follow flow-trembling power.
4. Rush force of body weight.
5. Whole body opposite power.
6. Faster and bigger Shi Li, using ground force and stance structure.

Target setting: Explosive power.

The way: By applying braking power.

Stage 7: Push hand, strikes, and free sparring

Push hand is a practice of feeling and sensitivity. Dun Sau is the real and ultimate target to be achieved:

1. Regular push hand to maintain structure.
2. Numerous punches and kicks training; apply the stance force.
3. Dun Sau Sparring for attack and defense; Fist Dance for enjoyment and flexibility.

Target setting: Speed, power, being cruel, and accuracy.

The way: Drilling.

Stage 8: Weapons

Develop characteristic Yiquan weapons such as broadsword and pole.

Stage 9: Strategies and tactics 戰術和戰略

1. The core of Yiquan is intent movement and whole body unity six directions opposite power.
2. Strategies rely on speed, shock power, rear leg prop, and explosive power.
3. Tactics are to set the guarding area and distance area. Use a straight line to protect and a curved line to avoid the direct attack of the enemy; counter-attack from the side.

Chapter 8

QUICK START

LIANG'S THREE TREASURES

Yiquan is a vast system with several levels, with the Static Stance just a basic exercise. However, if there are limited resources, training in Master Liang Zi Peng's system is the best for simplicity. Therefore, we introduce this system as a Quick Start for beginners.

THE "SOUTHERN YIQUAN"

Since the time when Master Liang Zi Peng was the first person to come to Hong Kong to teach Yiquan, the name of Yiquan has only gradually become known to the public. His system, derived from his teacher, You, is more concise and easier than the vast system nowadays; therefore some people call his system the "Southern Yiquan," because it has its own characteristics and movements and is mainly taught in South East Asia.

OVERVIEW OF LIANG'S THREE TREASURES SYSTEM 梁子鵬 梁氏三寶

Master Liang Zi Peng has three main stance trainings:

1. Dun Yao (Squat Waist)
2. The two techniques of Tuo Yao: Tuo Yao (Drag Waist) and Cuo Yao (Rub Waist)
3. Zhan Zhuang (Static Stance)

1. Dun Yao (Squat Waist) 蹲腰 *(*上下*)* = 正面神龜出水

1. Move Hands 手動試力
2. Turn Hands 手翻試力
3. Hands Stop 手定試力

2. Tuo Yao

a. Tuo Yao (Drag Waist) 拖腰 – 搖船 (左右) = 撥水試力

1. Fixed Step Drag	定步拖
a. Both Hands Drag	雙拖
b. Single Hand Drag	單拖
c. Left and Right Drag	左拖右拖
2. Move Step Drag	動步拖
a. Forward Drag	進步拖
b. Backward Drag	退步拖 – 雙拖、單拖、左拖右拖
c. Free Step Drag	活步拖

b. Cuo Yao (Rub Waist) 搓腰 (雙人拖腰)

1. Fixed Step Rub	定步搓腰
2. Move Step Rub	動步搓腰

3. Zhan Zhuang (Static Stance) 站樁

1. Front Stance	平樁
a. Hun Yuan Zhuang	渾元樁
b. Jian Shen Zhuang	養生樁
2. Side Stance	側樁
a. San Cai Zhuang	三才樁

The purpose of practicing Yiquan is to develop an instantaneous explosive force. The method is quite simple, and is advanced through practicing Static Stance. By training in Static Stance, you can build up a stationary Hun Yuan force and strengthen your structure and body resistance. Keep your arms soft, just like a snake winding through the grass. Sink your body weight and prop your legs strongly, so that you can receive the coming Fali.

After that, you can practice Dun Yao. Try to relax your chest. Both hips roll in and sink the Gua like sitting on a chair. To move up your body, your legs prop the ground while your chest is relaxing downwards. Then straighten your knees and strengthen your hips and chest. If you face an enemy as strong as you, remember to attack from the sides. Therefore, it is important to practice Tuo Yao. In combat, pull your enemy in order to destroy his balance, and then press your waist to send him flying.

THE ESSENCE OF STATIC STANCE

The requirements of the three main stance practices are:

1. *Dun Yao:* Spine upright, smooth buttocks, anus raised, three roundings.
2. *Tuo Yao:* Stomach leads waist to move, waist sits, hollow chest, back upright, Qi centralized to Dantian from top and down.
3. *Zhan Zhuang:* Chest hollowed and back raised, Qi linked upwards and downwards; this will generate the Hun Yuan Qi.

These three stance practices require the initiative to be in the spine and the abdomen, so that they can link up the whole body and achieve the following effects:

- Blood circulates freely, muscles relax, one is mentally and bodily happy and thus achieves the first stage of bodily fitness and health.
- Joints extend and physique separates to the point of skin separating from flesh and flesh separating from bones. Qi travels freely, so that the Qi deepens into bone and marrow. Then the whole body can withstand a beating in order to achieve self-defense.
- Qi travels freely, up to Xuan Guan (玄關) and down towards Yong Quan (湧泉). It travels full cycle so that Ren Du Mai (任督脈) are flowing freely. One will forget all about one's surroundings and other things, finally returning to one's origin and achieving the stages of enlightenment.

LIANG'S SYSTEM IN DETAIL

1. Dun Yao

Steps

To start, stand with feet apart at a width double that of the shoulders' width. Arms extend to the front and rise up to shoulder height; palms face the ground, with all fingers slightly apart and "tiger mouth" naturally spreading out.

Step 1

Slowly squat down, with both palms following suit. Retract both arms slowly towards the ribs. Spine and abdomen remain straight and aligned, with neck up straight, not moving about, and remaining in a position of upright spine. Squat until the knees and the Gua are aligned in a straight line.

At this moment, the internal and external shape should be the following:

1. The crotch should be open internally. Waist should be in the center of the crotch.
2. Kidney and intestines should be full of Qi so that they can be fully massaged.

3. Lungs contracted. Diaphragm moves downward.

Step 2

Straighten your knees slowly. Raise your hands up to shoulder height with palms facing down. Separate your hands, just like a flying airplane. Do the movement as slowly as possible.

At this moment, the internal and external shape should be the following:

1. Hips relaxed. Crotch should be moved downward.
2. Hands raised. Try to move your internal organs, especially intestines and kidneys, through the movement of the waist and ribs.
3. Back straight and hands separated. Shoulder blades should be open internally. Upper back, waist, and crotch have to be rounded out as a half moon. This is called "outer three circles."

This is one session. Afterwards, return to the starting position.

Points to note when practicing Dun Yao

1. Relax. Do not try to control your breathing. Let your bodily movements activate the contraction and extension of the lungs and diaphragm. Never hold your breath, stop breathing, or intentionally prolong your inspiration.
2. When performing squats and straightening your knees, remember to keep your body straight. Hold your head and upper back straight. When straightening your legs, try to use the force from your feet, through the knees, crotch, abdomen, and then neck, to the head. Keep your chest sunk and not stuck out. Keep your elbows and wrists soft.
3. Once you squat downwards, stand up immediately. Pull your hands up and forward. Once your legs are straightened, then squat immediately. Pull your hands back with palms facing down. Do not allow any interruption between the movements. This exercise strengthens many internal organs.
4. Please seek doctor's advice if you have hurt your knees or legs before.
5. Do the exercise regularly. Keep a slow motion. Try to finish the whole movement in 10 seconds. At the beginning, do ten reps each time. Each week increase this by five reps. The maximum reps is 30.
6. This exercise strengthens leg muscles, improves balance, and increases power. Bending the knees and pulling the hands are to pull your enemy forward. Straightening the knees and pushing the hands are to push your enemy. This is the powerful technique that makes the students of Liang so strong.

Advice from the master

When Liang taught Dun Yao, he always said the following:

- When you squat downwards, imagine there is something blocking you from the buttocks.
- When you raise up your body, imagine there is somebody pressing your head, not allowing you to stand up.

Remember four key words when practicing: relax, sit, push, and prop (鬆, 坐, 頂, 撐):

- *Relax:* First relax and sink your chest.
- *Sit:* Let the Kau sit; open your gap of Kau.
- *Push:* The head pushes up and hands relax; there is no movement on the chest.
- *Prop:* Hands stretch outwards in a V shape.

The imagery must be done with serious intent:

- When you squat down, relax your chest muscles and then sit until your thighs resist so that you feel the pressure on them.
- When you stand up, the top of your head feels like breaking through the roof of your house, with the shoulders supporting thousands of tons of material, the head rising up from deep water to the surface of the water, like the sun rising from sea level. The tightness presses up like a pump, with fingers like sharp knives, the back is contracted very tight, and thighs burst apart.

Frequency and quantity are the following:

- Two sessions each day.
- At the beginning, squat 10 times, then add 5 times each week, eventually building up to 30 times for each session.

Testing of Dun Yao by coach

- Stand in front of a wall and do Dun Yao with your back always sticking to the wall. If your buttock extends out then, when you squat down, your back cannot stick to the wall.
- The coach has to check that, when squatting downward, at least your thighs must reach horizontal level.
- When you squat downward, the coach places both arms below you. You should use your body power to stick his arm and lead him to fall towards you and downward.

- When you rise, your coach grasps your upper arms. Your power should rise up and you stretch your arms so that your coach will be pushed up and backward.

When you rise from the lower posture of Dun Yao, imagine you are doing weight-lifting and it is very difficult to rise.

Dun Yao movements

Front view

SIDE VIEW

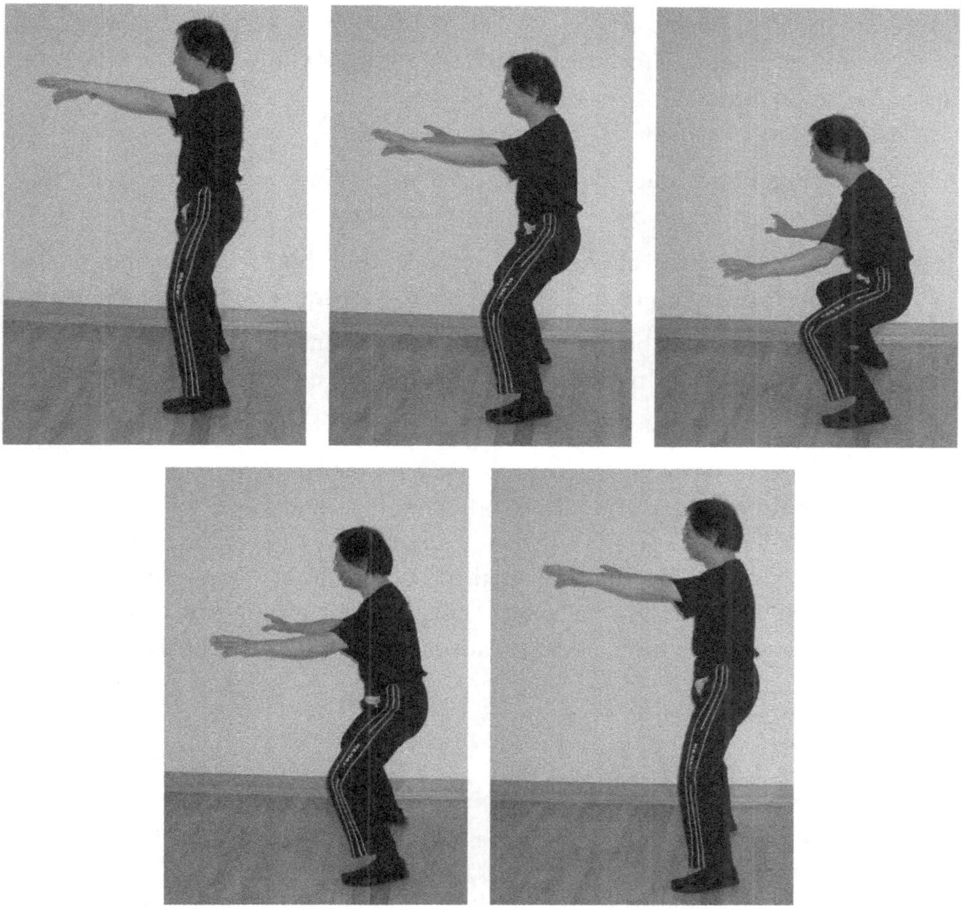

Dun Yao variations

1. HOLD THE SKY (托天式)

When moving up your body, raise your arms with the palms facing up, just like holding something. Imagine you are holding a heavy weight. Then bring the arms down with the palms facing down. Imagine you are pressing something downward.

2. FLYING BIRD (飛鳥式)

When moving up your body, raise up your arms from the side with the palms facing down. Imagine you are a flying bird. Then bring the arms down with the palms facing down. Bring the arms back to the flanks.

3. Squat Waist (神鰲出水式)

This is a technique using only your body, not your hands. Your hands are resting lightly on a table. Do not move your hands. Move your body by bending and straightening your legs. This is a traditional training method called Sea-tortoise Projecting from Water.

There are three kinds of movement:

- Stretch your arms up above your head with palms facing downward; stay there and do not move—just squat your body and waist.
- Stretch your arms outward in front of your body with palms facing downward; stay there and do not move—just squat your body and waist.
- Stretch your arms below your waist with palms facing downward; stay there and do not move—just squat your body and waist.

4. Holy Dragon Distributes Rain (神龍布雨式)

This is a hand-moving technique. Bend your legs and raise your hands up. Straighten your legs and press your hands down. This can produce an opposite force. It is the traditional training method called Front View Holy Tortoise Projecting from Water. It produces both shaking and rotating test force at the same time, which comes from the foundation of Dragon Distributes Rain.

Enlightening experience of Dun Yao

by Anthony Liu

One of my most impressive experiences of learning Chinese martial arts was the Dun Yao of Yiquan.

The Moving Training Exercises of Taiji, Walking Post of Bagua, Standing Post of Xing Yi, and Chen Style Taiji all have their own training effectiveness. Dun Yao makes Yiquan training become so special wholly because of its "micro-moves"—simple but never easy.

The movement starts from the standing position, which is 90 degrees perpendicular to the ground, similar to the Martial Post Stance, climbing inch by inch upwards, supporting from the roots of our feet with the ground. The process is a bit similar to the waist and abdomen (breathe in/out) practice of Yoga, or the Taming Tiger exercise of Eagle Paw, tough not to crack when you slow the movements down. The body control has to be spot-on at every single point; our nervous system sending each message ought to be concentrating and relaxing as well, and every inch of our muscles is in the status quo of contracting and expanding.

I still remember the time when I began the learning from Master Tang. The aches of the thigh and hip tendons became a kind of diplegia. It was impossible to complete more than three times in every attempt—it reminded me of the rough combat gym in the past.

Yiquan requires "Yi" (intention). The standard is that our minds have to ease up the ascending and descending flow in an extraordinarily slow movement, resulting in the acceleration of our metabolism, increased heart beat, and raised blood pressure. There is an obvious feeling of our body temperature rising and the thermolysis goes up. One of my wonderful experiences of practicing Yiquan was my sweat dropping, drop by drop in a leisurely manner, and it was so cozy sweating through every pore.

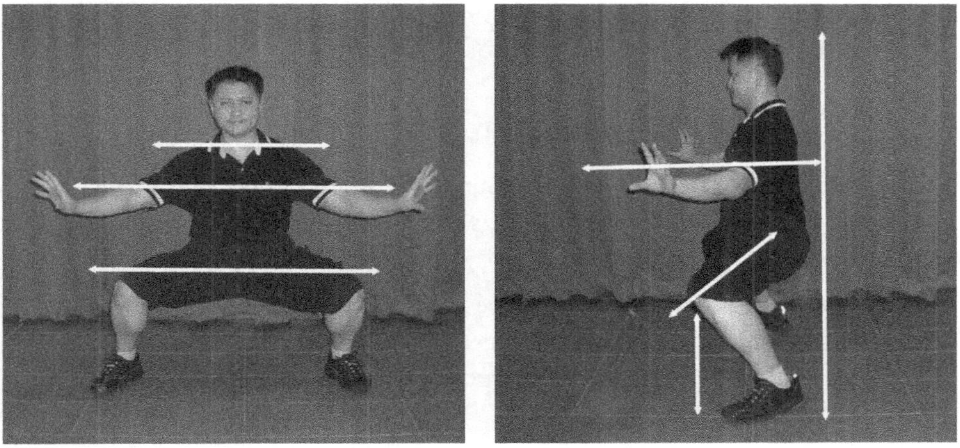

Anthony illustrating the technique of Dun Yao

From the front view, you need three horizontal lines to measure your standard. From the side view, your back must be straight

2a. *Tuo Yao*

Steps

Step 1

Stand with your legs forward and backward. The back foot is placed at 45 degrees to the front. The legs form a straight line. The front leg's toes point forward. Bend the knee of the front leg. The back leg keeps straight. Put your body weight on the front leg. The distance between the legs depends on the individual person. Raise the hands forward. Relax your shoulders and sink your elbows. Spread your "tiger mouth." The fingers of each hand are spread apart in the shape of claws.

Step 2

Contract your abdomen muscles to move your body backward. Straighten your waist and turn to the direction of your back leg. Coordinate your neck, waist, and crotch. Move your hands back to the front of your chest with palms facing down. Your hands pull down.

Step 3

Rotate your waist. Split your hands sideways. With your body facing to the front, keep your body straight. Keep your backbone straight and move forward slowly. Pull your hands forward. Your elbows drop down and wrists twist upward. All the fingers of each hand are spread out. Bend your front leg and straighten your back leg. Your body weight is placed on the front leg. Return to the starting position until your back and waist are totally stretched.

Points to note when practicing Tuo Yao

1. Relax. Do not try to control your breathing. Do not only focus on the movements of your hands or legs. All the movements should follow the movements of the waist.
2. When your body weight changes to your back leg, do not allow your hip to flop or hang. If your hip is relaxed, then your enemy can push you away easily. However, if the purpose of the practice is for healthy living, then you can still do this.
3. When your upper back is straight, use your abdomen muscle to pull it back immediately. When the waist is at the center of the crotch, rotate and pull forward immediately. Do not allow any interruption between the movements. When you are rotating, contracting, and extending the waist, at the same time your internal organs are also moving. At this very moment, the bodily movement seems soft. In fact, it is hard. It is highly recommended to use Qi to practice martial arts.

Advice from the master

Remember four key words when practicing: drag, sit, support, and close (拖, 坐, 撑, 合):

- *Drag:* Front leg presses the ground.
- *Sit:* Sink body downward and open Gau, with thigh flat.
- *Support:* Hands stretch sideways with power.
- *Close:* Rear leg presses the ground.

Frequency:

- Two sessions a day, morning and evening, preferably after Dun Yao and before Static Stance.
- At the beginning, 20 times for each side. One month later, 50 times each side.

Speed:

- The correct speed should be 12 seconds per movement—that is to say, 5 movements per minute. Doing it too quickly will not add resistance strength to the muscles of the legs and hips.

Tuo Yao movements

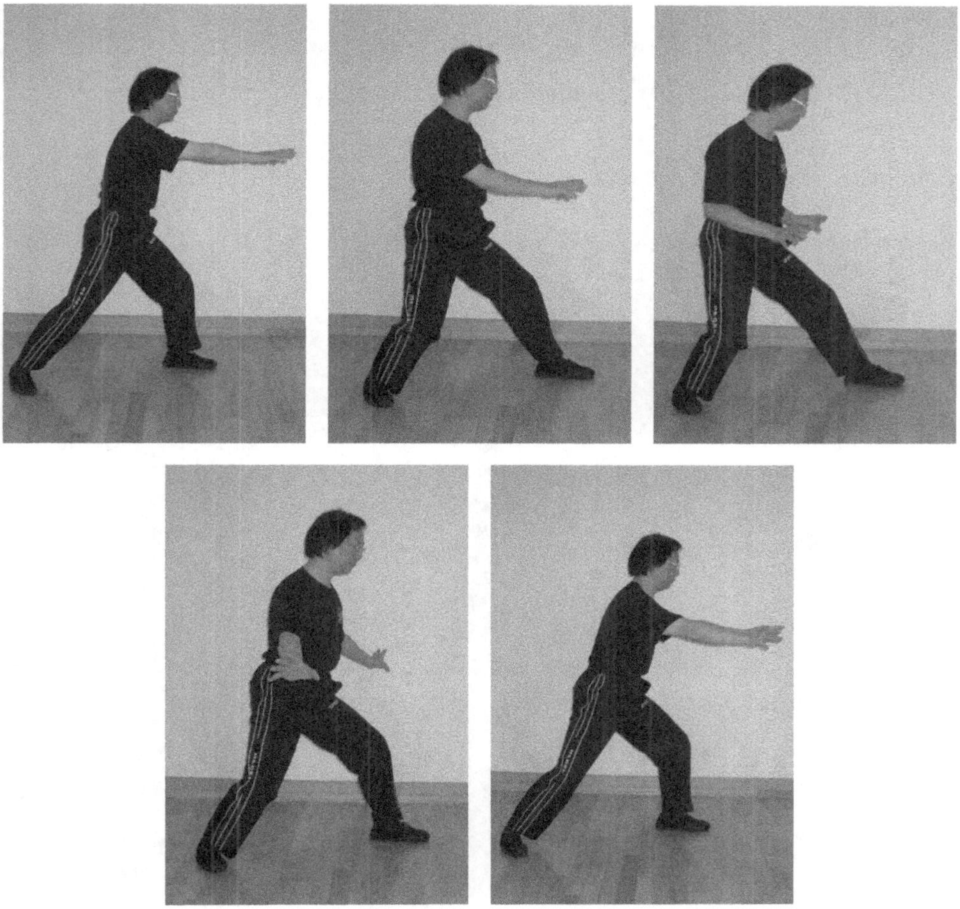

Tuo Yao variation—Moving Step

Moving Step is a movement form of Tuo Yao. It includes single hand and both hands Tuo Yao.

The requirement of Moving Step Tuo Yao

1. Step forward lightly.
2. Hands need to press down to keep balance.
3. When stepping outwards or backwards, move the feet horizontally.
4. When the back leg is moving forward, it feels like a horse pulling a carriage.

Moving Step—Tuo Yao movements

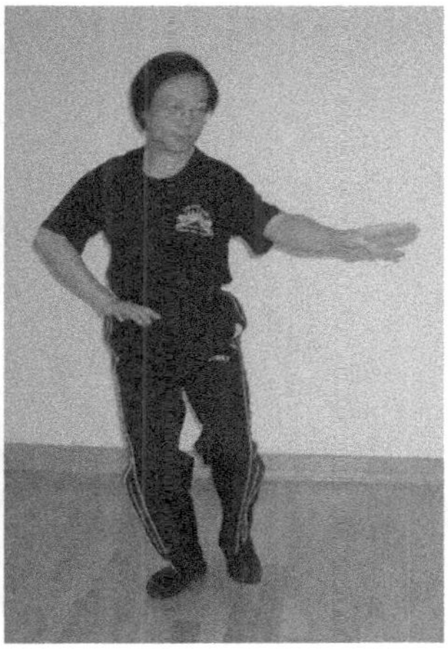

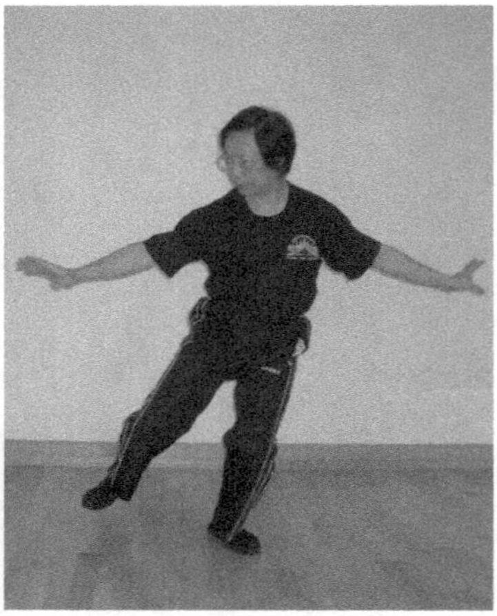

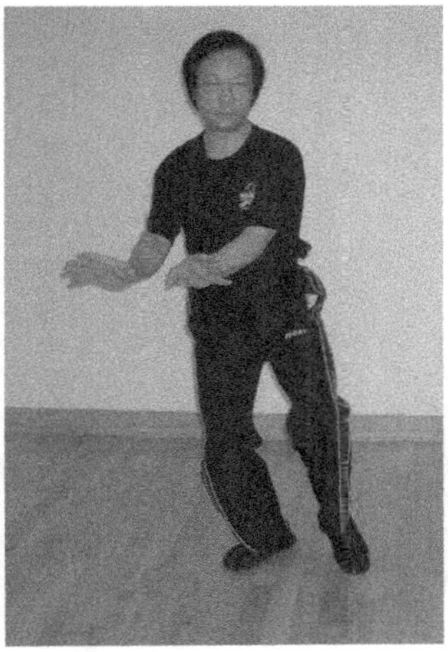

2b. Cuo Yao

Cuo Yao is Tuo Yao in pairs. Two persons stand face to face, doing Tuo Yao at the same time. They use their imagination to increase resistance. When partner A pushes forward, he needs to coordinate his whole body muscles together to increase the power, and partner B needs to sit back to absorb the force. By using this method, the quality of training can increase rapidly.

Steps

Step 1

Partners A and B practice together. The partners stand facing each other and both shift their body weight to their right foot and step their left leg forward. Each raises their hands forward with palms facing down. B puts his hands above A's hands.

Step 2

B pushes forward and A sits back.

Step 3

In order to release the force from B, A tries to pick up B's hand with palm facing up and sits back.

Step 4

A's hands drill upward, extending his arms by separating the elbows. Both hips roll out and draw strength.

Step 5

A rotates his hands and puts them above B's hands.

Step 6

A sits the Gua and separates the hands; the hands push forward.

Step 7

B does not push against A's hands, but merely follows B as he retreats. Repeat the movement.

Points to note when practicing Cuo Yao

1. Do not push against your partner's hands; merely follow him as he retreats. Focus on your mind and try to stay calm and relaxed.
2. Bend your knees. The body is vertically upright.
3. Try to stretch your hands and your legs. The force on the hands should come from the reaction force from the foot.
4. Keep practicing. Do not let your body rise or fall during the movement. Try your best to absorb the force from your partner.
5. Keep your shoulders and elbows relaxed and rounded. Make use of what you learnt in the Static Stance.

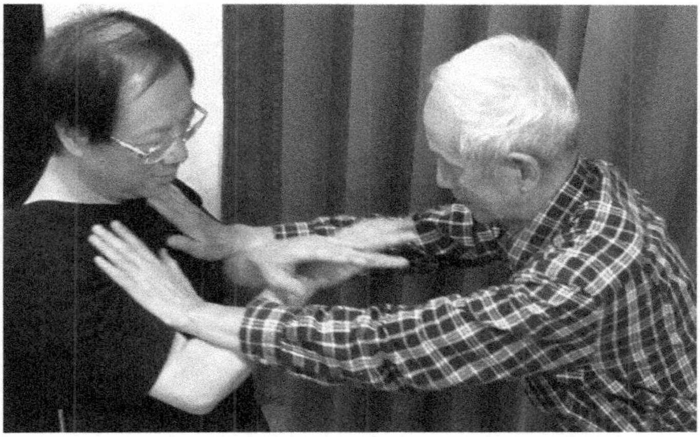

Cuo Yao movements

Top view

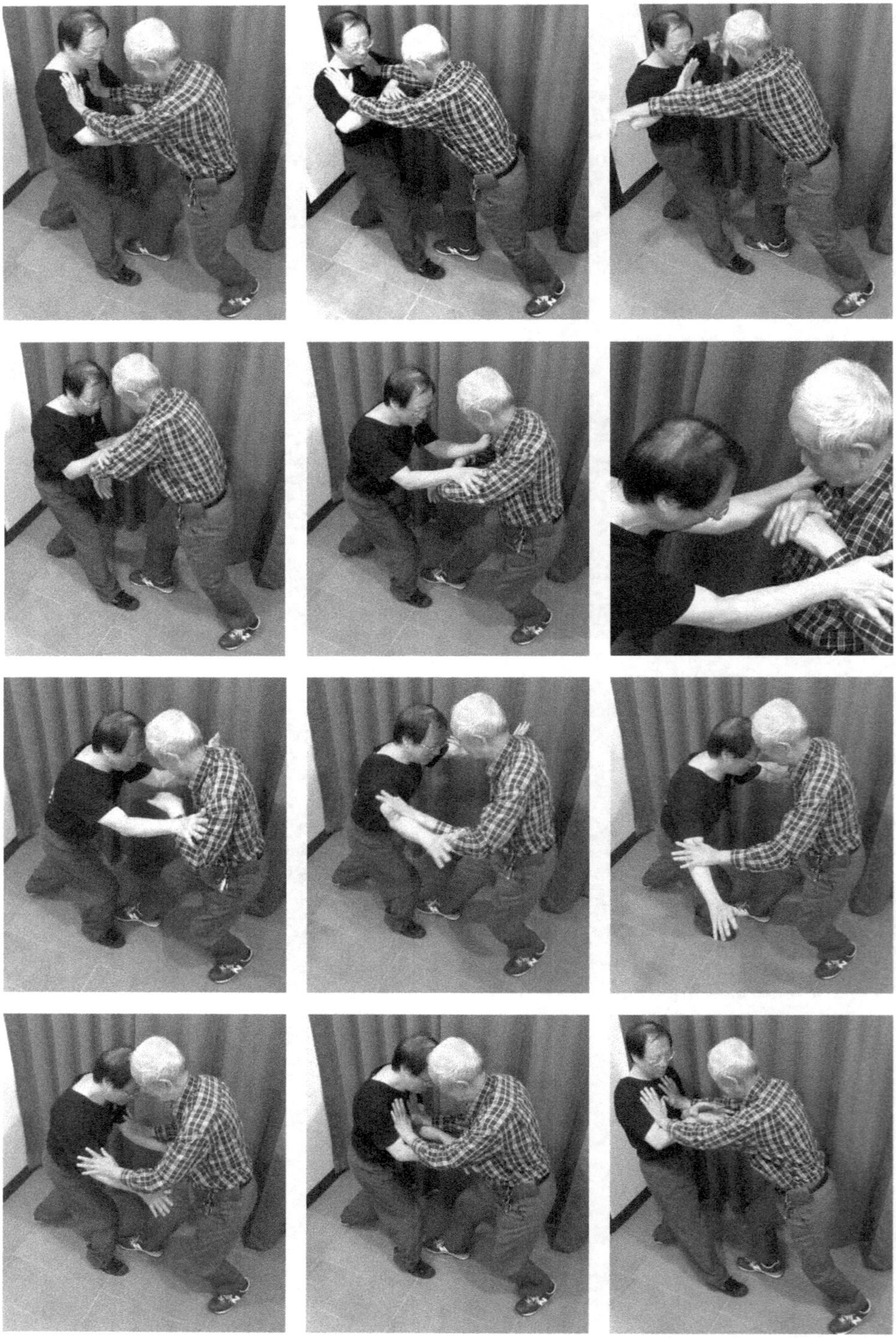

3. *Zhan Zhuang (Static Stance)*

This training should be guided by a qualified trainer or master. The Static Stance is all about the movement of Qi and proper structures; thus, students should be careful.

a. Wen Zhuang (Gentle Stance) 文樁

STEPS

1. Stand with your feet slightly wider than shoulder width, with toes pointing forward. Keep your body straight. Relax your chest and shoulders.
2. Put your arms by your sides. In the following, there are three standing methods:
    a. Holding Moon—Raise your arms to chest height, with palms facing your body.
    b. Loading Star—Place your hands at the side of your body.
    c. Support Sky—Raise your arms toward your head and rotate your palms so that they face outward and upward.
3. Breathe out slowly. The eyes stare forward. Try to maintain a peaceful mind. As a beginner, you should try to focus on the correctness of the posture and keep your body straight and upstanding.

MOVEMENTS

Wen Zhuang (Gentle Stance) 1: Cheng Bao Zhuang

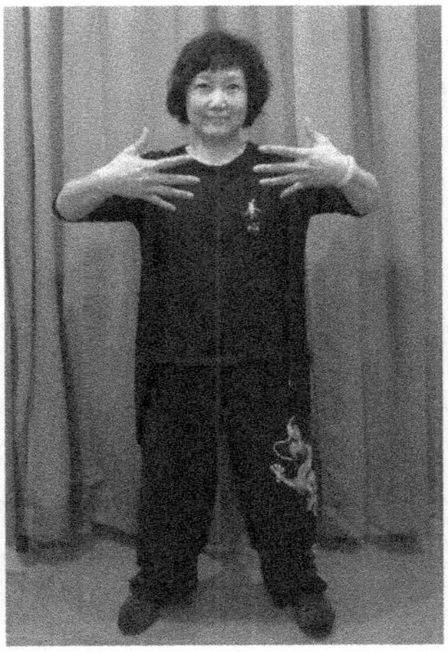

FRONT VIEW AND SIDE VIEW (FEATURING ERICA LIU)

Wen Zhuang (Gentle Stance) 2: Fu An Zhuang

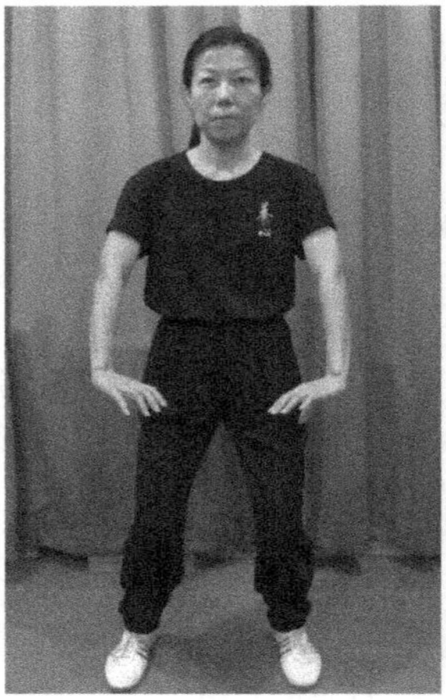
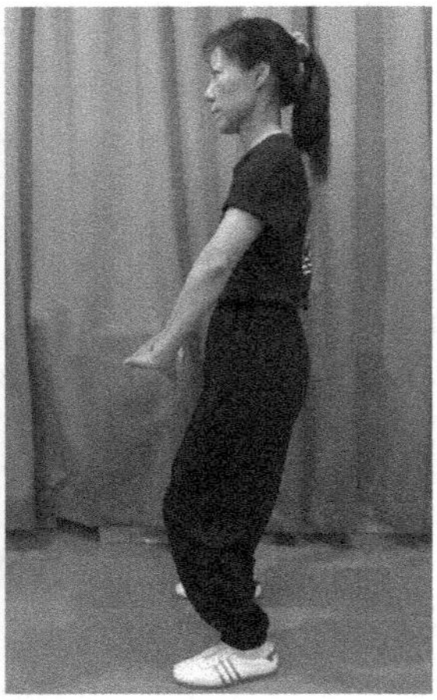

Front view and side view (featuring Joyce Wong)

b. Wu Zhuang (Martial Stance) 武樁

This stance is also known as San Cai Zhuang (Trinity Stance; old name: San Ti Shi).

Steps

1. Stand in a T-shape stance with body weight placed 60 percent on the back leg and 40 percent on the front leg.
2. The front hand pushes forward and stretches out straight while the other hand presses down.
3. Keep a vertically straight body without any inclination. The eyes stare just like an eagle. Focus and concentrate. The spine is erect and shoulders and chest relaxed. Both elbows drop down. Both hips roll in and draw strength.

Points to note while practicing Wu Zhuang

1. Do not try to control your breathing, for example breathing faster or slower. Do not focus on the contact of the tongue with the upper palate. Do not focus on only using the nose for breathing because it will be easy to feel uncomfortable if you close your mouth. Do not try to control the extension and contraction of your chest and Dantian.
2. Hold your head and upper back straight. Allow all the tension to leave your body. The body weight is equally shared on each foot. Your head, Dantian, and legs should coordinate perfectly.

3. Empty your mind; it should hold nothing. Try to control your thoughts and emotions. Reach a full extension of your body. The mind is naturally going to calm and settle down without any inclination. There is no thought or intention, no figure or image, and no self or others; only Qi exists in the body.

Advice from the master

Instruction on the steps of the movements:

- *Relax:* Set the structure, then relax from top to bottom.
- *Resist:* Hold the structure; do not collapse.
- *Sit:* Sink the Kua, fold into the Gua, and the buttocks really sit back.
- *Full:* Get Qi and the whole body to swell.
- *Conscientious:* The spirit must be serious and used internally to support and hold.

Movements

San Cai Zhuang or Santi Stance

PRINCIPLES FOR THE SANTI STANCE

The traditional eight essences

1. San Ding—Three Pressing:
    a. Head Must Press
    b. Tongue Must Press
    c. Palms Must Press
2. San Kou—Three Arching:
    a. Both Shoulders Arch
    b. Backs of Palms Arch
    c. Backs of Feet Arch
3. San Yuan—Three Round:
    a. Back Round
    b. Chest Round
    c. Tiger's Mouth Round
4. San Min—Three Quick:
    a. Mind Should Be Quick
    b. Eyes Should Be Quick
    c. Palms Should Be Quick
5. San Bao—Three Embracing:
    a. Mind and Intention Embraced
    b. Ribs Embraced
    c. Courage Embraced
6. San Chui—Three Dropping:
    a. Qi Should Drop
    b. Shoulders Should Drop
    c. Elbows Should Drop
7. San Qu—Three Bent:
    a. Both Arms Bent
    b. Both Legs Bent
    c. Both Wrists Bent
8. San Ting—Three Straightening:
    a. Neck Should Be Straightened
    b. Waist Should Be Straightened
    c. Knees Should Be Straightened

ONCE YOU PRACTICE SANTI STANCE, KEEP ALL EIGHT ESSENCES;
IMAGINE YOU ARE AN UNBREAKABLE FORTRESS, READY TO RUSH LIKE A TANK

Fortress

I have met a very important Xing Yi Quan teacher called Master Niu Sheng Xian (牛勝先). He is the student of the famous internal martial artist, Li Tian Ji (李天驥). He lived in Beijing, though I met him in Guangzhou. He gave me very clear instruction about the proper way of practicing Xing Yi Quan and internal martial arts. He emphasizes "built-up power."

He said to me, "Santi Shi is a fortress. The fortress is so firm that no one can push or pull you. Every part of your body is linked; people cannot move arms, hands, legs, or any part of your Stake."

He added, "When you rush forward to attack, no one can stop you by pulling your hands and legs from your back. There is also no one who can block you from rushing in; they will collapse and be broken into pieces."

Master Wang Xiang Zhai has a similar description in his writings: "The whole body looks like it is melted" (整體如鑄).

PROSTRATION 磕大頭

Introduction

The exercise of Yiquan prostration was brought to Hong Kong by Liang Zi Peng. He learnt this exercise from Master You Peng Xi (尤彭熙).

Prostration is a general term describing a gesture of homage and respect. There are many different ways to do prostrations, and the traditions vary from place to place. However, knowingly prostrating in the wrong way, whether out of pride or in order to make it easier, is an act of disrespect and a demonstration of contempt.

Proper prostrations, on the other hand, bring immeasurable benefits. The Buddha once said: "A single prostration is so powerful that if, as a result, one were to become a universal emperor as many times as the number of grains of dust beneath one's body down to the lowest depths of the earth, the benefits of that act would still not be exhausted."

Originally prostration was a religious act of respect and form performed by all traditions of Buddhism, but in particular Vajrayana Buddhism. Master You learnt from a reincarnated rinpoche, and felt that this exercise would improve the conditioning of the body and help to strengthen the power. So he decided to include this exercise in the Yiquan system. This has become one of the secret conditioning exercises for Yiquan practitioners of Liang's linkage.

The practice in Buddhism

In Vajrayana Buddhism, prostrations are often performed before meditation or teachings, but can form a separate practice by themselves. Prostrations are seen as a means of purifying one's body, speech, and mind of karmic defilements, especially pride.

Prostrations are used in tandem with visualization and can be used to express reverence to Guru Rinpoche and others. In the context of offering homage to Guru Rinpoche, prostrations are to be performed as follows:

> Bring your hands together in the "lotus bud" mudra (the base of the palm and the fingertips together, and thumbs slightly tucked in) and place them on the crown of the head, then to the throat and heart. As you place your hands on your crown, you offer homage to Guru Rinpoche's enlightened body, purify defilements and obscurations incurred through the avenue of your body, and establish the potential to realize Nirmanakaya. At your throat, you offer homage to his enlightened speech, and establish the potential to be the realized Sambhogakaya. Bringing your hands to your heart, you offer homage to his enlightened mind, purify your mind's obscurations, and establish the potential to realize Dharmakaya.

The actual prostration

The actual prostration is performed by putting your hands together and placing them on the crown of your head, then at your throat, and then at your heart, to purify the obscurations of body, speech, and mind respectively. Then touch the floor with your body at five points—the forehead, the palms of the two hands, and the two knees—in order to purify the obscurations of the five poisons and obtain the blessings of body, speech, mind, qualities, and activity. Then stand up straight, put your hands together again, and continue to the second round.

Then once again drop the body forward and stretch it full length on the floor, with the arms outstretched in front. Again, with hands in the lotus bud mudra, bend your arms back and place your hands on the top of your head, a gesture that acknowledges the blessing flowing from Guru Rinpoche. Then stretch your arms out once more and push yourself up. Bring your hands into the lotus bud mudra for the third time and touch your heart in a gesture of reverence. Then, with a smooth motion, bring your hands to your crown and perform the next prostration.

This type of prostration is done normally at least 108 times. A prostration mala can be used to facilitate counting.

Pilgrims regularly prostrate at the Jokhang Temple. The Lhasa Tibet prostrations, which are done there in large numbers, such as 100,000, can be part of the preliminary practices to the practice of tantra. Other practices like this can be reciting the Refuge prayer, mandala offerings, and Vajrasattva mantras.

Prostrations could be likened to an "emergency measure" for clearing the mind. They are a very powerful technique for seeing the karma of a situation because both the mind and the body are involved. Something that might take days of sitting and contemplating in order to digest may be done in a much shorter time with prostrations. The usual practice here is to do 1080 bows a day. This can be done all at once or, as is usually the case, spread out throughout the day.

Preparing for practice

- The practice must be done before meals or one and a half hours afterwards, so that your stomach is not full of food that will cause your body pain.
- Wear soft pants without a leather belt, otherwise it will hurt the stomach when you hit the ground.
- Prepare a soft pillow with straps on the top.
- Spray talcum powder on the ground for your practice.
- Purify your mind and concentrate before you practice.
- Have full confidence in your success during practice.

The procedure

- Stand straight with your feet together and hands in front of your body before the area that you sprayed with talcum powder.
- Bend down as if you are going to jump into water. Inhale deeply.
- Either holding a pillow or wearing gloves, slide your hands on the ground and stretch your arms. Push your body forward to the ground quickly, with the stomach hitting the ground with sound. Exhale lengthily.
- Be careful not to hit your chin on the ground, or else you will be injured badly.

- Fully stretch out so that your elbows and knees will not crash against the ground.
- Do not stand up immediately; drag your arms and elbows back to the position of your chest. Then using deep breathing, stretch and extend your back. Hold your knees and use your waist to raise your body. This will tighten the muscles of your abdomen.
- Stand upright, step back to your starting position, relax, and do the prostration a second time.

Numbers and duration

At the beginning, practice ten times and take a rest. Every time, add three repetitions until you can practice 20 times per session. Practice one session in the morning and one session in the afternoon.

You may feel an ache in your abdomen and forearms, but after adequate rest you will recover quickly. So be patient and practice hard. When you practice continuously, the muscles of your arms and legs will grow stronger and you will feel that you are full of power.

Keep at it for half a year and your Qi will become strong and your fajin energy will be very powerful and fierce.

Common errors

1. Not stretching out your hands enough so that your knees will hit the ground.
2. Not enough coordination, resulting in your knees hitting the ground first.
3. Not having your hands in front of your body when you are dropping down.
4. Raising your hands above the chin, resulting in your chin hitting the ground.
5. Opening your mouth or intending to talk when you drop down. This is very dangerous as you may bite your tongue.
6. Not raising your head enough when you drop forwards so as to avoid your forehead and chin hitting the ground.
7. Not bowing and arching your back to stand up, which means that you will lack one procedure of training your back and abdomen.
8. Dropping and sliding too slowly like an actual Buddhism prostration, which is not applicable here. Your movement must be quick and powerful, treating this as a hard practice.

Photos showing the actual practice

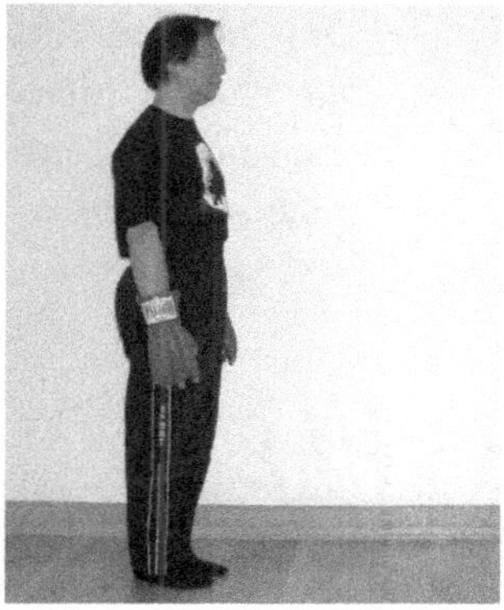

1. Stand upright and concentrate

2. Bend and ready

3. Drop and stretch

4. Push forward

5. Hit abdomen on the ground

Practice at High Mountain, below Holy Tree, absorbing fresh Qi and energy, will increase your strength quickly
Photo taken at Shen Nong Jia, Natural Park of Hu Bei, 2006

CONCLUSION

When training Static Stances, the time and frequency should be decided according to one's ability and body structure. When a beginner practices Dun Yao and Tuo Yao, normally the frequency should not exceed ten times. One should focus on the quality of a movement rather than the quantity of the movements. One should practice Static Stance in a relaxed way. If one feels uncomfortable or bored, it is better to stop and do some jogging in order to relax.

Quick Start practice program for a 60-minute class

	Duration	**Movements**
1.	2 min	Warm up —Single swing arms —Double swing arms forward and backward —Stretch legs
2.	3 min	Dun Yao—Perform slowly 15 times within 3 min
3.	10 min	Static Stance—Fu An Zhuang
4.	10 min	Static Stance—Cheng Bao Zhuang
5.	5 min	Static Stance—Santi Zhuang—Left side
6.	5 min	Static Stance—Santi Zhuang—Right side
7.	5 min	Tuo Yao—Both/single hands drag
8.	2 min	Cuo Yao
9.	3 min	Prostration
10.	3 min	Receive and emit strength training
11.	10 min	Push hand
12.	2 min	Cool down

Chapter 9

STATIC STANCE

GENERAL ASPECTS

The core is Static Stance

The core or the nucleus of Yiquan is Static Stance. Static Stance is the source to obtain the strength, and Test Strength is the application of Static Stance. During Static Stance, large movements are worse than small movements; and even better is not to move and remain in Static Stance.

What is Static Stance and why is it so called?

Static Stance is a form of movement in which the practitioner holds his posture in a particular way for a certain time. The purpose of the stance is to develop and strengthen the skeleton in a flexible and relaxed manner. The skeleton becomes a fortress and guarding posture. Through the practice of tension and relaxation, the body develops static expansion strength and six directions Hun Yuan strength (靜態張力, 六面爭力之混元力).

What are the benefits of these stances in health and combat?

In old books of war, there lies the concept of strengthening ourselves first before we can have enough strength to attack others.

The Art of War by Sunzi

CHAPTER IV TACTICAL DISPOSITIONS

1. Sunzi said: In ancient times, the good warriors first put themselves beyond the possibility of defeat, and then waited for an opportunity of defeating the enemy.
2. To secure us against defeat lies in our own hands, but the opportunity of defeating the enemy is provided by the enemy himself.

3. Thus the good fighter is able to secure himself against defeat, but cannot make certain of defeating the enemy.
4. Hence it is said: One may know how to conquer without being able to do it.
5. Security against defeat implies defensive tactics; ability to defeat the enemy means taking the offensive.
6. Standing on the defensive indicates insufficient strength; attacking, a superabundance of strength.
7. The general who is skilled in defense hides in the most secret recesses of the earth; he who is skilled in attack flashes forth from the topmost heights of heaven.

Thus on the one hand we have the ability to protect ourselves; on the other, a victory that is complete.

孫子兵法》形篇第四 - 形篇

孫子曰：昔之善戰者，先為不可勝，以侍敵之可勝。不可勝在己，可勝在敵。故善戰者，能為不可勝，不能使敵之必可勝。故曰：勝可知，而不可為。不可勝者，守也；可勝者，攻也。守則不足，攻則有餘。善守者，藏于九地之下；善攻者，動于九天之上。故能自保而全勝也。

It is Chinese philosophy that one should strengthen himself first before planning to attack or trying to defend. Therefore, if one wants to be a good fighter, one must build up the body into iron and improve one's conditioning and sports abilities.

Yiquan is both an excellent martial art and a very effective system of health cultivation (一, 求衛生身體健康； 二, 講自衛； 三, 尋理趣).

1. Yiquan for health

- A completely natural system with no harmful side-effects.
- Builds up leg and arm muscle, enables smooth breathing, and enriches the spirit for work and combat.
- Suitable for building and maintaining health.

2. Yiquan for self-defense

- Develops whole body strength in a comparatively short time.
- The system is clear, reachable, and measurable.
- It is simple and effective, with no difficult movements or complicated linking forms.
- Anyone can learn it.

3. Yiquan for mind

- It is fascinating.
- It builds strength through mind–body integration.
- The journey of discovery through its practice is never-ending.

What is Empty Stance and why is it so called?

When you practice a stance, it is not just for relaxation—you have to keep in mind that you are training. Every time you practice, there should be benefit for every minute of the stance. So you must use your intent to practice. The intent is stretch and contract, and to get the six directions strength. All processes of the stance should be full of internal movements. This is called Life Stance.

If one just stands there and closes their eyes, opening their mouth, and relaxing even, as if all the skeleton is falling down, this is called Empty Stance or Dead Stance. It would be better to go to bed to sleep and rest comfortably there. The result would be much better than standing.

THEORIES OF YIQUAN STANCE

1. Essential points

- Keep basic body requirements for steps, body, arms, waist, and eyes correctly.
- Principles: shoulder stretch, elbows stretched to the sides, with 30 percent holding and 70 percent stretching.
- Mind requirement: tense and relaxed.

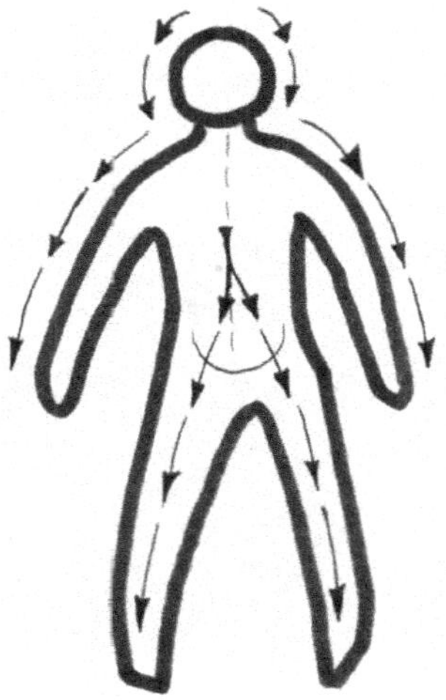

THE WAY OF RELAXING

2. Body scanning

As you hold a standing posture, make sure your body shape is adjusted in an appropriate alignment:

- Head is straight, without bending left or right.
- Chin is pushed close to your neck, so that your neck feels tension.
- Shoulders are rounded towards the front.
- Back is rounded and stretched sideways.
- Chest is hollow but not pressed downward.
- Armpits do not press down and should stretch outward.
- Forearms extend forward.
- Elbows are supported and stretched to the sides.
- Hands have the power of pushing out but holding inwards.
- Buttocks sink like sitting on a high chair.
- The front thigh shows a folding line.
- Kua sits on a fallen round tree.
- Knees bend at 45 degrees.
- The soles of the feet are hollow and the toes claw the ground.

You must check and make sure all body parts are in the proper position before you come into silent meditation. If not, all the time you spend in standing will be wasted and will even be uncomfortable, painful, and difficult to amend in future practice.

YOUR MIND HAS TO BE VERY CALM, LIKE THE SURFACE OF A QUIET POOL; BUT UNDER THE SURFACE, WATER FLOWS

3. Mind movements

- Floating in water
- Showering in warm water
- Holding paper balls
- Penetrating and holding up in sand
- Stretching skin and tendon
- Walking in mud
- Stretching silk in the whole body
- Swimming in air
- Listening to quiet rain
- Observing stars under moonlight.

4. How to test and measure achievement

For this there are six phenomena. Seek the first four initially, and then add the final two:

1. Heat
2. Numbness
3. Distension
4. Heaviness
5. Shaking
6. Resistance.

5. Mind achievement

1. Unity
2. Heavy
3. Coordination
4. High spirit.

(論四形: 體整如鑄, 身如鉛灌, 肌肉如一, 毛髮如戟)

6. Common error and correction in practicing

- Muscles becoming too hard or too soft.

7. Testing of the stance

Test the strength and stability of the structure. This should be handled by your instructor or coach in order to test the strength of the six directions power kept by your skeleton (間架).

PRACTICE IN HIGH MOUNTAINS: YOU WILL FEEL THE STRENGTH OF THE AIR, SO SOLID LIKE SWALLOWING THE QI INTO YOUR BODY AT EVERY BREATH

ZHAN ZHUANG (STATIC STANCE) 站樁

When Master Wang first learnt the Static Stance from his teacher, Master Guo, according to his daughter Guo only taught him one combat stance, side push up. In addition every punching posture of Xing Yi Quan was to be kept for a long duration. This also applied to the Santi Stance, which was normally practiced by his early students.

The Santi Stance was practiced among the lineage of Liang Tse Peng, Han Xing Yuan, and Han Xing Qui as a major stance.

At the early founding stage of Wang's stance, there were very few postures: two front stances and one side stance—that is, the Santi Stance. Then, later, according to different strength requirements, the system became more complete. According to Han Xing Qui, in Shanghai there was a Qigong of one-finger Zen, with different postures to generate the Qi to different parts of the body. Master Wang analyzed the different needs of the parts of the body and summarized them in 24 postures. These postures were shown in Han's book *Yiquan Xue*.

Wang designated all the stances as Huen Yuan Zhuang. But in order to distinguish different postures, followers named the postures themselves and hence different lineages had different names. The Yiquan Association is trying to standardize these names, but different names have been used for such a long time that this has proved difficult. So people are still using different names for the stances and movements.

Program of standing

There are procedures for keeping the stances, similar to using a computer system:

Boot up

Log in

Enter

Search for virus

Set up

Input and output

Reset

Turn off.

Thus, for the Static Stance, the procedures are as follows.

Preparation

Warm up: perform the five relaxation exercises, circling exercise, and hand and leg stretches.

Setting up

Step wide, hold a stone ball at a low position, bend downward, and then lift up and enter into the posture.

Scanning

- Check the three parts and nine sections 檢查三段九節.
- Check the width of steps.
- Check the gesture of the hands—height and distance; stretch outwards and then hold back.
- Check the angles of arms and legs forming triangles.
- Check the eight balls in the body, squat Kua to sit on a high chair, press your lower jaw, really press the eight balls, and expand your abdomen.

Enter into status

- *10 minutes:* (1) Correct your postures continuously; (2) fix the posture (定型), keep it, and do not collapse or let the structure change.
- *10 minutes:* Be silent; concentrate, like standing in a dark room.
- *10 minutes:* Relax; prolong breathing, and be totally relaxed and flexible; tense and relax at intervals; feel the Dantian expand and contract when

coordinated with the breathing; and feel the Qi passing from chest to abdomen, deep and long.

- *10 minutes:* Body shaking and numb (modify bones).
- *10 minutes:* Concentrate on stretches to train the small muscles (modify tendons).

Imagining

- *10 minutes:* Imagination movements (意境意念): listening to rain and wind, standing in a swimming pool, standing at the top of a hill, taking a shower, etc.
- *10 minutes:* Practice small movements (摸劲); stretch to improve opposite power:
    - Simulate (動感意念) push and pull trunk, palms grasp bird, rubber band power, etc.
    - To feel the changes inside the body, blood reaches tips of fingers and Qi passes from spine to brain.
- *10 minutes:* Mind leaving body (out of body—OFB) to look back and travel (optional).
- *10 minutes:* Mind returns to body.

Log out

Retrieve from stance, and tell the body to relax and be ready.

Ending

By Guan Qi, penetrating Qi.

Release power and cool down

Patting method.

Actual practice

- Health Stance—eight main patterns.
- Stand at least five minutes for each posture, if you are busy.
- Timing of stance: increase time of stance by five minutes each week for each stance, extending to 60 minutes for each stance.

Follow-up

1. Do not go on if:
   a. you feel pain from the chest, shoulders, knees, or back
   b. breathing is not comfortable, there is choking, or Qi cannot pass through
   c. posture is not balanced, like something pressing down
   d. you feel shaky or are swaying; in this case open your eyes.
2. Enhancement:
   a. Add timing.
   b. Stand in posture lower.
   c. Add stretches and twists.
3. Need to get the feeling:
   a. Four phenomena: heat, numb, swollen, and heavy.
   b. For Health Stance, feel the body is full of strength like a balloon.
   c. For Combat Stance, get eyesight as sharp as a leopard.
4. Measurement by Test Stance:
   a. Set the timing for each different posture according to their difficulty.
   b. Test four appearances/likes (出四如) by:
      i. pressing and pushing—skeleton does not collapse
      ii. hitting hips, back, and thigh for training of resistance
      iii. pulling and pushing different parts of the body that are still non-movable
      iv. pinching muscles that are hard like iron.

Benefits from Static Stance

Primary

- Balanced posture.
- Props strength of arm joined with shoulder (連通).
- Head props upward, with neck straight.
- Three locks:
  - Perineum
  - Dantian
  - Throat.

Secondary

- Develops Hun Yuan strength.
- When both arms are held in circles before your chest, if the opponent presses on them, they have an expanding force and elastic strength.
- Evolution of strength (樁法換勁).

THREE INSUFFICIENCIES 三不夠—WHY AM I NOT PROGRESSING?

Suppose you have been standing for the same duration as others in your group, or even longer, but still cannot experience any sensations in the body. Why is this? Doctor Yu Yong Nian has suggested the following "three insufficiencies."

1. Insufficient duration

- The duration of each session is not enough. Standing for a short period is relatively easy and more comfortable, but the endurance is not enough and the reactions of the body will be lesser. Standing for 40 minutes is better than 20 minutes. However, the results will vary according to body fitness. At the same time, standing once a day will yield less progress than standing three to four times daily.
- There must be progress to achieve results. Normally, it will take three to four months to change the body structure. Change will vary according to the duration, quality, and frequency of standing, as well as to body structure.

2. Insufficient angle

This means that the legs are not bent enough at the knees, which will affect the quality of the training. Maintaining a suitable angle will tense the muscles correctly and promote the effectiveness of the training.

3. Insufficient intent

Different stages require different intents during standing. An alert intent will strengthen the nervous system, increase blood circulation, and provide training preparation for attacking and guarding. Different intents will bring about different sensations in the skin and body.

A fairy mountain, full of Qi and spirit, a place which must be visited by international martial arts practitioners, Wudang Shan of Hebei, 2006

Photo of Master C S Tang taken at the old palace where Zhang San Feng practiced Taiji Quan, Wudang Mountain, 2006

Chapter 10

YIQUAN GENERAL STANDARD REQUIREMENTS

OVERVIEW

The following are essential requirements of the Yiquan stance, but have not previously been available to the general public:

1. Hand shapes
2. Leg shapes
3. Body shapes
    a. Grasp eight balls
    b. Triangle fitness
    c. Lifting the large tendon
    d. Open and round your back
    e. Swell your abdomen
4. Spiritual attitude requirements.

THE STANCE IN DETAIL

1. Hand shapes

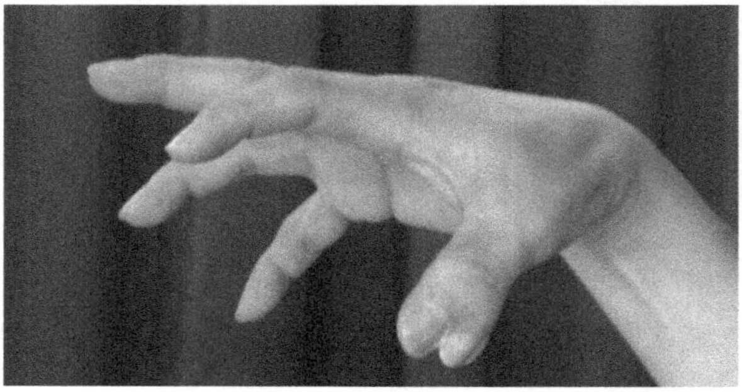

FUNCTION OF FIVE FINGERS: TI, ZHI, CHA, XUAN, AND MO

a. Function of the five fingers

Five terms are key: ti, zhi, cha, xuan, and mo:

1. 提 Thumb: Ti, lift—lift up and curve.
2. 指 Index finger: Zhi, point—point straight.
3. 插 Middle finger: Cha, stick—penetrating.
4. 旋 Ring finger: Xuan, rotate—curve back.
5. 抹 Little finger: Mo, wipe—can wipe backward.

Fingers have individual duties, and are usually under conscious control. In Yiquan, each finger processes its own functions. Most masters of Yiquan have kept this secret; however, Zhang Hong Cheng and Master Wang Yu Fang have revealed these previously hidden functions.

b. Hanging function

Zhang Hong Cheng and Master Wang Yu Fang especially revealed the functions of the following:

- Thumb: like a hook that pulls the enemy's hand.
- Little finger: like a clothes hanger.

(掌如覆碗，虎 撑圓，拇指如鉤，五指要夾.)

Master Wang said: "The palm is in the shape of a bowl turned upside down." He added: "Tiger mouth stretches in a circle, the thumb is like a hook, and the fingers must grip."

That means the fingers are in a grasping mode and the center of the palm has a hollow shape.

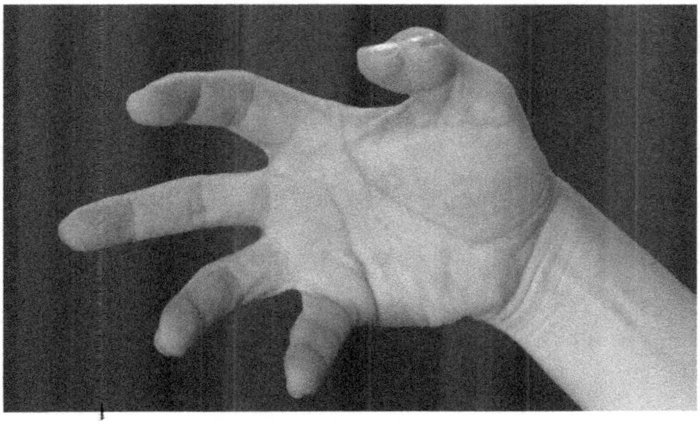

c. Fingers grip pearls

Imagine gripping pearls in between the fingers. Hold with power and do not let the fingers close together.

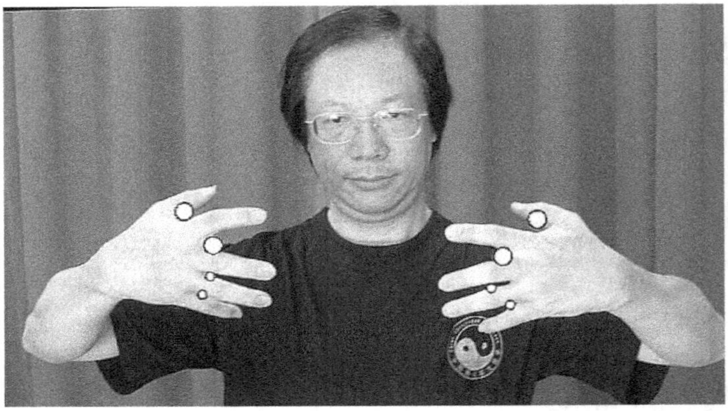

d. Arm shape

1. 頂 Ding: The outside wrist must support.
2. 提 Ti: The upper wrist must be raised.
3. 撕 Si: Both palms must push out sideways as though you are tearing cloth.
4. 抱 Bao: Both arms hold two balloons and must not pop them.
5. 墜 Zhui: Both elbows must droop in a relaxed manner.

e. Position of the hands

The principles are:

1. height not higher than the eyebrows
2. height not lower than the navel—that is, the waist belt
3. close to but not touching your body
4. apart, but not more than a foot.

f. Fist shape

GRASPING SHAPE OF FIST

PUNCHING SHAPE OF FIST

No matter whether you punch with the fists or palms, the elbow must not be totally stretched, and must force downward. We say, "Shape is curved, but the power is straight" (形曲力直).

2. Leg shapes

The leg should keep the following points when practicing:

1. Knees:
   a. 縮 Suo: Knees contract.
   b. 提 Ti: Knees raise towards abdomen.
   c. 夾 Jia: Knees grip against both legs.
2. 頂 Ding: Legs prop against the ground.

3. 扒 Pa: Toes claw to fit on the ground.

3. Body shapes

In order to strengthen the skeleton, practitioners should understand clearly the structure of their own body in terms of martial arts training. Our body is divided into three parts and nine sections (三段九節):

- Upper part: head, chest, stomach.
- Middle part: stomach, abdomen, Kau.
- Lower part: Kau, knee, leg.

a. Grasp eight balls (抓八個球)

To locate eight balls in our body:

- Throat: 1 ball
- Armpits: 2 balls
- Palms: 2 balls
- Kau: 2 balls
- Crotch: 1 ball.

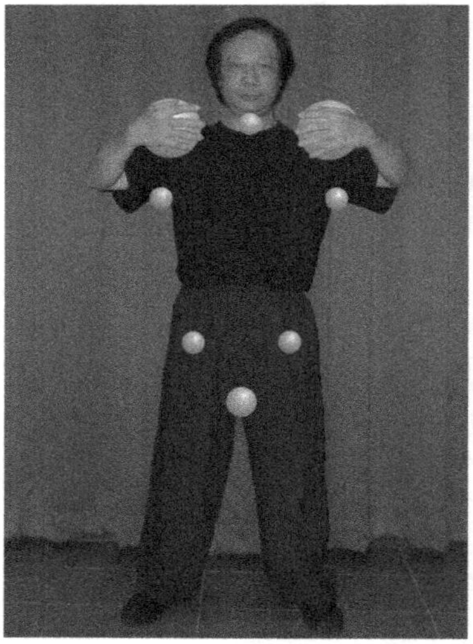

GRASP EIGHT BALLS

3 GRIPS, 2 PROPS (三夾兩頂)

1. Throat, armpits, and crotch must grip.
2. Head and tongue must be lifted up.

By insisting on the "3 grips, 2 props" to fix the eight balls at your structure, the body becomes a whole.

These apply to both front and side stances.

b. Triangle fitness

The most powerful skeleton has triangle shapes at the joints. Avoid your structure having flat surfaces; always keep limbs and body in triangle shapes so that you have a strong supporting power and your structure will not collapse.

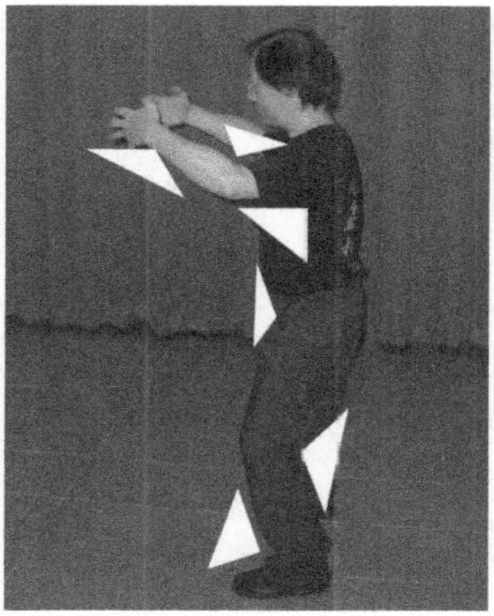

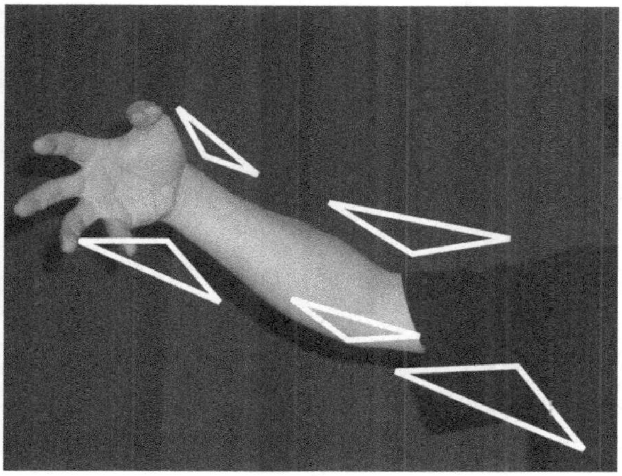

ARMS HELD IN TRIANGLE SHAPE TO ENHANCE SUPPORTING POWER AND STRIKING STRENGTH

MASTER WANG YU FENG ALWAYS MENTIONED THAT, WHEN STANDING, YOU SHOULD IMAGINE THAT YOU STAND ON A FALLEN TREE OR CANNON, AND THAT YOUR HIP KUA SHOULD KEEP AN INWARD PRESSURE AND BE TIGHT

c. Lifting the large tendon (Tiao Dai Jin) 挑大筋

This practice is normally taught at a later stage; practitioners subsequently think it is a secret that the masters do not want to tell them.

It is a little bit difficult to perform, but it is a fundamental requirement because the purpose of Static Stance is not to build up muscle, but to stretch and strengthen the tendons so that they can release powerful Fali.

The tendons include tiger mouths of the hands, wrists, inside of the elbows, armpits, necks, hips, inside of the knees, ankles, and surface of the feet. They should be explicitly seen to be lifted up when doing the stance, and this lifting should be maintained throughout all the time of standing.

d. Open and round your back

Round your shoulders by extending your arms from the shoulder joints; your back will now be open and round.

e. Swell your abdomen

The internal organs of your chest sink to the stomach and your abdomen will expand. This is an important part of internal martial arts: we have to keep this structure so that we can emit strength.

4. Spiritual attitude requirements

The Principles of Trust

信條：尊長，護幼，信義，仁愛，智勇，深厚，果決，堅忍。

The Principles of Trust are to respect the elderly, to protect the young, integrity, love and benevolence, courage and wisdom, strength of character, decisiveness, and endurance.

The Four Countenances

四容：頭直，目正，神莊，意靜。

The Four Countenances are the head straight, the eyes fixed, the spirit strong, and stillness of intention. Keeping to these countenances will enhance concentration.

The Eight Essences

八要：靜，敬，虛，切，恭，慎，意，和。

The Eight Essences are stillness, reverence, emptiness, earnestness, respect, care, intention, and harmony.

FOUNDATION

Only with a strong foundation of the above can one talk about the training of the body and mind. Training first involves the standing poses or standing meditations, and at the same time involves an analysis of how to control the joints and the muscles, and how to utilize the tension and relaxation of single and double weight. Single and double weight is not limited to referring only to the weight of the hands and the feet, but can also be extended to include the head, the hands, the body, the feet, the shoulders, the elbows, the knees, and the hips as well as the large and small joints, the four limbs, and the entire skeleton. Even the smallest points of energy contain a distinction between single and double weight, tension and relaxation, emptiness and firmness, and lightness and heaviness. The ratios of 30 percent of your energy in outward expansion and 70 percent inward embracing, and 40 percent of the weight on the front foot and 60 percent on the back foot, can also be reversed. This is not something that can be easily described by the written word. In summary, we have to work from the abstract to the concrete.

SUMMARY FOR PRACTICING STATIC STANCE

1. Static Stance and Test Strength should be practiced as a whole.
2. Keep to the Four Countenances and Eight Essences.
3. Keep to the body requirements of the above and remember that your throat must not jut forward. Apply 3 grips, 2 props to hold the eight balls.
4. The body must be hollow and flexible; stand erect and lift—Xu Ling Ting Ba (虛靈梃拔).
5. The tips of the limbs must have power, so that one can hang clothes off them.
6. Train to inhale, not expel. Train to lift, not stamp.

Standing lower will increase base power and footwork.

STEP SHAPES

1. Horse stance

2. Bow stance

3. Empty stance

4. Sit stance

5. T-shape stance (Ding Ba Bu) 丁八步驟

6. Tiger stance

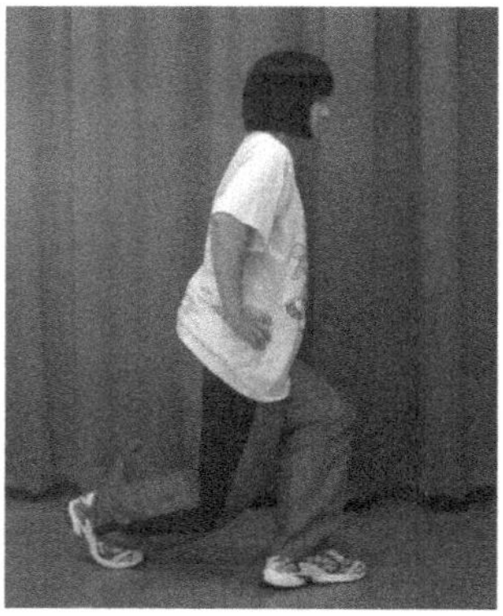

7. Dragon stance

Chapter 11

PREPARATION, CARE, AND WORKOUT

PREPARING FOR PRACTICE

INTRODUCTION TO PRACTICING YIQUAN

If you do not get enough healthy exercise in your life, then you will experience fatigue, unwanted weight gain, and possible ill health. You will not have a healthy outlet to rid yourself of stress and anxiety, which builds up in you in the normal course of living. Therefore, it is very important that we spare some time to exercise daily.

Benefits of practicing Yiquan

Practicing Static Stance training and sensing dynamic movement can improve our health and provide us with many benefits—for example:

1. It improves our cardio-respiratory functioning, physical strength, and blood circulation; and at the same time it reduces our blood cholesterol.
2. It reduces our chances of having cardiovascular disease, high blood pressure, and diabetes in later years.
3. It strengthens our immune system and reduces our chances of having a stroke.
4. It strengthens our muscles and increases bone density, so decreasing our chances of getting osteoporosis.
5. It improves joint flexibility and body balance so as to reduce our chances of getting hurt.
6. It slows down the aging rate.
7. It burns excess fat and helps control our body weight.
8. It enables us to enjoy memorable moments with friends and family by practicing push hand and partner training.

9. It helps us to manage stress, which is good for preventing sleep disorders.
10. It releases tension, increases self-confidence, builds up a positive self-image, and improves interpersonal relationships and social networks.

Tips for practicing

Consult your doctor before doing exercise in order to be aware of the condition of your health. During exercising, you need to pay attention to several things—for instance:

1. Select suitable sports and the amount of exercise according to your abilities.
2. A place that is too hot, too cold, or too stuffy is not suitable for doing exercise. Do not do exercise when you are too full or hungry.
3. Wear comfortable sports clothes and shoes.
4. Remember to do warm-up and cool-down exercises.
5. Be careful of doing too vigorous exercise, especially exercise for the neck, lower back, and knee.
6. A professional trainer is needed for involvement in some advanced training, such as push hand and free sparring.
7. Remove any obstacles, be careful of wet areas, and avoid doing exercises in dark areas in order to prevent accidents happening.
8. Make sure you breathe well during exercising.
9. If you are suffering from chronic diseases such as heart trouble or diabetes, please consult a doctor before doing any sports.
10. If you do not feel well, for instance you feel dizzy, are breathing very hard, or your heart is painful during exercising, you should do some cool-down exercises and have some rest. If the situation does not improve, you should stop doing any exercise and consult a doctor immediately.

Some guidelines for practicing

1. Those who are sick or infirm can practice the following Static Stances:
    a. *Lying-down Static Stance:* suitable for those who cannot move freely; they can practice on their own or ask someone to assist them.
    b. *Sitting Static Stance:* suitable for those who cannot stand for a long time; they should sit on a comfortable chair with their feet on the ground and their back flat against the chair.

c. *Standing Static Stance:* suitable for those who have good body balance and do not need assistance.

If necessary, you can ask people to assist you during exercising.

2. Breathing exercise. A method that is suitable for everybody is: close your mouth, breathe in slowly, and try to feel your lungs expanding. Then breathe out with your mouth.
3. Exercising time and frequency. For beginners, it is suggested that a suitable frequency is four times a week, with each session lasting for 15 minutes and increasing gradually to 30 minutes per day. Advanced practitioners should extend standing to two hours per day.

Daily workout capacity

According to some research, we can improve our health if we exercise for at least half an hour a day. Therefore, we should schedule at least three to five hours a week to enjoy suitable sports activities.

Suggested formats might be one of the following:

- At least a half-hour exercise each day.
- At least a one-hour exercise within two days.
- At least half an hour of accumulative exercises each day (each time at least 10 minutes).

For example:

- Every day do 15 minutes of exercise before and after work.
- Divide the 30 minutes of exercise into three parts: morning, afternoon, and evening. Each part should last 10 minutes for practicing Static Stance or footwork training.

Increased exercise in daily living

1. Use stairs instead of an elevator.
2. If you have to use an elevator, do some static stances when you are in it.
3. Walk instead of using a vehicle. You can do footwork training while you are walking.
4. Do some static stances or power and leg muscle training while you are watching TV.
5. Practice push-hand and Yiquan training with classmates frequently. Maintain Yiquan training as a habit.
6. Participate in some outdoor extra-curricular activities.

Set a target

Set an achievable target—for example:

- *Frequency.* Should be 5 to 7 times a week. Doing exercise daily is the best; if this is not possible, do it at intervals.
- *Intensity.* You should reach your target heart rate and feel that you are working hard, but at an acceptable level.
- *Time.* Each exercise program should be maintained for at least 30 minutes. Beginners can divide it into several parts; for example, divided into three parts, with each part lasting for 10 minutes. However, you can only burn fat if you do exercise for more than 20 minutes.
- *Type.* Select the type of exercise that fits your fitness purposes. Exercise can be divided into aerobic exercises, stretches, and building muscle. The best exercise is jogging or some low/medium-intensity whole body exercises.

Procedure of practicing Yiquan

- Warm-up exercises:
    - Stretching
    - Relaxation.
- Main training tasks:
    - Static body balance training: Static Health Stance
    - Muscle and spiritual training: Static Combat Stance
    - Power training: Shi Li—Testing dynamic strength movement
    - Advanced leg muscle and body balance training: Mo Ca Bu—Footwork training
    - Advanced strength and speed training: Fali—Emitting of dynamic strength
    - Advanced Qi and spiritual training: Fa Sheng—Emitting of sound
    - Whole body coordination and rhythm training: Fist Dance routine
    - Actual combat training: Free sparring.
- Cool-down exercises:
    - Breathing
    - Stretching
    - Relaxation.

COMMON WORKOUT MISTAKES

Skipping the warm-up

Warming up is one of the key elements to a successful program because muscles stretch most efficiently when they are warm. Going from normal activity straight into high-impact exercising puts tremendous stress on the body—stress that could ultimately slow you down. When the muscles are cold and still, you will be more prone to injury. You may suffer from long-term damage to muscles, bones, and ligaments. Overworking the body and ignoring its need to recuperate often causes painful problems.

Just as a car engine needs oil to prevent the damage of metal rubbing against metal, so the body has its own lubricating fluid—called the synovial fluid—which helps prevent wear and tear of the joints. When we become inactive after sleeping or sitting for a long time, we should perform a sequence of stretches to help lubricate the body.

Do the five body relaxation exercises below to improve circulation and relieve stiffness in the joints.

Failing to stretch

Stretching is not the same as warming up. Three to five minutes of stretching provides greater flexibility and range of motion. Properly executed stretches should be gentle, easy, and sustained. Avoid bouncing and stretching injured muscles.

Condensing your routine

Many people are "weekend warriors," who cram their entire routine into the weekend and skip working out during the week. People cannot do all their athletic endeavors in two days of intensity and expect it to make up for the rest of the week. These exercisers have a tendency to overdo it, which strains the body and can result in painful musculoskeletal damage.

Believing in "No pain, no gain"

It is normal to experience some muscle soreness during and after a routine. You should feel tension and stress, but if what you are doing is really painful, you are not doing yourself any favors. This is Master Wang's principle of training: exercise must be done in a comfortable way.

Forgetting to mix it up

No professional athletes do the same exercise every day. Muscles break down during a workout and can take up to 36 hours to heal, so do not always subject them to the same work. Instead, switch your routine. It is important to know what exercises are most appropriate for your body type.

INTRODUCTION TO THE RELAXATION EXERCISES

Headaches and pain from the neck and waist are symptoms of stress that come from working in a fast-paced, competitive environment. They are the result of tensing up the neck and shoulder muscles, which reduces blood flow and oxygen supply to the brain.

Working on a computer with your head frozen in one position for a long time can cause a tension headache. Exercising the neck and shoulders frequently and keeping a good posture can help prevent this.

Perform the warm-up exercises every two to three hours to improve blood flow to the neck and waist. Always do the exercises in a controlled manner and breathe easily throughout the process.

The following relaxation exercises can be done alone as a separate program. You should always practice this when you are tired or feel stressed. It is also a very good program to perform before doing the main program.

FIVE BODY RELAXATION EXERCISES 鬆身五法

This is a good warm-up program, in five parts:

1. Arm swings, front and back.
2. Arm swings, both hands in front.
3. Arm swings, forward and backward.
4. Squat, arm sweeps, shoulder rolls, and waist twists.
5. Alternating bow stances with heel/toe arcs.

1. Arm swings, front and back

- Starting position: arms are held out at the sides, shoulder height, with legs straight.
- Exhale, bend knees, and lightly swing the arms in a relaxed manner so the front hand touches a shoulder; the rear hand swings across the back.
- Inhale and straighten the legs as you swing out the arms to the position at the beginning.
- Alternate sides, swinging both arms in front of and behind the body.
- Key points: arms should be relaxed to swing; bend and straighten the knees.

2. Arm swings, both hands in front

- Arms are held out at the sides, shoulder height, with legs straight.
- Exhale and bend the knees as you swing both arms across the front of the body like folding arms.
- Inhale and straighten the legs as you swing out the arms to the position at the beginning.
- Swing alternate arms in front and outside.

3. Arm swings, forward and backward

- Inhale and swing one arm directly in front of the body at the same time as swinging the rear hand behind the body.
- Exhale, bend the knees, and drop the arms in a swimming stroke action and alternate sides.
- The arms should be moved in a light scooping action.

4. Squat, arm sweeps, shoulder rolls, and waist twists

- Horse stance: both hands hold a big ball. Inhale, up and to the top, and then fold down to the center of the body, exhale, and sink. Repeat the circles.
- Legs stand wide apart. Inhale, swing the body forward away from the legs, and then exhale, back towards the center of the legs—continue in a rhythmic fashion rocking backward and forward.
- In the same position bend forward, keep the back straight, and hold the body still. Bring the arms close to the body and make a cross. Roll the shoulder joints and elbows softly forward. Repeat in the opposite direction.
- With legs still apart, keep the back straight and roll the body from left to right, side to side, relaxing the arms. This is like "wind sweeping through the willow" (搖風擺柳).
- Finish in horse stance. Relax to allow the blood to flow down your body.

5. Alternating bow stances with heel/toe arcs

- Rock the body from a rear-weighted stance to a forward stance, concentrating on keeping the center and transferring the weight through the heel to the toe.

Take a rest and return to the starting posture.

The movements

ARM SWINGS, FRONT AND BACK

ARM SWINGS, BOTH HANDS IN FRONT

Arm swings, forward and backward

Squat, arm sweeps, shoulder rolls, and waist twists

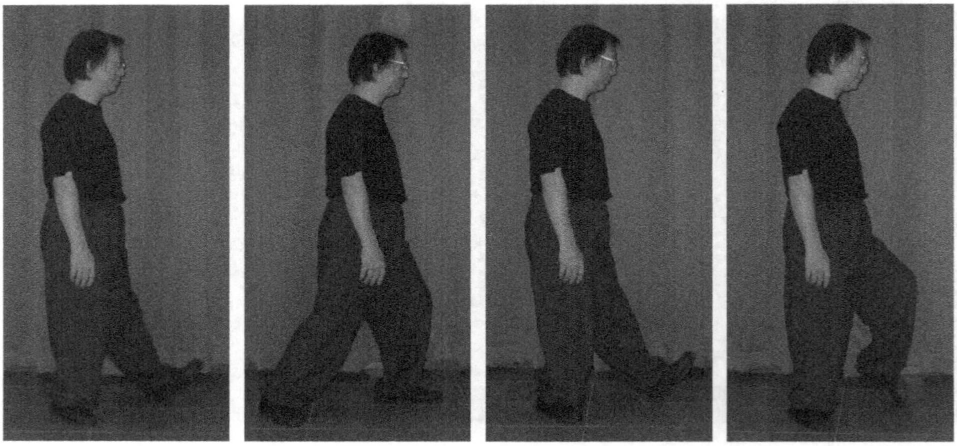

Alternating bow stances with heel/toe arcs

CIRCULAR FLEXIBILITY EXERCISES

1. Cross Wrist Turning 十字功轉腕
2. Towel Elbow Turning 巾字功轉肘
3. Fan Arm Turning 扇字功轉膊
4. Dai Shoulder Turning 大字功轉肩
5. Wrist Turning 轉腕功轉腕

1. Cross Wrist Turning 十字功 轉腕

WITH ARMS STRAIGHT, JUST TURN WRIST

2. Towel Elbow Turning 巾字功 轉肘

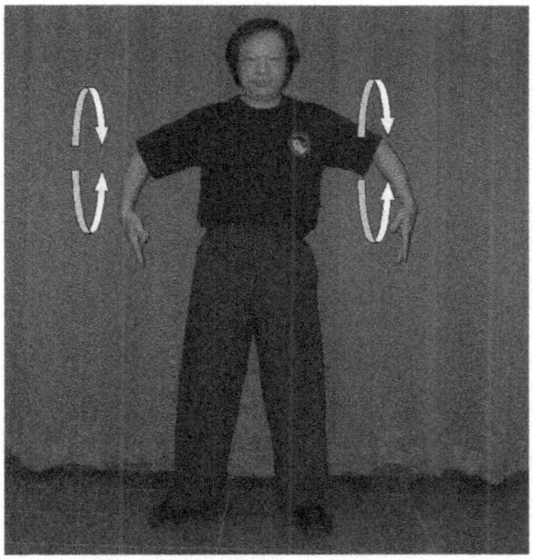

WITH UPPER ARMS FIXED, JUST TURN LOWER ARMS

3. *Fan Arm Turning* 扇字功 轉膞

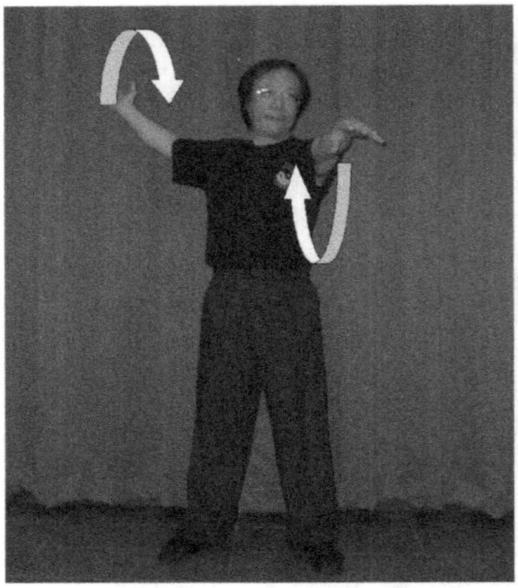

One arm moves forward, one arm moves backward

4. *Dai Shoulder Turning* 大字功 轉肩

Swing one arm forwards with fingers pointing out

5. *Wrist Turning* 轉腕 功轉腕

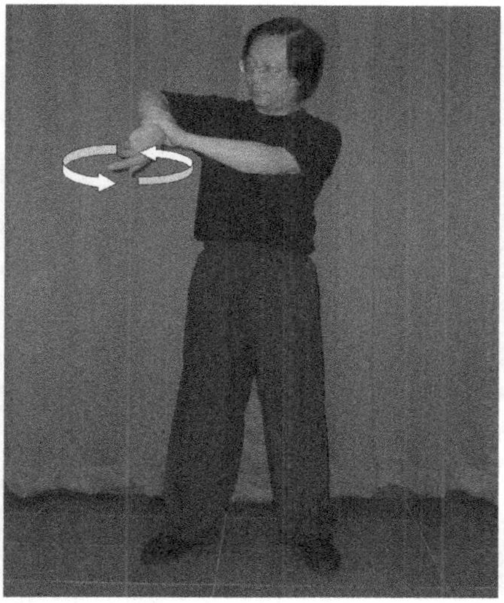

1. Hold left hand to turn wrist

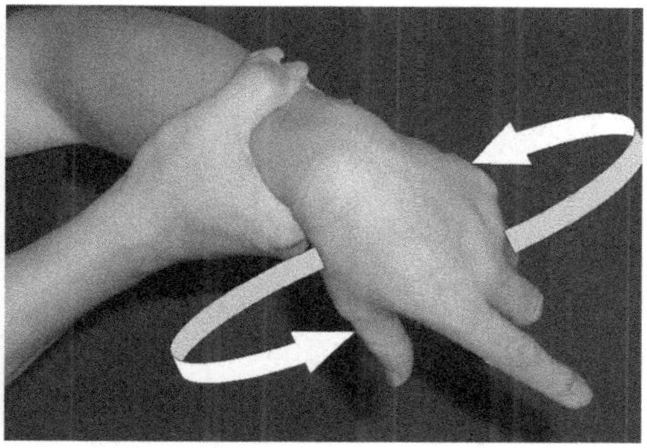

2. Hold right hand to turn wrist

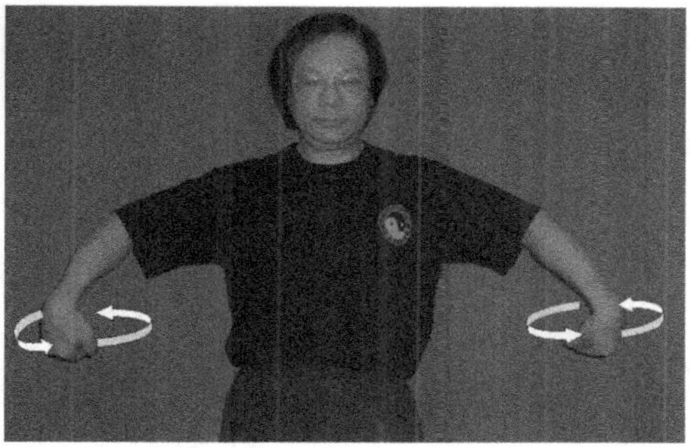

3. Both wrists turn

COOL-DOWN ENDING EXERCISES

Penetrate Qi 貫氣

1. Prepare to end the exercise of stances or movements by telling yourself that you are going to end the exercise.
2. Open your eyes, place your legs together, and calm yourself down.
3. Stretch your hands widely along both sides of your body with palms up, and then raise the hands over your head; inhale. Press the hands to the position of the stomach and exhale. Do it slowly and repeat three times until your spirit is calm.
4. Rub both hands till they are warm and then rub them all over your face several times.

The art of the patting system 拍打藝術

This cool-down exercise is very important. It will relax the stiffness of your muscles after holding a posture for a long time or performing strong Dun Yao and Fali. It will add flexibility and speed up the regeneration of torn tissues. This patting system was taught by Master Wang Yu Fang, and he insisted on the students completing this exercise after every standing session and hard movements.

Your hands are full of energy. By rubbing them after Static Stance, they can deliver the stored energy to the required pressure points.

The patting must follow a sequence along the meridian of the body. The important points to consider are:

- Hand shape
- Location of pressure points
- Patting heavy or light
- Frequency
- Quantity
- Precision
- Patting hand techniques.

Order

1. Left and right of neck, shoulder, and arm
2. Chest and hips
3. Front and back of legs.

Hand shapes

There are four kinds of hand shapes for patting the body:

1. Dragon Fist
2. Tiger Fist
3. Phoenix Fist
4. Leopard Fist.

1. Dragon Fist

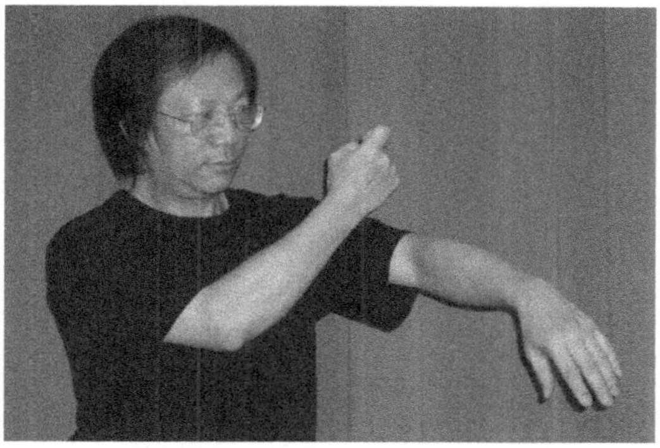

Clench your fist; use the bottom of the fist to slap from above

2. Tiger Fist

Clench your fist; use "tiger mouth" to slap from below

3. Phoenix Fist

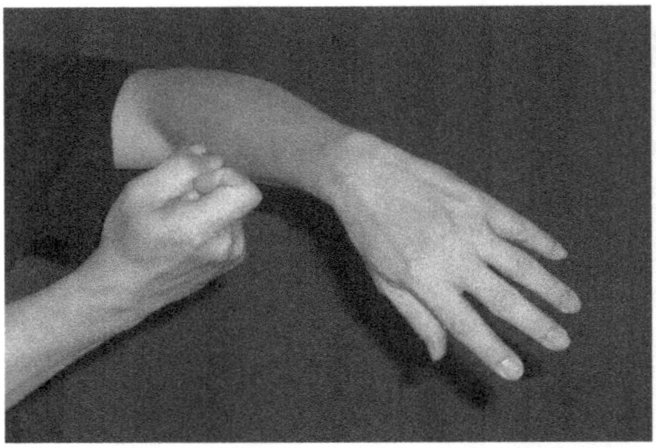

Bend your index finger; use the sharp point to slap

4. Leopard Fist

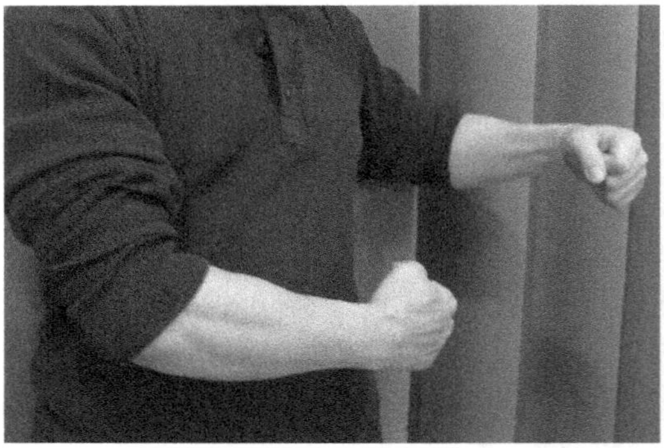

Use the heart of your fist to slap the hips

Procedure

1. Use your right Leopard Fist to pat your left neck and vice versa.
2. Use your right Dragon Fist to pat your left shoulder and vice versa.
3. Use your right Dragon Fist to pat your left arm from the shoulder to the upper arm and use Phoenix Fist to pat the lower arm. Repeat three times. Then use your left hand to pat your right side with the same fist and manner.
4. Use your right Tiger Fist to pat the underneath of your left arm from the shoulder to the hand. Repeat three times, and then do the left-hand side.

5. Use your right Dragon Fist to pat your left chest to the stomach and then use your left Dragon Fist to pat your right chest.
6. Bend down and use your right Tiger Fist to pat your left leg from top to bottom, from the outside first and then to the inside of your leg. Repeat for the other side three times.
7. Straighten up your body, hold both Dragon Fists, and pat your stomach 36 times. This patting is to strengthen your resisting power and stabilize the Qi in the Dantian.
8. Use both palms to rub your stomach 36 times.
9. Repeat the movement of forcing the Qi to flow.
10. Walk around to totally calm down before you come back to your daily life.

Master Wang Xiang Zhai performing Ti Bao Zhuang

Chapter 12

ZHAN ZHUANG

STATIC STANCE POSTURES

A. FRONT STANCE 正椿 (平椿、文椿、三才椿)

Yang Sheng Zhuang (Health Stance) (養生椿, 健身椿)

1. Fu Bao Zhuang (Float Hug) 浮抱椿 (手抱乾坤)
2. Fu An Zhuang (Float Press) 浮按椿 (頂天立地)
3. Cheng Bao Zhuang (Prop Hug) 撐抱椿 (懷抱嬰兒) (養心椿)
4. Tui Tuo Zhuang (Push Prop) 推托椿 (掌托天門)
5. Fun Shui Zhuang (Split Water) 分水椿 (白鶴展翅)
6. Ti Cha Zhuang (Lift Jab) 提插椿 (入地三尺)
7. Ti Bao Zhuang (Lift Hug) 提抱椿 (提抱日月)
8. Yang Shen Zhuang (Cultivating Spirit) 養神椿

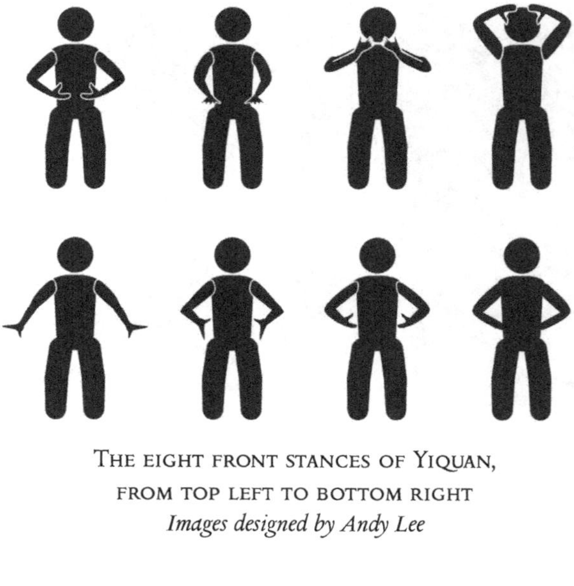

THE EIGHT FRONT STANCES OF YIQUAN,
FROM TOP LEFT TO BOTTOM RIGHT
Images designed by Andy Lee

Difficulty scoring system:
∗ = 20 degree difficulty
○ =10 degree difficulty

1. Fu Bao Zhuang (Float Hug) 浮抱樁

FRONT VIEW

SIDE VIEW

Names: Also called Hun Yuan Stake or Lean Hug; it is the overall basic stance.

Difficulty: ∗ ∗ ○○○

Key: Suitable as a starting posture for morning, afternoon, and evening, each time for 10–20 minutes.

REQUIREMENTS

Breathe in deeply and sink the Qi to the lower abdomen (the Dantian). Bend forward to relax the chest, and then straighten the back to let the Qi flow up the back without any obstacles. Try to maintain the lower abdomen in a ball shape.

STAKE REQUIREMENTS

The chin is tucked inwards, the top of the head is upright, the neck is strengthened, the eyes are half open. You should have a smiling face.

Benefits

- Stretches the backbones
- Stretches the shoulders and chest
- Strengthens the muscles of the stomach and limbs
- Reduces the fat of the thighs and stomach
- Strengthens the joints of the legs
- Strengthens the organs of the lower abdomen.

Improves

- Bad backbone alignment
- Poor and wrong standing postures
- Weak muscles of the legs and joints
- Constipation.

Steps

From the standing posture, step the left leg sideways to shoulder width. Bend the body forward, stretch, and circle both hands in front of the body, like holding a heavy stone ball. Hold it up to the position of the stomach against resistance. Then stay there, so that you can keep your buttocks forward. Keep the elbows extended sideways. The palms hang up as if holding a small ball. The back of the palms feel as if they are floating on the surface of water.

Expected feelings

Stomach burning, hands swelled, and heat emitted.

Imagery

Imagine holding two stone balls in the hands. They are heavy and you have to support them at the position of the waist without dropping them. Try to make use of this visualization to let your body weight sink to the Gua and feet. This will really make you relax and feel heavy. Your Qi will sink from your chest to deep into the ground.

2. Fu An Zhuang (Float Press) 浮按樁

FRONT VIEW

SIDE VIEW

Difficulty: ＊＊○○○

Key: Suitable for morning, afternoon, and evening, each time for 10–20 minutes.

STAKE REQUIREMENTS

Breathe in deeply and sink the Qi to the Dantian. Press the palms downward so that you get an opposite force to stretch your head upright. Try to feel your body weight sinking downwards. Your elbows must stretch and point sideways. The fingers point to the front, with the index finger pointing upward. The palms are hollow.

BENEFITS

- Stretches the backbones and helps with concentration
- Keeps the body balanced and stable
- Strengthens the waist and finger power.

IMPROVES

- Bad backbone alignment
- Dizziness
- Weak muscles of the legs and hands

- Finger penetration strength
- Breathing and digestive system problems.

Steps

From the previous stance, every part of your body stays still; the wrists and elbows maintain their position. Just turn your palms downward, with fingers pointing forward.

Expected feelings

The palms will feel hot, the fingers like ants crawling on them, and with Qi penetrating through to the fingertips.

Imagery

The fingers penetrate and extend when the Qi feeling becomes stronger, and Qi feels as if it is coming out from your fingertips. Imagine your palms are placed on a wooden plate on the surface of the water in a swimming pool.

Advanced movements

Press the wooden plate downward into the water, and feel the buoyancy resist your pressure until you cannot press anymore. The power floats your palms upward. Repeat this action again and again.

3. Cheng Bao Zhuang (Prop Hug) 撑抱桩

Front view

Side view

Names: Cheng Bao Zhuang is the general name used by most practitioners. Previously, it was called the Middle Hun Yuan Stance or Hands Holding the Baby.

This is the most essential stance of Yiquan. Some practitioners will just stand in this posture daily.

Difficulty: ∗ ∗ ∗ ○ ○

Key: Suitable for morning, afternoon, and evening, each time for 20–30 minutes.

Requirements

Breathe in deeply and sink the Qi to the Dantian. Do not let the breathing stay stuck in the chest. Straighten the back to let the Qi flow up the back without any obstacles.

Stake requirements

The arms hold a big paper ball with both elbows pushing out sideways. The posture of bending should cause an ache in your thighs. The hands must not be held too far away from the chest, or else your body will lean forward and the position of the arms will not be tight enough to generate Qi. The arms are like iron pincers. The abdomen inhales as if it is the warrior general of China.

Angles: Your arms must not be held horizontally and flat. The position of the palms must be higher than the elbows, so that the arms become sliding. This is very important, because if your arms are placed flat and the opponent strikes them, you risk breaking them. Sliding arms provide more protection and added flexibility.

Benefits

- Stretches the backbones and helps concentration
- Extends the chest and enhances explosive power
- Strengthens the muscles of the back and chest
- Strengthens the organs inside the chest and waist
- Develops an iron-clad resistance.

Improves

- Bad backbone alignment
- Weak muscles of the legs and hands
- Guarding and protective power for the arms
- The nervous system and lung disease.

Steps

From the previous posture, do not move your elbows; raise your hands and palms to the level of the chest. Let the palms face your chest and then apply the requirements.

Expected feelings

With Qi pushing up to the top of the head, the arms have strong power to press inwards to contract the holding ball. The groin feels hot and burning. The back feels as if it is on fire.

Simulation

The arms hold a big paper ball or balloon. If it is held too loosely, the ball will drop to the ground; too tight, and it will burst. Make the imaginary real. Really hold the ball tight and press it to your chest. This will strengthen your upper structure.

IMAGERY

Half close your eyes and feel the light blowing wind; warm, fresh air flows along your body. When you are calm and feel you are full of energy, open your eyes and try to press your arms inward with more strength, extend your neck and head, and breathe in deeply to pump the Qi into your body and arms, so that your body and arms swell like the tire of a car.

Remember the standard stance requirements, especially the following:

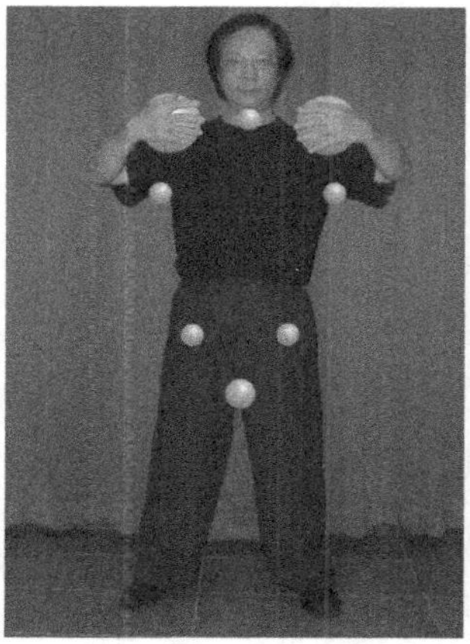

1. GRASP EIGHT BALLS

2. TRIANGLE FITNESS

HAND REQUIREMENTS

- Maintain a triangle
- Keep the elbows lower than the palms
- Hold and keep the hands two palms distance apart
- Hold the hands lower than the nose and higher than the shoulders.

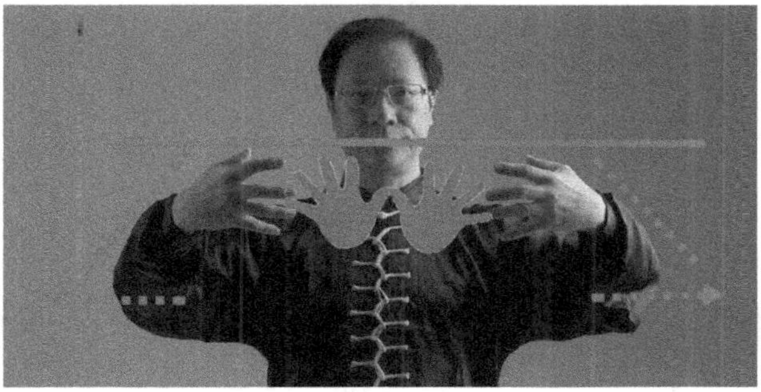

BE STRONG

Imagine you are a tree, and your legs are roots that are planted into the ground. Your body is like the trunk of the tree, straight and strong. Your arms and hands are branches of the tree

4. Tui Tuo Zhuang (Push Prop) 推托樁

FRONT VIEW

SIDE VIEW

Names: Also called Palms Prop the Gate of Sky. This is a difficult stance.

Difficulty: * * * * *

Key: Suitable for morning, each time for 10 minutes.

REQUIREMENTS

Breathe in deeply and strongly to generate enough Qi to support this strong stance.

Stake requirements

Must maintain the propping position of the hands.

Benefits

- Reduces stress and tiredness
- Enhances breathing
- Strengthens the muscles of the shoulders and forearms
- Reduces abdominal fat.

Improves

- Stiffness of backbone and joints
- Discomfort of the respiratory system
- Weak physical strength and spirit
- Gastroenteritis (胃潰瘍及腸炎)
- Power and breathing capacity of lungs.

Steps

Turn your palms upward to face the sky, with elbows stretched with force. Sink your body, thighs and Kua, and then push upward. Remain in this posture.

Expected feelings

Both palms become swollen. Both upper arms feel like a pumped tire, very strong and elastic. After standing for a long time, Qi pushes up to the top of the head, and the back feels very hot with a burning sensation.

Imagery

Imagine that the big refrigerator of your home is falling towards you. You must immediately push it back. Retain this image. You have to bend your knees and use the thighs and feet to generate an upward pushing force.

5. Fun Shui Zhuang (Split Water) 分水樁

Front view

Side view

Names: Also known as Split Press. This is also a difficult stance.

Difficulty: * * * * *

Key: Suitable for morning, each time for 10 minutes.

Requirements

Breathe in deeply and strongly to generate enough Qi to support this strong stance.

Stake requirements

Maintain the propping position of the hands. The hollow of the upper elbows must be facing upward as if they can hold teacups. Sink the elbows and extend the fingers outward.

Benefits

- Reduces stress and tiredness
- Strengthens the muscles of the shoulders and fingers.

Improves

- Stiffness of backbone and joints
- Weak arms
- Hemiplegia (半身麻痺).

Steps

Turn your hands to the side of your body, palms facing down, with hands and elbows pushed sideways with force. Sink your elbows, thighs, and Kua.

Expected feelings

The shoulders should feel a slight pain because of stretching sideways. You should feel heat spread from the arms to the whole body quickly.

Imagery

You think you are standing on a roof, looking downward. It is very high and you feel so great! The palms are like pressing on two tables by your side.

6. Ti Cha Zhuang (Lift Jab) 提插樁

Front view

Side view

Difficulty: ＊＊＊○○

Key: Suitable for morning, each time for 10 minutes.

Stake requirements

Maintain the supporting position of the arms. Raise the elbows and drop the arms with the fingers pointing downward. The arms are grasping as if they are holding balls. Keep your natural breathing.

Benefits

- Reduces stress and tiredness
- Strengthens the muscles of the shoulders and upper arms.

Improves

- Strength of the internal organs of the abdomen
- Weak arms and weak hand structure.

Steps

Raise the elbows and drop the hands to the side of your body, palms facing your body, with fingers spread and pointing to the ground.

Expected feelings

The deltoids feel pain because of the high position of the elbows. Try to move and stretch your body to release the pain. You should feel heat spread all over your back.

Imagery

The fingers point and penetrate through to the soil. Then apply opposite power to raise up your elbows. The poles of the whole body feel as if there is a light wind blowing through the room.

Stance is like a cowboy with guns

7. Ti Bao Zhuang (Lift Hug) 提抱桩

Front view

Side view

This is a very important posture that Han Xi Wan insists beginners practice as the main beginning posture. He requires students to resist pain and gradually hold the posture for 45 minutes. Han's whole process is to concentrate on standing at the beginning of training and not practice any other stance for three months. If one can do this, the structure of one's skeleton will be fixed and becomes very powerful and full of energy.

Names: This stance can also cure heart disease and shoulder pain, and so it is also called Yang Xin Stance or Cherish Stance (養心樁).

Difficulty: * * * * *

Key: Suitable for morning, each time for 10–30 minutes.

Stake requirements

Maintain the supporting position of the arms. Raise the elbows and drop the arms with the palms bending upward. The shoulders are brought forward and the back is rounded. Raise your head upright and slightly tense your neck. It is difficult to keep this stance for long, but try your best. Keep breathing naturally.

Benefits

- Injects energy into your body
- Strengthens the muscles of the shoulders and arms.

Improves

- Stiffness in the backbone and joints
- Weak arms and weak hand protections
- Body structure and Qi flow through the whole body.

Steps

Raise the elbows and drop the hands to the side of your body, with palms facing your body, and bend your wrist.

Expected feelings

The deltoids feel pain because of the high position of the elbows. The palms become hotter and hotter.

Imagery

The palms are positioned as if holding two iron balls, or like holding two canisters of water as you are going to wash your car. Some say that doing this holding stance is like holding a rugby ball at each side of your body, walking out onto the playing field. Others liken it to somebody who walks as if they have rolls of carpet under each of their arms, with their elbows tensed to the sides and their forearms pointed straight to the floor.

8. Yang Shen Zhuang (Cultivating Spirit) 養神樁

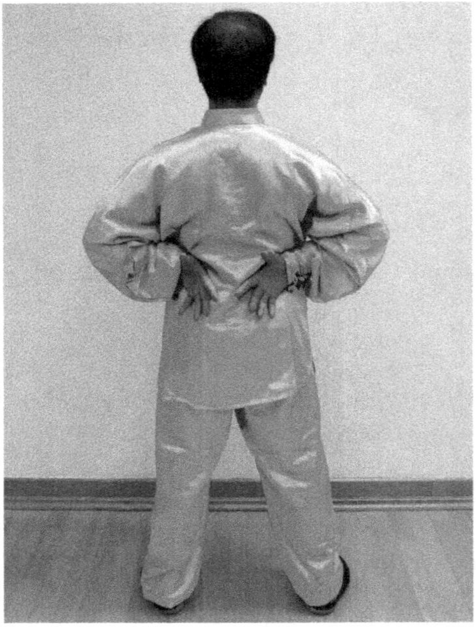

Names: Also called Yang Shen Zhuang (Cultivate Kidney Stance) 養腎樁 or Xiu Xi Zhuang (Relax Stance) 休息樁.

Difficulty: ＊○○○○

Key: Suitable for morning, evening, and after every stance, each time for 5–10 minutes.

Requirements

Breathe in deeply and calmly as in relaxation mode. The back must be upright.

Stake requirements

The back of the hands should touch the back, transmitting Qi from the hands to the Ming Men (命門).

Benefits

- Stretches the stomach muscles sideways
- Expands the chest
- Strengthens the muscles of the shoulders and forearms

- Reduces abdominal fat
- Increases blood circulation to the head.

Improves

- Stiffness of backbone and joints
- Discomfort of the liver, spleen, and intestine
- Diabetes and thyroid gland disorder (糖尿病及甲狀腺)
- Weak strength and spirit
- Migraine and insomnia (偏頭痛及失眠).

Steps

With legs apart, place the back of your hands behind your back, at the position of both kidneys. The palms face away from the body, with fingers spread apart, like grasping a ball. Lean back. Breathe naturally, relax, and calm down.

Expected feelings

Both palms become swollen. Both upper arms feel like a pumped tire, very strong and elastic. After standing for a long time, Qi pushes up to the top of the head, and the back feels as if it is burning.

Students' feedback: This is the stance which gets the fastest feeling of Qi. The palm feels numb and swollen. The whole body heats up quickly and the feeling is very strong (快麻脹).

Imagery

You stand in a dark room, without any light. All is quiet and silent; you can hear your own breathing. Then lean backward as if touching the wall. You are now like a warrior approaching the gate of his enemy's castle, standing there, raising his head to utter war cries.

The spirit of Static Stance

動似山飛 力如海溢 神猶霧豹 氣若靈犀

In 1947, Chou Jian Nan (周劍南), a famous Taiwanese martial artist, approached Master Wang Xiang Zhai, Yiquan's founder, at the old palace of Beijing and asked him for advice. Master Wang wrote to him using these four phrases:

- Move like flying mountain
- Strength like the overflowing sea
- Spirit like the leopard in the fog
- Energy like a clever rhinoceros.

Front stance practice program for a 60-minute class

	Duration	Movements
1.	2 min	Warm up—Five relaxation exercises
2.	2 min	Dun Yao—Perform slowly 15 times within 3 min
3.	10 min	Fu Bao Zhuang
4.	10 min	Fu An Zhuang
5.	10 min	Cheng Bao Zhuang
6.	5 min	Tui Tuo Zhuang
7.	5 min	Fun Shui Zhuang
8.	5 min	Ti Cha Zhuang
9.	5 min	Ti Bao Zhuang
10.	5 min	Yang Shen Zhuang
11.	1 min	Cool down

FRONT STANCE SEQUENCE FOR 60 MINUTES

B. SIDE STANCE 側樁 (戰樁、武樁、混元樁)

DRAGON STANCE OF MASTER C S TANG

As described in the previous section, the basic stance is the front stance. After practicing so that one can handle front stances and can meet the requirements, the next stage is to perform the side stance. There are several different side stances, with every stance needing specific effort and purpose.

Front stances provide practice for balanced postures. In contrast, side stances provide practice for non-balanced postures. Most of the side stances are mainly postures that turn aside from the front postures.

The main side stance is called Mao Dun Zhuang, although since 1960 some practitioners have called this posture Hun Yuan Zhuang.

The degree of difficulty of side stances is harder than front stances, because most of the time the body weight is placed on the rear leg. At the same time, in order to practice in a guarding manner, alertness and tension are required; the Kua has to be sunk lower.

Side stances will lead to many different Shi Li according to their different postures.

Ji Ji Zhuang (Combat Stance) 技擊樁

1. Hun Yuan Zhuang (Sphere) 混元樁 – 側浮抱樁
2. Mao Dun Zhuang (Spear and Shield) 矛盾樁 – 小步樁
3. Fu Yun Zhuang (Float Cloud) 浮雲樁
4. Gou Gua Zhuang (Hook Hang) 勾掛樁
5. Ping Bao Zhuang (Even Hug) 平抱樁 – 扶按樁
6. Dun Bao Bei Zhuang (Hold Treasure) 墩寶貝樁
7. Tui Tuo Zhuang (Push Prop) 推托樁 (托天樁)

1. Hun Yuan Zhuang (Sphere) 混元樁 – 側浮抱樁

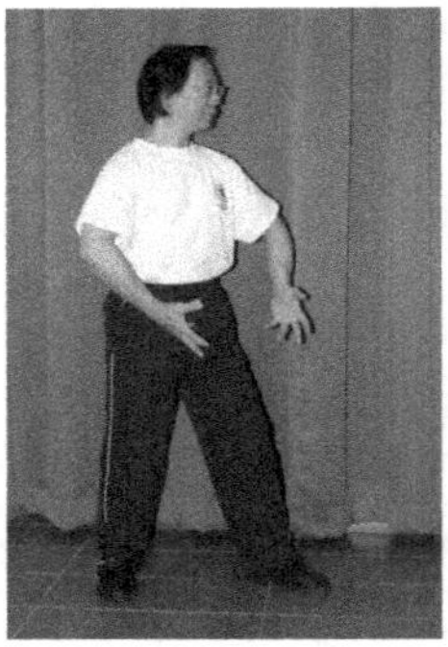

2. Mao Dun Zhuang (Spear and Shield) 矛盾樁 – 小步樁

3. Fu Yun Zhuang (Float Cloud) 浮雲樁

4. Gou Gua Zhuang (Hook Hang) 勾掛樁

5. Ping Bao Zhuang (Even Hug) 平抱樁

The hand position of this stance can be at the level of the chest or in front of the abdomen. When placed at the lower position, it is also called Fu An Zhuang (Float Press) 扶按樁.

The elbows stretch sideways and the fingers of both hands point to each other

6. Dun Bao Bei Zhuang (Hold Treasure) 墩寶貝樁

THE SHAPE OF THIS STANCE LOOKS LIKE HOLDING A BABY IN YOUR ARMS
A baby is classed as treasure in Chinese custom

7. Tui Tuo Zhuang (Push Prop) 推托樁 (托天樁)

Detailed description of Mao Dun Zhuang (Combat Stance) 技擊樁

Among all the side stances, Mao Dun Zhuang is the most important, so we explain it here in more detail. It is a Guarding Stance and is the product of much experience and of many Yiquan masters.

LEFT POSTURE

RIGHT POSTURE

Names: Also called Hun Yuan Stake or Warrior Stance. It is also called Spear and Shield Stance. With the left posture, your left arm is held in front of your body, simulating a shield to protect your face and chest. Your right arm is held at your right chest, ready to shoot towards the front.

Difficulty: ✻ ✻ ✻ ○○

Key: Suitable for morning, afternoon, and evening, each side stance lasting for 10–20 minutes.

STAKE REQUIREMENTS

The chin is tucked inwards, the top of the head is upright, the neck is strengthened, and eyes are fully open and staring without blinking. The face should be dignified.

BENEFITS

- Stretches the backbones
- Stretches the shoulders and arms
- Strengthens the muscles of the lower abdomen to resist strikes
- Reduces the fat of the thighs and stomach
- Strengthens the joints of the legs.

Improves

- Incorrect standing postures
- Weak muscles of the legs and joints
- Constipation.

Steps

From the standing posture, step the left leg forward at 45 degrees to your front. The front leg is just touching the ground, with your ankle raised. All the weight is placed on your back leg. Raise your front hand with your arm in a circle. Raise your back hand at the side of your body, nearly flat, with fingers spread like holding arrows, ready to shoot.

Expected Feelings

Stomach burning, and hands swollen and burning red.

Imagery

Imagine your arms are holding the trunk of a tree. You want to push it up and then press it down deeply into the earth. After you have practiced for a period of time, you have to test your structure by moving the trunk left and right. Your imagining must be real, so that your arms, palms, surface of your chest, thigh and Gua, and knees are all touching the trunk. Just think that you are a koala, resting and holding the trunk of a tree.

1.

2.

3.

4.

Look far away and extend your eyesight to make yourself seem bigger and bigger; this will help you to develop more self-esteem and confidence. Also, when you face your enemy or are ready to do push hand, you will not be frightened.

When you perform this stance, move your front leg up and down to test the air resistance and expand your skeleton so that you can train your power.

Simulations

1. Lights

Eyes

This is a combat posture, and so therefore you must not close your eyes for this stance. In addition, you have to stare to the front, as if looking far away to the hills beyond the river opposite. The eyes sparkle and light comes out from the eyes.

Whole body lights up

Your whole body releases light, and a sphere covers your whole body. As you move your front arms a little bit, the hill opposite seems to be dragged towards you. As you move your right arm forward, it appears as if there are hundreds of arrows shooting out towards your enemy.

2. Hedgehog 刺猬

The spines of a hedgehog are hollow hairs, made stiff with keratin. He will try to ram into any intruder with his spines.

When a practitioner performs a combat stance, he must keep alert so that all his hairs stand up and are sensitive. He looks like an angry cat who is ready to fight with another cat.

Once your enemy touches or presses on your arms, you react and either emit upwards by turning your hands to throw him far away or press downwards to shock him.

3. Archer

This stance is also called Drawn Bow to Shoot the Jade or Drawn Bow to Shoot the Wall. The stance can be summed up in the phrase, "The rear hand stretches like holding a baby, the front hand stretches like pushing the big mountain."

So when you practice this stance, you should stretch your arms fully and expand your structure with Qi.

The following is also important: "When drawing the bow, you should draw a strong bow. When shooting an arrow, you should use a long arrow." That means you should use the best and strongest weapon. If you want to shoot an enemy, shoot his horse first.

C. POWER STANCE 功力樁

Gong Li Zhuang (Power Stance) 功力大樁

1. Xiang Long Zhuang (Descending Dragon) 降龍樁
2. Fu Hu Zhuang (Taming Tiger) 伏虎樁
3. Du Li Zhuang (Chicken) 子午樁 (又名金雞獨立)
4. Ying Zhuang (Eagle) 大步鷹樁 (大式樁)
5. Cheng Tui Zhuang (Stretch Leg) 撐腿樁 (蛟龍出海)

1. Xiang Long Zhuang (Descending Dragon) 降龍樁

Xiang Long painting on the wall of Shaolin Monastery

Subdue the Dragon Stance

Names: Also called Dragon Stance, meaning Subdue the Dragon. The name comes from Buddhism, and shows the strong power of the posture. The stance itself is derived from traditional Chinese wrestling. It stretches and twists the body and spine and strengthens the waist.

Difficulty. * * * * *

Key: Suitable for morning, each side for 5–10 minutes.

Stake requirements

The front palm, spine, and rear leg lie on the same line. Stretch the front arm fully above your head. The eyes look at your rear leg. Bend as low as you can for increasing strength. Do the other side of this stance after the first practice to balance the muscles of your body.

Benefits

- Stretches the backbone and spine
- Strengthens the muscles of the neck and limbs.

Improves

- Bad backbone shapes
- Weak muscles of the legs and joints.

Steps

From the standing posture, split your legs as wide as possible. Step the left leg forward; the front leg bends down and the foot is placed at 45 degrees. All the weight is placed on your front leg. Lean your whole body forward. The rear leg treads with the ankle raised. Raise your front hand with palms facing outward and stretch as much as you can. Extend your back hand at the side of your body towards the rear leg. Bend your wrist. Then turn your head and eyes to look at the ankle of the rear leg.

Expected feelings

The arms are swollen and burning. Beginners will feel difficulty on the twisting and bending forward posture.

Imagery

Imagine you are a big dragon with high spirit and power.

C S Tang illustrating Xiang Long Zhuang to a group of American students

2. Fu Hu Zhuang (Taming Tiger) 伏虎樁

Fu Hu painting on the wall of Shaolin Monastery

Tame the Tiger Stance

Names: The full name of this stance is Tame the Tiger Stance. The name also comes from Buddhism. Some explain it as if riding a tiger, with both hands pushing its head down to the ground. Others describe it as if catching the tiger at the side, with one hand pushing its back and the other hand pressing its head downward.

Difficulty: ＊＊＊＊＊

Key: Suitable for morning, for each side for 5–10 minutes.

Stake requirements

The chin is tucked inwards and the forehead is pushed forward. Stretch the head and neck upright, with eyes fully open and staring without blinking, like a tiger. Both legs are spread widely. Sink your Gua, with the back and waist held upright. Use the power of both hands to press downwards.

Benefits

- Strengthens the muscles of the limbs, especially the legs.

Improves

- Power of your base.

Steps

From the standing posture, step the front leg forward widely into a big T-stance. The step is equal to double the width of the shoulders. Place all the weight on your back leg. Sink your body downwards.

Press your front hand with palms downward. Bend your elbow and twist the wrist so that the thumb points to your body. Press your back hand in front of your back leg and remain at the level of the belt. The fingers stretch apart like a tiger's claw. Fold your hip forward so that your back is full of power.

Expected feelings

At the beginning, the legs tremble. Try to lengthen the time for each session so that you can remain in this posture for longer.

Imagery

Imagine your arms are pressing a wild animal. It struggles and you must press hard to stop it from moving. Sink your Gua to sit firmly on the tiger. Press it tight, until it stops breathing. Let your eyes stare and your imagining be realistic. Do not slacken off.

Tame the Tiger Stance performed by Master Li Jiang Yu in Hong Kong

3. Du Li Zhuang (Chicken) 子午椿 (又名金雞獨立)

Chicken Stance

Names: Also called Stand-alone or Golden Chicken Stance with One Leg. Its old name is Meridian Stance.

Difficulty: ＊＊＊＊＊

Key: Suitable for morning and evening, each time and each side for 10–20 minutes.

Stake requirements

The gua is depressed inward. The head is upright, the neck is strengthened, the eyes are staring to the front. Stretch the upper hand fully to the sky. Press down the lower hand to keep your balance. Raise your leg as high as possible to the level of your ribs. Fold your hip forward.

Benefits

- Stretches the backbone
- Stretches the shoulders and chest
- Strengthens the muscles of the limbs
- Strengthens the resistance strength of the joints of the legs
- Reduces the fat of the thighs and stomach.

Improves

- Bad backbone shape
- Weak muscles of the legs and joints.

Steps

From the standing posture, raise the left hand up over your head with fingers pointing upward. Press your right hand downward in front of your stomach. Raise and bend your left leg in front of your body to the level of your stomach.

Stand like a chicken

4. Ying Zhuang (Eagle) 大步鹰桩 (大式桩)

Eagle Stance

A closer look at this stance

Names: Also called Big Step. This is again a very important stance because, according to Madam Wang Yu Fang, this was one of the main stances that her father learnt from his teacher.

Difficulty: ＊＊＊＊○

Key: Suitable for morning and evening, each time and each side for 10–20 minutes.

Stake requirements

Stretch the head and neck upright, with eyebrows contracted together and eyes staring like a leopard seeking his food. Both legs are spread widely. Sink your Gua, with the back and waist held upright. Use the power of both hands to prop upwards. Maintain the angles of the elbows and palms.

Benefits

- Strengthens the muscles of the upper arms
- Strengthens the power of the legs.

Improves

- Weak muscles of the legs and joints
- Resistance power of the body and the legs.

Steps

From the standing posture, step the left leg forward for a wide stance. Place most of the weight on your back leg. Raise your front hand with the arm in a circle, with palms outward beyond your forehead. Raise your back hand at the side of your temple, with fingers spread like grasping birds. Sink your body.

Expected feelings

The legs tremble and the arms will soon be tired. If you persist, you will build up your power.

Imagery

Imagine your arms are supporting the sky. The sky is blue. Look a little bit upward. Develop your own power.

5. Cheng Tui Zhuang (Stretch Leg) 撑腿椿 (蛟龍出海)

Names: Also called Dragon Came Out from the Sea.

Difficulty: ＊＊＊＊＊

Key: Suitable for morning, each side for 5 minutes.

Stake Requirements

Place the front hand as though taking a shield, and stretch the back hand backwards as though holding an arrow and ready to shoot. Extend both elbows until you feel the muscle tense. Raise the back leg as high as your belt and push forward. The toes should turn towards the body as much as you can. Stretching the hands can help balance the stance.

Benefits

- Strengthens the muscles of legs and increases stability.

Improves

- Increases the power of your leg for strikes.

Steps

From the combat stance posture, step the front leg forward, raise the back leg and stretch it outward. Bring your hands together as though holding a ball.

Expected feelings

Beginners will find their legs start trembling. Try to hold the posture for longer each session, so that you begin to be able to stand in it for longer.

Imagery

Imagine you are kicking the body of your enemy. Try to stretch your hanging leg outwards as though you are pressing on him. Continue to push outwards little by little.

Let your eyes stare and ensure your imagery is realistic. Do not lose focus.

Madam Wang Yu Fang's stance

This is the stance that Madam Wang Yu Fang mentioned that her father learnt from his teacher, Master Guo Yun Shen.

More illustrations of postures from different angles

1. Xiang Long Zhuang (Descending Dragon) 降龍樁

2. Fu Hu Zhuang (Taming Tiger) 伏虎樁

The hand shapes of this tiger stance vary according to different masters. Some have their front palm curved inwards, others will pull inwards, while still others will press straight downwards. These can be practiced according to your preference.

3. Du Li Zhuang (Chicken) 子午椿

D. DAI BU ZHUANG (BIG STEP STANCE) 大椿

1. Bao Zhuang (Hug) 正抱 – 三平混元椿
2. Cheng Zhuang (Prop) 側撐 – 大式椿

See Chapter 24 for descriptions of these postures.

E. ZUO ZHUANG (SITTING POSTURES) 坐式椿

1. Fu Bao Zhuang (Float Hug) 浮抱椿
2. Fu An Zhuang (Float Press) 浮按椿
3. Cheng Bao Zhuang (Prop Hug) 撐抱椿
4. Tui Tuo Zhuang (Push Prop) 推托椿
5. Gou Gua Zhuang (Hook Hang) 勾掛椿

For those who are weak, cannot stand for too long, or even cannot stand at all, it will be easier for them to practice Static Stance in a sitting manner. Those who have to work for long hours in an office looking at a computer could perform these sitting stances to reduce their stress and recharge their body energy. Those who just aim for combat can still practice these stances for relaxing and a release from their hard training.

The chair you use must not be too high—when you stretch your legs, they should easily touch the ground. Sit at the edge of the chair to make sure your back is straight and your buttocks are turned towards the front.

Any posture of front stance can be applied to the Zuo Zhuang. Timings will be applied according to individual body conditions.

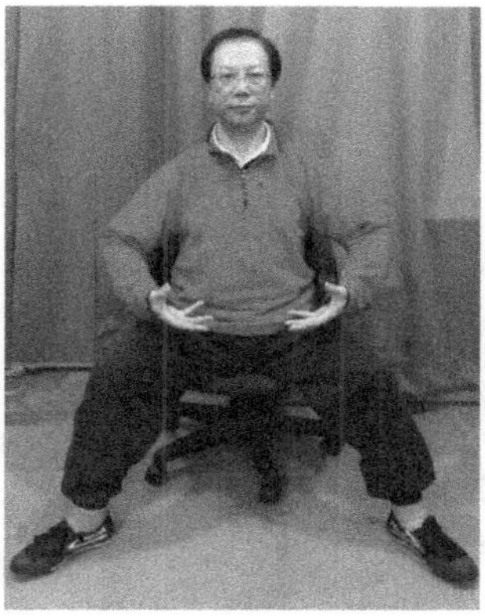

1. Fu Bao Zhuang

2. Fu An Zhuang

3. Cheng Bao Zhuang

4. Tui Tuo Zhuang

5. Gou Gua Zhuang (left and right)

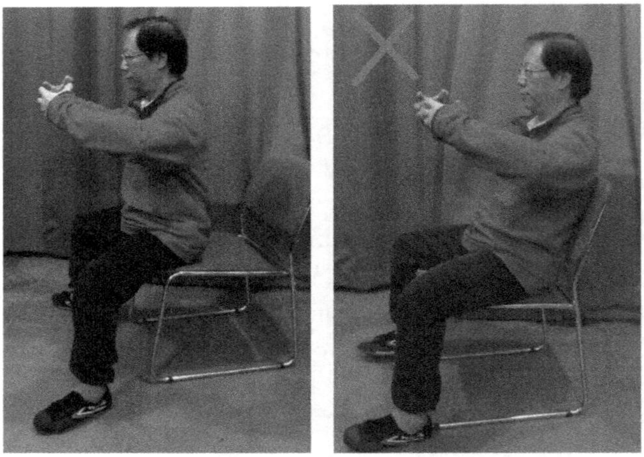

YOUR BACK SHOULD BE STRAIGHT. SIT ON THE EDGE OF THE CHAIR WITH GOOD SPIRIT. DO NOT LIE BACK ON THE CHAIR—LYING BACK IS NOT A TRAINING MODE

F. WO ZHUANG (LYING POSTURES) 臥式樁

1. Fu Bao Zhuang (Float Hug) 浮抱樁
2. Fu An Zhuang (Float Press) 浮按樁
3. Cheng Bao Zhuang (Prop Hug) 撐抱樁
4. Tui Tuo Zhuang (Push Prop) 推托樁
5. Gou Gua Zhuang (Hook Hang) 勾掛樁

Wo Zhuang is for weak and handicapped patients. These stances have been proven to be very effective during the group practice introduced by Master Wang Yu Fang and Master Wang Xiang Zhai when they taught in the hospitals.

Those who are strong can skip these postures, because lying down to practice will make you sleepy, and it is better to go to sleep to recharge your energy instead.

Guidance is important for sitting and lying postures; your coach can adjust and give you the correct timing control, and the enhancement and correction of postures.

STATIC STANCE PRACTICE PROGRAMS FOR A 60-MINUTE CLASS

There are many different patterns of stances and each has its own characteristics and functions. Of these, there are four basic stances which are always practiced by the old masters and which you should also always practice:

1. Cheng Bao Zhuang (Prop Hug) 撑抱桩
2. Mao Dun Zhuang (Spear and Shield) 矛盾桩
3. Fu Yun Zhuang (Float Cloud) 浮雲桩
4. Dun Bao Bei Zhuang (Hold Treasure) 墩寶貝桩

These four stances are important because of the following:

1. As a result of their range of training intensities, they are suitable for all groups of people.
2. Through these four stances, one can obtain most of the basic combat strength skills and structure. It will then be easier to advance your strength through the systematic integrated training of Yiquan.

Group training

	Duration	Movements
1.	3 min	Warm up—Five relaxation exercises
2.	3 min	Dun Yao

Total: 6 min

a. Health Stance

	Duration	Movements
3.	2 min	Fu Bao Zhuang
4.	2 min	Fu An Zhuang
5.	4 min	Cheng Bao Zhuang
6.	2 min	Tui Tuo Zhuang
7.	2 min	Fun Shui Zhuang
8.	2 min	Ti Cha Zhuang
9.	2 min	Ti Bao Zhuang
10.	2 min	Yang Shen Zhuang

Total: 18 min

b. Combat Stance

	Duration	Movements
11.	2 min	Hun Yuan Zhuang (left and right)
12.	4 min	Mao Dun Zhuang (left and right)
13.	4 min	Fu Yun Zhuang (left and right)
14.	2 min	Gou Gua Zhuang (left and right)
15.	2 min	Ping Bao Zhuang (left and right)
16.	4 min	Dun Bao Bei Zhuang (left and right)
17.	2 min	Tui Tuo Zhuang (left and right)

Total: 20 min

	Duration	Movements
18.	4 min	Tuo Yao (left and right + moving steps)

Total: 4 min

c. Power Stance

	Duration	Movements
19.	2 min	Xiang Long Zhuang (left and right)
20.	2 min	Fu Hu Zhuang (left and right)
21.	2 min	Du Li Zhuang (left and right)
22.	2 min	Ying Zhuang (left and right)
23.	2 min	Ying Tui Zhuang (left and right)

Total: 10 min

	Duration	Movements
24.	2 min	Cool down, patting exercises

Total: 2 min

Individual training

This is a program for individuals who need to perform daily practice, so that they can go through all the important stances. Once a week, practice the whole sequence as in the group class, so that you will still be familiar with all the stances.

	Duration	Movements
1.	3 min	Warm up—Five relaxation exercises
2.	3 min	Dun Yao

Total: 6 min

a. Health Stance

	Duration	Movements
3.	5 min	Fu Bao Zhuang
4.	5 min	Fu An Zhuang
5.	10 min	Cheng Bao Zhuang

Total: 20 min

b. Combat Stance

	Duration	Movements
6.	5 min	Mao Dun Zhuang (left and right)
7.	5 min	Fu Yun Zhuang (left and right)
8.	10 min	Dun Bao Bei Zhuang (left and right)

Total: 20 min

	Duration	Movements
9.	4 min	Tuo Yao (left and right + moving steps)

Total: 4 min

c. Power Stance

	Duration	Movements
10.	2 min	Xiang Long Zhuang (left and right)
11.	2 min	Fu Hu Zhuang (left and right)
12.	2 min	Du Li Zhuang (left and right)
13.	2 min	Ying Zhuang (left and right)

Total: 8 min

	Duration	Movements
14.	2 min	Cool down, patting exercises

Total: 2 min

Concise program: Individual intensive training

	Duration	Movements
1.	3 min	Warm up—Five relaxation exercises
2.	3 min	Dun Yao

Total: 6 min

a. Health Stance

	Duration	Movements
3.	15 min	Cheng Bao Zhuang

Total: 15 min

b. Combat Stance

	Duration	Movements
4.	20 min	Mao Dun Zhuang (left and right)

Total: 20 min

	Duration	Movements
5.	10 min	Tuo Yao (left and right + moving steps)

Total: 10 min

c. Power Stance

	Duration	Movements
6.	6 min	Xiang Long Zhuang (left and right)

Total: 6 min

	Duration	Movements
7.	3 min	Cool down, patting exercises

Total: 3 min

As mentioned before, if you want to enhance your strength and structure, try to keep standing in one posture for a long time, so that you really enter into the shape and fix your structure. Do not change your pattern too quickly.

Keep practicing the most basic and important stances; you can then change your posture at intervals, on different days and at different stages. Try to maintain the basic stances and then practice other stances too.

YIQUAN STANCES ILLUSTRATED

a. Health Stance

Front Stance 1
Fu Bao Zhuang

Front Stance 2
Fu An Zhuang

Front Stance 3
Cheng Bao Zhuang

Front Stance 4
Tui Tuo Zhuang

Front Stance 5
Fun Shui Zhuang

Front Stance 6
Ti Cha Zhuang

Front Stance 7
Ti Bao Zhuang

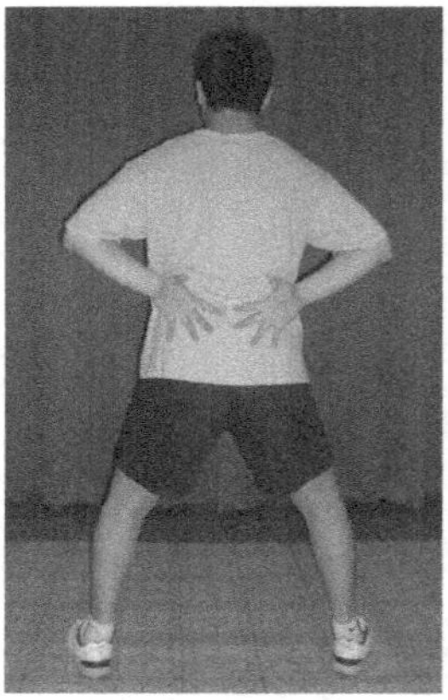

Front Stance 8
Yang Shen Zhuang

b. Combat Stance

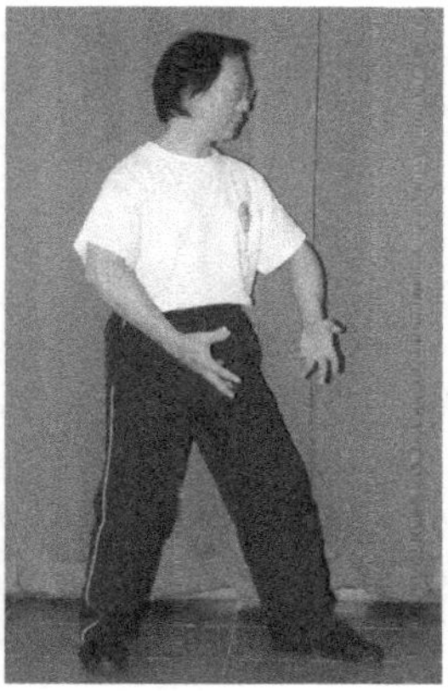

SIDE STANCE 1
HUN YUAN ZHUANG

SIDE STANCE 2
MAO DUN ZHUANG

SIDE STANCE 3
FU YUN ZHUANG

SIDE STANCE 4
GOU GUA ZHUANG

SIDE STANCE 5
PING BAO ZHUANG

SIDE STANCE 6
DUN BAO BEI ZHUANG

SIDE STANCE 7
TUI TUO ZHUANG

c. *Power Stance*

POWER STANCE 1
XIANG LONG ZHUANG

POWER STANCE 2
FU HU ZHUANG

POWER STANCE 3
DU LI ZHUANG

POWER STANCE 4
YING ZHUANG

POWER STANCE 5
CHENG TUI ZHUANG

Chapter 13

SHI ZHUANG
TEST STANCE

A good instructor should know how to check and test the standards of his students. These tests can be applied from different angles to each stance.

Tests include the following:

- *Firm and solid:*
    - The instructor presses on both arms strongly and the practitioner should not collapse. The practitioner should use zhuang expanding power, not resisting by tensing the muscles, but should drop the scapula and extend the arm socket to support the chest.
    - The instructor tries to pull back and the practitioner holds without breaking his shape or breaking his balloon, or moving fully forward.
- *Elastic force like pressing on a spring:*
    - The instructor presses on both arms; the practitioner should bounce the instructor's whole body away, like a ball hitting the wall and bouncing away. Then the instructor tests several parts of the practitioner's body and experiences the bouncing power from him.

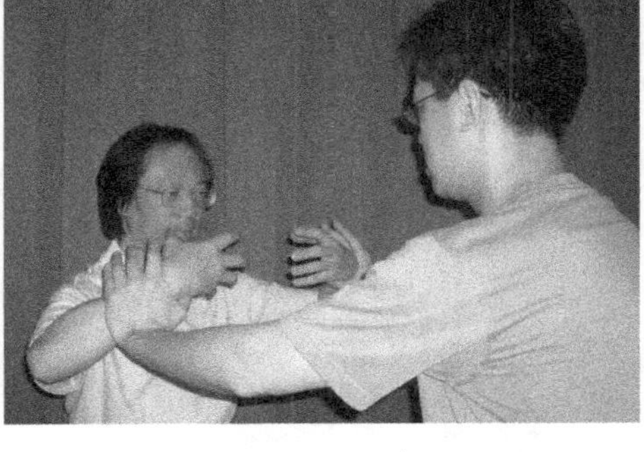

1. The practitioner's posture should not collapse

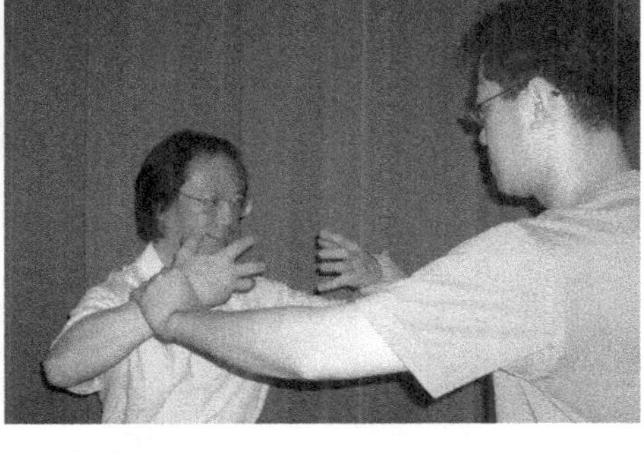

2. Opponent wants to pull back; I still keep the posture and will not be pulled by him and fall towards him

THE WAY TO PRACTICE TEST STANCE

Procedure

Test the following:

1. Cheng Bao Zhuang
2. Mao Dun Zhuang.

The instructor holds the practitioner's arms; the practitioner has to feel the six directions of strength:

1. Drag (pull)
2. Hold (pull back)
3. Press downward
4. Stretch forward
5. When pulling backwards, the toes grasp the ground, the knees and Kua grip tightly, and the bottom contracts and pulls up
6. The instructor tries to feel the muscles of his leg, and checks that they tense and relax like the leg of a frog.

Resistance power and bouncing power

- The instructor hits the practitioner's hips, chest, back, and legs to test his resistance power.
- The instructor tries to push the arms, hands, elbows, shoulders, back, buttocks, and legs. The practitioner will sink and try to apply a small Fali to bounce the instructor away.

The power of the stance should enable you to support a person standing on your legs.

Showing Ma Pu Stance

Showing Kung Pu Stance

The strong frame made by the arms should elevate a person

The front and side stances should be strong to resist pushes

Seek power 摸勁

After you stand for a while in each stance you will reach a stage of silence and feel very quiet. You are fully concentrated on the flow of Qi inside your body; you can then start to seek power. The purpose is to seek an unbalanced or tense part of your body and bring it into balance. Another purpose is to seek the feeling of opposite power (爭力). Stretch one side of your hand and try to feel the reaction of the other side of your hand. The third purpose is to find coordination between the upper and lower body. Once your hand extends and engages power, the leg will automatically pump against the ground to link up (連通) all parts of your body and participate in this ready posture.

However, your movements must be as small as possible so that even the person next to you is not aware you are moving. Your skeleton will then be more strong and developed in six directions strength.

TEST POWER BY INSTRUCTOR

1. For side stances

1.

2.

3.

2. For two big stances

1.

2.

3.

Chapter 14

MASTERS' POSTURES

MASTER WANG YU FANG 王玉芳老師

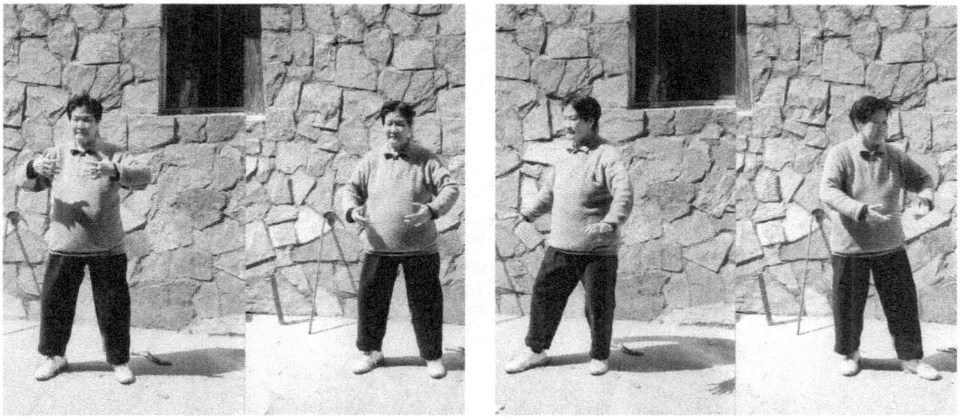

FRONT AND SIDE STANCES

Side stance

MASTER YU YONG NIAN 于永年老師

MASTER YAO ZONG XUN 姚宗勳老師

MASTER HAN XING YUAN 韓星垣老師

Eight postures of stance

SIDE STANCES

MASTER HAN XING QIAO 韓星橋老師

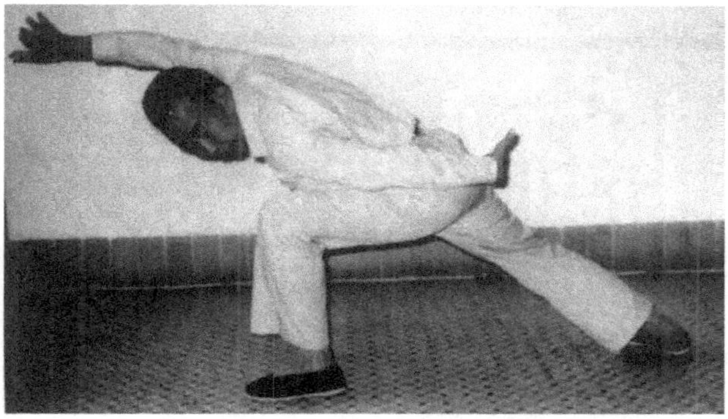

MASTER LI JIANG YU 李見宇老師

  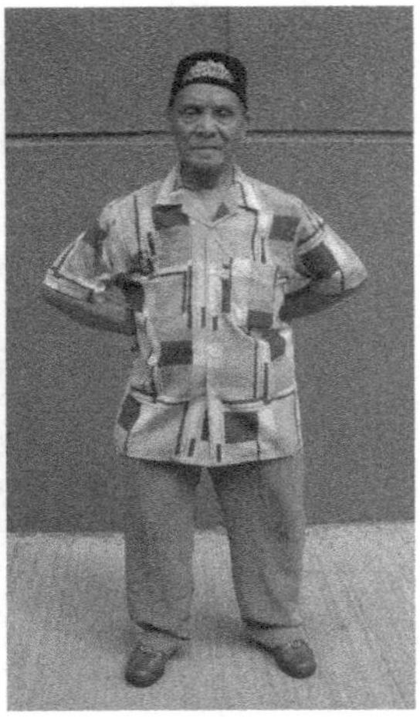

MASTER HAN SI HUANG 韓嗣煌老師

MASTER WANG BIN KUI 王斌魁

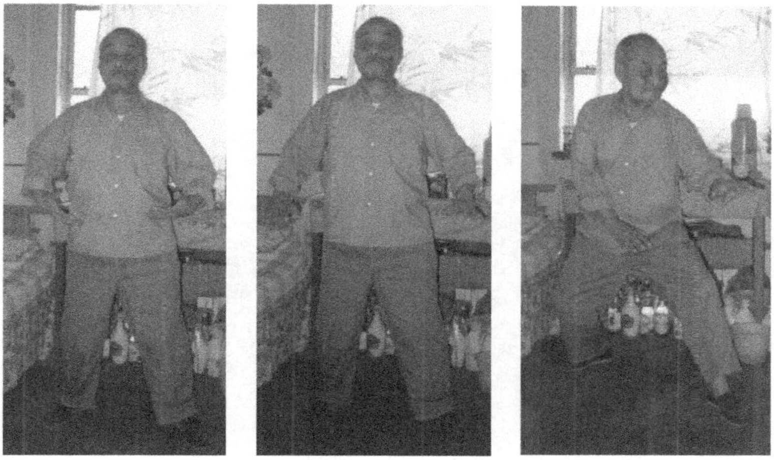

MASTER WANG AN PING 王安平

YAO CHENG GUANG AND YAO CHENG RONG 姚承光 及 姚承榮老師

1988, Hong Kong

Chapter 15

SHI LI

TEST STRENGTH

A. FRONT STANCE SHI LI 正面試力

Basic Test

1. Pin Yi Test 平移
2. Li Yao Test (Vertical Wave) 立搖
    a. Cheng Ba–Tui Tuo Stance Test 神龍布雨
3. Ping Xuan Test (Horizontal Rotate) 平旋
    a. Fu An–Ti Cha Stance Test 烏龍攪海/風擺荷葉

Main Test

1. Up and Down 上下
    a. Fu An Shi Li (Float Press) 浮按
    提按試力 (搖轆轤)(吞浪捲浪/波浪試力)
2. Forward and Backward 前後
    a. Ping Tui Shi Li (Level Push) 平推
    推拉試力 – 勾掛 (插糖膠)
3. Left and Right 左右
    a. Ba Shui Shi Li (Pushing Water) 撥水
    分水試力 (風帆試力/搖船試力)
    b. Shun Shui Tui Shou (Push Boat) (順水推舟)
    單手推前拉後

Background

Test Strength is the enlargement of the Static Stance. It is a test to see whether your requirements of Static Stance can be maintained properly under moving conditions. When speed and power are added to Test Strength, it becomes Fali.

Therefore they are related in a chain. A pair, or a group, of Static Stance practices, linking together and slowly seeking strength, is called Shi Li. When these individual Shi Li are acted out quickly and violently, they burst out and become Fali. You emit the strength and feel that a pressure inside your chest and body has to burst out through your throat; when you moan out loud, it is the sound of thunder.

Master Wang said, "Strength is obtained from testing." Test Strength is a kind of feeling and seeking of energy, and experiencing the contact of the body with the resistance of air.

In the *Heart Sutra*, it is said, "Forms are empty; emptiness is form. Apart from form, there is no emptiness; apart from emptiness, there is no form. Likewise, feelings, perceptions, mental formations, and consciousness are all empty."

The six faculties are the eyes, ears, nose, tongue, body, and mind. The six external factors are form, sound, smell, taste, texture, and mental objects.

This is a Chinese cultural tradition that says that Chinese martial arts have the same theories as the *Heart Sutra*. You cannot touch the Ching and Qi inside your body, but you can feel them. Others cannot see what you feel. In Static Stance, the external structure is not moving; but inside, your body is burning. Even someone next to you cannot observe your internal experience.

It is the same with Test Strength. All movements of intent are making use of all the objects of earth and heaven as examples. It is one's feeling not to learn its form but its intent, until you can ignore the form and shape, become melted with the world, and forget yourself. Body and space become a unity.

The movement of Test Strength requires imagination to imitate non-existing power movement. The main imagination used is resistance strength.

The relationship between Zhan Zhuang and Shi Li

The purpose of Zhan Zhuang is to build up and firm the structure of your guarding posture and develop the Hun Yuan six directions strength for protection and attack. Shi Li is a follow-up training to seek and try to use the two opposite directions force (二爭力). During movement of the hands and body, try to coordinate and link the limbs and body into perfect, strong movements.

The most important things are the following:

1. The supporting and curved angles of your arms and body are so strong after training in Zhan Zhuang that they are like a balloon and the tires of a car; every point of your body is like a spring (全身無點不彈簧).
2. Your gesture can look very strong in the posture of Zhan Zhuang, but once you move are you still able to keep the requirements of maintaining your structure? Test Strength means to try to find out, during movement,

how to keep all the supporting power and angles in the right manner, so that the emitting of strength can be maximized.

Fali shortens the process of the emitting of force by speeding up the strength that is tested in Shi Li and, at the same time, your whole body is compressed to its limit so that it explodes into explosive force.

The formation of Shi Li

Cheng Bao Zhuang → Fu An Zhuang = Fu An Shi Li

Gou Gua Zhuang → Ping Bao Zhuang = Ping Tui Shi Li

Dun Bao Bei Zhuang → Fun Shui Zhuang = Ba Shui Shi Li

The formation of Fali

Cheng Bao Zhuang → Tui Tuo Zhuang = Upward Fali

Basic Test

1. Pin Yi Test 平移

MOVEMENTS

Hold a Tui Tuo Zhuang (Push Prop) front stance. The palms are facing outwards and held still without moving. Move your body horizontally from side to side.

The purpose of the test is to hide and avoid the punch of your opponent with your palms; hold them in a fixed position.

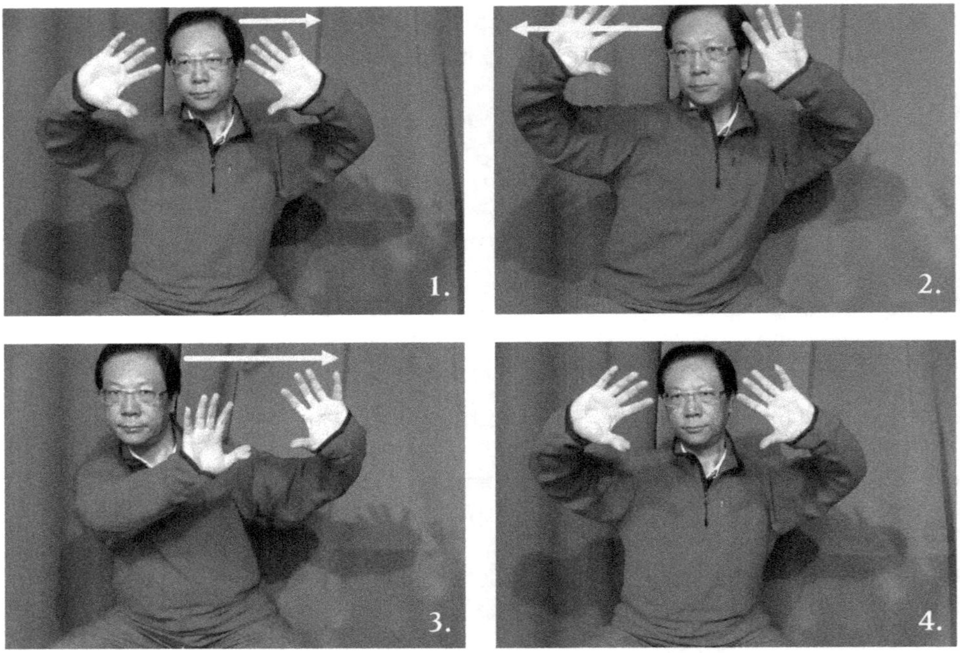

2. Li Yao Test (Vertical Wave) 立摇

a. Cheng Ba–Tui Tuo Stance Test 神龍布雨

Movements

Hold a Tui Tuo Zhuang (Push Prop) front stance. The palms are facing outwards and held still without moving. Move your body in vertical circles in a clockwise direction for 10 circles, and then turn your body anti-clockwise for another 10 circles. These movements simulate a window cleaner washing a window.

The purpose of the test is to block the opponent with your palms; hold them in a fixed position. Then move your body and enter the opponent's guarded zone.

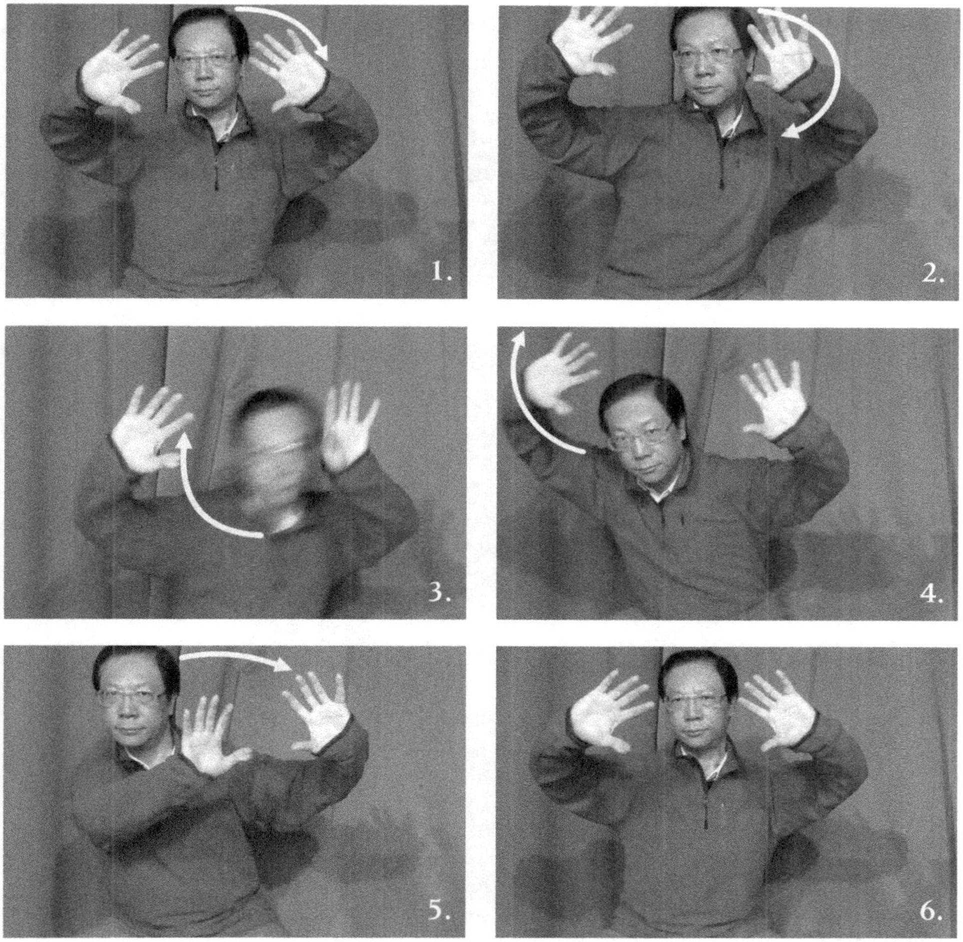

3. Ping Xuan Test (Horizontal Rotate) 平旋

a. Fu An–Ti Cha Stance Test 烏龍攪海/風擺荷葉

Movements

Hold a Fu An Zhuang (Float Press) front stance. The palms are facing downwards and held still without moving. Move your body in horizontal circles in a clockwise direction for 10 circles, and then turn your body anti-clockwise for another 10 circles. These movements simulate playing Ma Que (Chinese gambling game on the table).

The purpose of the test is to turn the attack of your opponent sideways with the strength of your waist.

The circle movement of vertical wave

The circle movement of Rotate Shi Li

Main Test

1. Up and Down 上下

a. Fu An Shi Li (Float Press) 浮按—also called Wave Lulu 提按試力 (搖轆轤) (呑浪捲浪/波浪試力)

Movements

Hold a Fu An Zhuang side stance. The palms are facing downwards. Swing the hands upward and forward in vertical circles. The body leans forward. The hands press down with the fingers like claws and the body leans backward. These movements simulate a wave surf.

The purpose of the test is to lift up the opponent's pressing hands on your arm, followed by striking on his chest and then clawing back to press his arms so that he falls towards you.

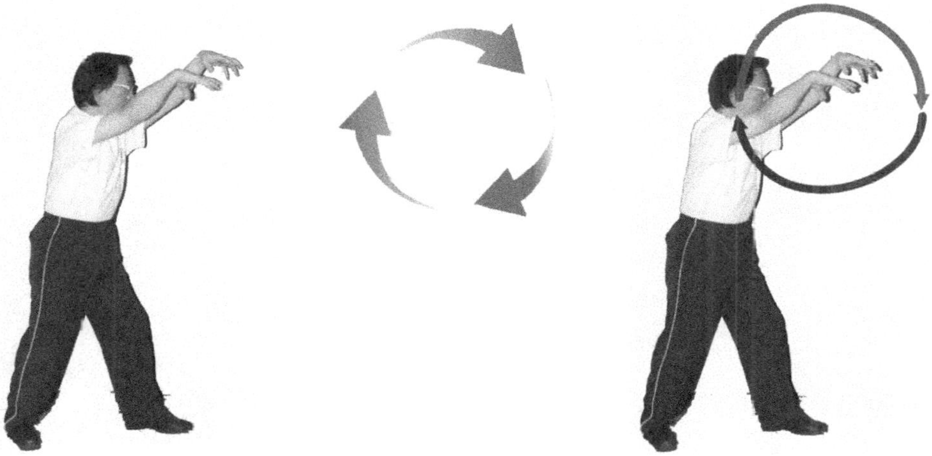

The circle path of Lulu Shi Li

2. Forward and Backward 前後

a. Ping Tui Shi Li (Level Push) 平推
推拉試力 – 勾掛 (插糖膠)

Movements

Hold a Gou Gua Zhuang side stance. The palms are facing each other. Claw the hands backwards and then turn the palms downwards into Ping Bao Zhuang. Push the hands forwards with the fingers pointing to the front. These movements simulate dipping your fingers into a pot of treacle.

The purpose of the test is to "stick" the opponent's hands so that he falls towards you. If he grasps you, you turn your palms downward and then push him back as you move forward.

3. Left and Right 左右

a. Ba Shui Shi Li (Pushing Water) 撥水分水試力 (風帆試力/搖船試力)

Movements

Hold a Fun Shui Zhuang (Split Water) side stance. The palms are split at the two sides of the body. Both hands move forward till the palms are facing each other.

The purpose of the test is to build up whole body strength. Both arms push forward with Hun Yuan strength.

b. Shun Shui Tui Shou (Push Boat) 順水推舟
單手推前拉後

MOVEMENTS

Hold a Fun Shui Zhuang (Split Water) side stance. The palms are split at the two sides of the body. The right hand moves to the front and then moves backward. The other hand will do the same separately and alternately.

The purpose of the test is to strike your opponent with one hand.

Ping Tui Shi Li illustrated

1.

2.

Intention and power control

Front Test Power

Imagine that your opponent is holding your hands and will not let you drag back. In response you need a strong force to drag back; keep your muscles relaxed, and just use a strong bone and tendon action.

Next you divert his power by turning your palms downwards. However, your arms must not collapse; still maintain the Zhuang's skeleton and frame. Pretend that your opponent holds you very tight and that you need a big effort to move.

Forward and backward testing method

The instructor holds the practitioner's hands tightly so that he requires great strength to pull back. When the practitioner pushes forward, the instructor will try to stop him and he will feel resistance and need to use rear leg and unity power to push. After the instructor releases his hands, and the practitioner practices Test Strength on his own, he will imagine that his instructor is blocking him.

Split Water Power

THE APPLICATION: 1. BREAKING HIS GUARD

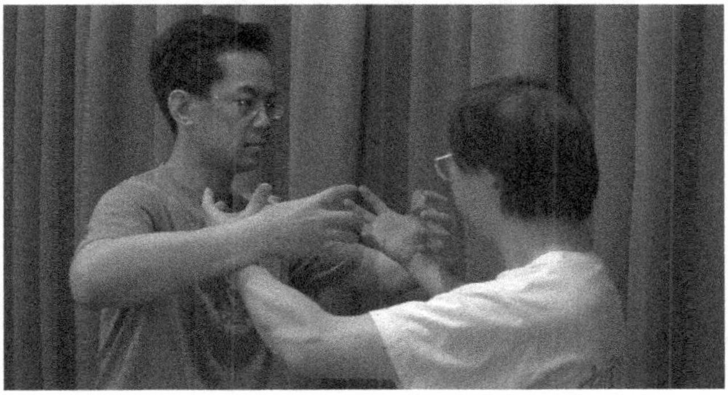

Both persons have a strong structure, so the opponent's fortress will need to be broken. Use split water power to separate his hands to both sides.

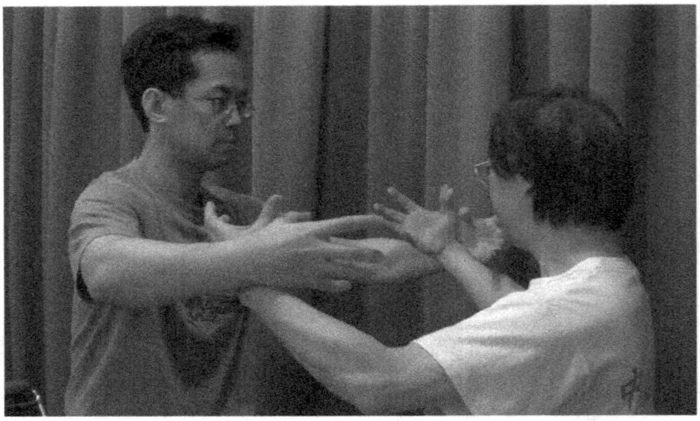

THE ATTACK: 2. THE COUNTER-ATTACK

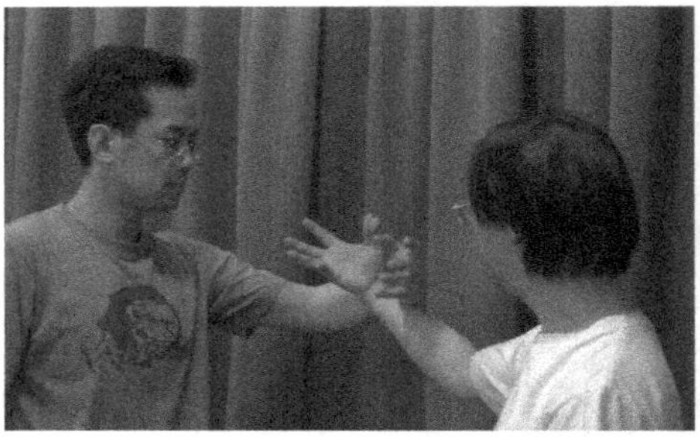

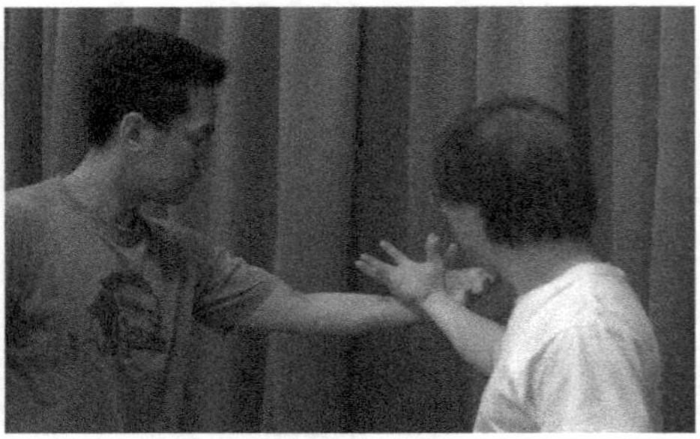

In single hand mode, apply split power to break open the opponent's center line and then use the palm to hit back.

The different hand shapes in applying Test Strength

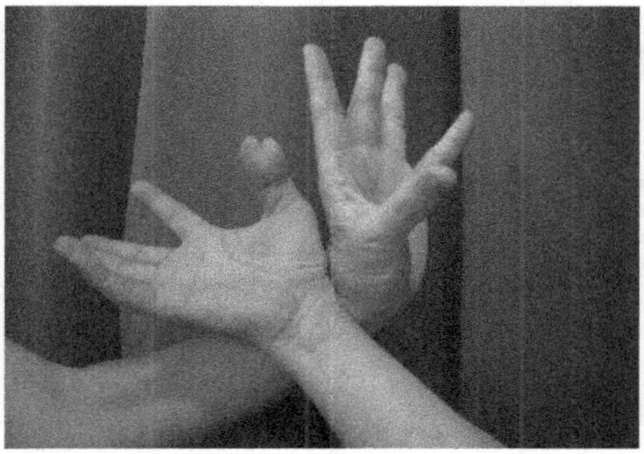

Applying split strength (the right hand illustrating)

Applying Gou Gua Zhuang (Hook Hang) for forward and backward Test Strength

B. ADVANCED SIDE STANCE SHI LI

Special Directions

1. Qing Ting Dian Shui (Dragonfly Skims Water) 蜻蜓點水
2. Shen Gui Chu Shui (Holy Turtle Comes from Water) 神龜出水
3. Ling Xi Pi Shui (Clever Rhinoceros Splits Water) 靈犀劈水
4. Xuan Shou Shi Li (Rotate Slash) 旋手試力
5. Fu Pu Shi Li (Tiger Throw) 虎撲試力

Vertical Movements

1. Shen Long Bai Wei (Dragon Swings Tail) 神龍擺尾
2. Ling He Tong Tian (Clever Crane Reaches Sky) 靈鶴通天

Special Directions

1. Qing Ting Dian Shui (Dragonfly Skims Water) 蜻蜓點水

Hold a Fu An Zhuang side stance. The right hand swings upward and forward. The left hand then swings again. Twist your body with the movements and raise your left ankle when you swing up your right hand.

Master Wang Yu Fang demonstrating Qing Ting Dian Shui in a very gentle and beautiful manner

2. Shen Gui Chu Shui (Holy Turtle Comes from Water) 神龜出水

Hold a Fu An Zhuang side stance with wide steps. Both hands are held up and stay in the same position. Move your body forward and backward.

A. Backward direction

B. Backward direction—moving individual hands

C. Forward direction

3. Ling Xi Pi Shui (Clever Rhinoceros Splits Water) 靈犀劈水

Hold a Gou Gua Zhuang side stance. Raise the right hand up and press the left hand down with Fu An. The right hand then strikes downward.

Master Yao Zong Xun demonstrating Ling Xi Pi Shui

4. Xuan Shou Shi Li (Rotate Slash) 旋手試力

Hold a Fu An Zhuang side stance. Both hands are turned and strike forward.

5. Fu Pu Shi Li (Tiger Throw) 虎撲試力

Hold a Fu An Zhuang side stance with a wide stance. Hold both hands up and press down. Bend your body forwards.

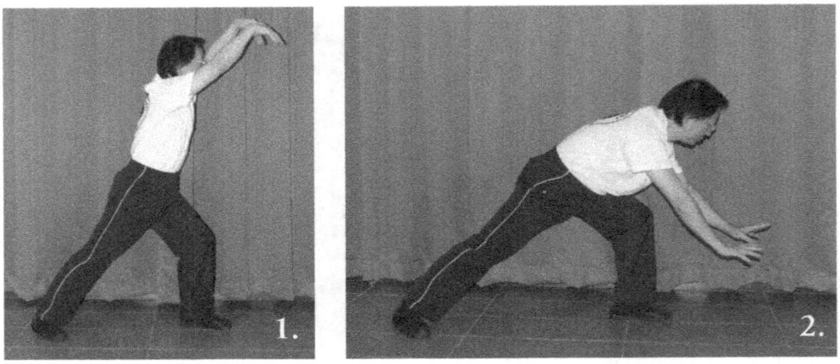

Vertical Movements 立圓試力

1. Shen Long Bai Wei (Dragon Swings Tail) 神龍擺尾

Hold a Fu An Zhuang side stance with a wide stance. The right hand twists and penetrates at the right hip. Turn upward. Repeat for the left hand.

2. Ling He Tong Tian (Clever Crane Reaches Sky) 靈鹤通天

Hold a Fu An Zhuang side stance with a wide stance. The right hand twists with palm upwards; extend up. The left hand presses downward, fully extended. Repeat for the left side.

TEST STRENGTH PRACTICE PROGRAM FOR A 60-MINUTE CLASS

	Duration	Movements
1.	2 min	Warm up—Five relaxation exercises
2.	3 min	Dun Yao

Total: 5 min

Static Stance

	Duration	Movements
3.	5 min	Cheng Bao Zhuang

Total: 5 min

Front Stance Shi Li

	Duration	Movements
4.	5 min	Li Yao Test
5.	5 min	Ping Xuan Test
6.	5 min	Fu An Shi Li
7.	5 min	Ping Tui Shi Li
8.	5 min	Ba Shui Shi Li

Total: 25 min

Side Stance Shi Li

	Duration	Movements
9.	3 min	Qing Ting Dian Shui
10.	6 min	Shen Gui Chu Shui
11.	3 min	Ling Xi Pi Shui
12.	3 min	Xuan Shou Shi Li
13.	3 min	Fu Pu Shi Li
14.	3 min	Shen Long Bai Wei
15.	3 min	Ling He Tong Tian

Total: 24 min

	Duration	Movements
16.	1 min	Cool down

Total: 1 min

C S Tang meeting Master Wang Yu Fang and Master Li Jiang Yu in Beijing, 2001

Chapter 16

THE POWERFUL TEN COMBAT SHI LI

OVERVIEW

These ten movements of combat Test Strength are as taught by Master Wang Yu Fang in April 2001.

Ten Special Movements of Combat Test Strength	王薌齋技擊試力十節功
1. Pull Up Tree	1. 拔樹試力
2. Filter Air	2. 空中濾氣試力
3. Press Spring	3. 按彈簧試力
4. Split Water	4. 分水試力
5. Dragon Turns Arms	5. 回龍轉臂試力
6. Hook and File	6. 鉤銼試力
7. Rub Ball	7. 揉球試力
8. Open and Close	8. 開合試力
9. Elbow Filing	9. 銼力試力
10. Bird Can't Fly	10. 鳥難飛試力

THE MOVEMENTS IN DETAIL

1. Pull Up Tree 拔樹試力

Stand at Hun Yuan Zhuang or Ding Ba Bu. Raise the hands to the chest, with palms facing each other. The fingers penetrate downwards, as if dipping into a pot of syrup (糖漿、糖稀). Both palms then uproot slowly.

Key points

In the downwards direction, the hands lead the elbows. Upwards, the elbows lead the hands.

Imagery

Penetrating downwards and rising upwards, with the intent of resistance and pulling.

Simulation

The downward movement is like planting a tree into the ground, deep into the soil. Upward is like pulling a tree with strong force.

2. *Filter Air* 空中濾氣試力

Stand at Ding Ba Bu with the upper hand placed above your head and the lower hand placed beyond your face. Then close both hands into an empty fist, as if grasping something, and pull and press downwards.

IMAGERY

The head pushes upright, and the legs step heavily.

3. Press Spring 按彈簧試力

Stand at Ding Ba Bu. Raise the hands, with palms facing downward, are then press downwards. Raise up, and repeat.

Simulation

As if pressing down on a spring. You meet resistance, then release and raise up, but feel the spring pulling your hands down.

4. *Split Water* 分水試力

SIDE VIEW OF SPLIT WATER TEST STRENGTH

Stand at Ding Ba Bu, with weight on front foot at 30 percent and back foot at 70 percent. Stretch hands sideways, and open the palms facing the front. Wave the hands forward and backward.

IMAGERY

Half of your body is dipped in a swimming pool.

SIMULATION

Push forwards; feel the water's resistance and flow through your fingers.

5. Dragon Turns Arms 回龍轉臂試力

Stand at Hun Yuan Zhuang. The palms are facing upwards, as if holding a ball uo to the chest, with the elbows pulled inwards. Turn the palms downward, then stretch forward.

Simulation

When turning the palms downward, imaging you are parting cotton or that a dragon is turning its body in the cloud.

6. *Hook and File* 鉤銼試力

Stand at Ding Ba Bu, with palms downwards. The movement is like pushing a floating ball on the water outwards; then turn the palms to face each other, as if holding the ball. Pull backwards.

Imagery

The fingers point out, and the elbows and hands pull back with opposite power.

Simulation

Stretch out like a rasp, pressing hard. Pull back like hooks pulling back an object.

7. *Rub Ball* 揉球試力

Stand at Ding Ba Bu. Raise your hands as if holding a ball. Push the ball outwards with force with the back of the front hand, so that it feels resistance. Repeat, changing directions and hands.

Imagery

When holding the ball, do not press it flat or hold it so loosely that it drops.

8. Open and Close 開合試力

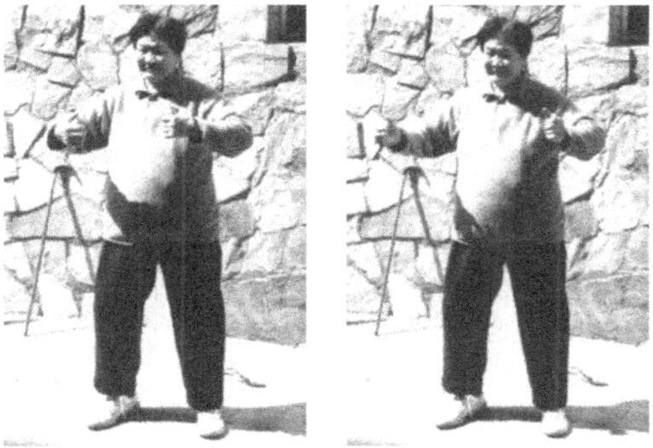

Stand at Ding Ba Bu, with palms facing each other, arms held in a half circle, and armpits in half-empty mode. Use the elbows to lead the hands and stretch outwards and inwards.

IMAGERY

You feel resistance and difficulty in splitting the hands or pressing inwards.

9. *Elbow Filing* 銼力試力

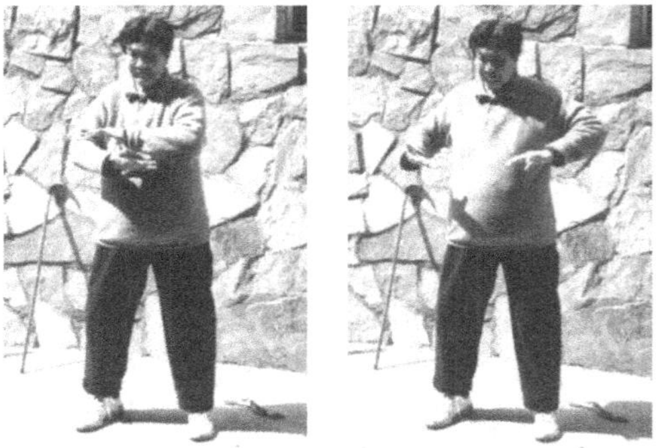

Stand at Hun Yuan Zhuang, with palms facing downwards or one palm facing up and one facing down, and with one palm placed upon the top of the other palm. Then stretch both elbows sideways.

IMAGERY

Both hands stretch with opposite power. Perform with both short and sudden power.

10. Bird Can't Fly 鳥難飛試力

Stand at Hun Yuan Zhuang. Raise the hands to shoulder level, with both hands held as empty fists. Use the back of the fists to push outward. Release and then push again.

IMAGERY

As if grasping birds in both fists; do not release them.

High Dragon Stance by Master Wang Yu Fang

SUMMARY OF THE TEN MOVEMENTS OF COMBAT SHI LI

1. Pull Up Tree 拔樹試力

2. Filter Air 空中濾氣試力

3. Press Spring 按彈簧試力

4. Split Water 分水試力

5. Dragon Turns Arms 回龍轉臂試力

6. Hook and File 鉤銼試力

7. Rub Ball 揉球試力

8. Open and Close 開合試力

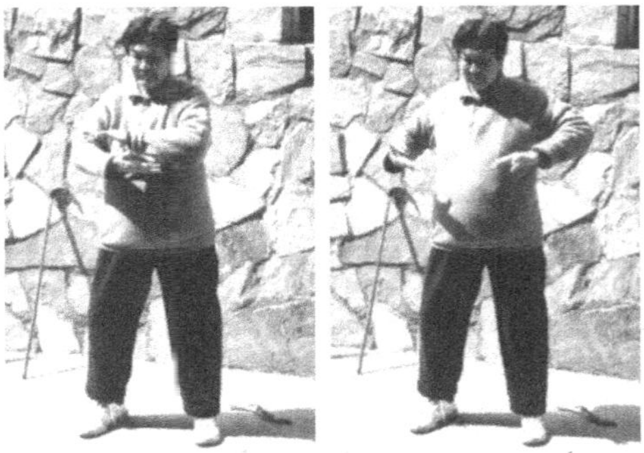

9. Elbow Filing 銼力試力

10. Bird Can't Fly 鳥難飛試力

Simulation on Filter Air 空中濾氣試力

Yao Lu Shi Li (Pushing the Oar) 搖櫓試力示意

TEN COMBAT TEST STRENGTH PRACTICE PROGRAM FOR A 60-MINUTE CLASS

	Duration	Movements
1.	2 min	Warm up
2.	2 min	Dun Yao
3.	5 min	Cheng Bao Zhuang
4.	5 min	Pull Up Tree
5.	5 min	Filter Air
6.	5 min	Press Spring
7.	5 min	Split Water
8.	5 min	Dragon Turns Arms
9.	5 min	Hook and File
10.	5 min	Rub Ball
11.	5 min	Open and Close
12.	5 min	Elbow Filing
13.	5 min	Bird Can't Fly
14.	1 min	Cool down

Chapter 17

MO CA BU
FOOTWORK

Footwork is called "Test Strength for legs." Sometimes this can also be classified within the topic of "Test Strength."

In Yiquan, footwork is similar to the mud walking mode of Bagua Zhang and the triangle footwork of Xing Yi Quan.

In Yiquan, footwork is called Mo Ca Bu, meaning rubbing steps. When practicing, the rear foot when passing by the front leg will rub the side of the front shin.

OVERVIEW

1. Basic Practice: Ding Bu (Fixed Steps) 定步
    a. Up and Down Pressing 原地上下踩步
    b. Four Directions Sliding 原地四面趟步
    c. Cheng Bao Zhuang (Prop Hug) 撑抱樁
2. Don Bu (Moving Steps) 動步
    a. Mo Ca Bu (Friction Steps—Rubbing and Sliding Step) 摩擦步
        i. Cheng Bao Zhuang Step 撑抱樁走步
        ii. Hands at Sideways Step 分撑手上下按走
        iii. Hands at Split Water Step 提趟扒縮步 – 分水
        iv. Hands at Skim Water Step 提趟扒縮步 – 點水
    b. Driving Boat Step 陸地行舟
        i. Gou Gua (Push Drag and Hook Hang) 推拉勾掛手, 雙點步走
        ii. Forward and Backward Free Stepping 進退活步走

3. Footwork together with Shi Li 走步試力

Up and Down	上下
Pull In	內撥
Split Water	分水
Rotate Hands	旋手
Flying Bird	飛鳥
Big Eagle Spreads Wings	大鵬展翅

Stories of Mian Zhai (Exert Workshop) 勉齋物語

Chinese calligraphy and footwork

The theories of Chinese calligraphy are in common with Chinese martial arts. The basic requirements of brushwork are the following:

- Strength penetrates to the back of the writing paper.
- All brushwork must use the center tip portion for writing.
- Eight directions must be supported.
- Back and forth must have snap and stops.

It is the same for kung fu, for which you need:

- a stable stance, sinking the body weight like roots into the ground
- a straight back, good spirit and full of power, and with a shining gaze
- the glutes wrapped and buttocks dropped, with legs propped in all directions, and be stable as a mountain
- back and forth brushing, which must have snap and stops.

Then for every movement, you can show your momentum.

When I first encountered Chinese calligraphy, my teacher was Wang Wei Chang, a famous master. He always said, "Learning from the higher level, you achieve the middle rank; learning from the middle, you get the lower material; if you learn from the lower level, you will always stay at the lowest level."

That was why he required us to learn Li Shu, a Han dynasty style. We would develop to the later dynasty and trace back to the ancient styles. He required us to imitate Li Qi Bei, the ceremonial Implement Stele. This is a style which is slim and stiff with no vulgarity. The wise man said, "Concerning calligraphy, only bad taste is the most difficult to cure."

In the first lesson, at the end of the class, Wang held up my writing, turned it to the back, and showed it to all the students. There were a few signs of ink at the back of my writing paper. Then he held a classmate's example up and everyone saw that the back of her writing paper was just like looking at the front: the ink penetrated to the back. He said she had practiced for three years already, so this was the difference between a beginner and an experienced practitioner.

In order to do this, you need to know why and how. Wang taught us the way of brushwork. When holding the brush, the fingers must be tight, but gripping it loosely. The inside of the palm must be hollow, the shoulder must stretch, the elbow across, and the wrist erect. When pressing the brush, strength comes from the body to the shoulder, to the elbow, the wrist, and then to the fingers; strength then reaches to all brush hair. If the brush tube is held too tight, in contrast, strength is blocked and cannot be delivered to the paper.

During writing, the brush must keep using the center tip. If not, the strength is weak and floats on the surface of the paper only. When performing strokes, the brush must be stable and the tube must not bend sideways. It should always be straight so that it can support in all directions with strength.

Also, when writing, the brush should not skim across the page, but must stop and write with rhythm.

My seal engraving teacher, Feng Kang Hou, taught us the engraving secret: "The composition and design of writing and engraving, the artwork, involves observing carefully and bringing emotions. If not, the artwork will become like sleeping in the same bed, but having different dreams."

THE STEPS ILLUSTRATED

1. Basic Practice: Ding Bu (Fixed Steps) 定步

a. Up and Down Pressing

1. Fun Shui Zhuang, T-step stance. Both hands are placed sideways

2. One leg presses downward

3.

b. Four Directions Sliding

1. Fun Shui Zhuang, T-step stance—both hands are placed sideways

2. Raise right leg—flat foot

3. Right leg slides to right side

4. Draw back and slide to front

5. Draw back and slide to back

2. *Don Bu (Moving Steps)* 動步

1. Right leg steps to right corner

2. Move weight to right leg

3. Move left leg forward

4. The hands keep balance

THE STEPS IN DETAIL

1. Basic Practice: Ding Bu (Fixed Steps)

We will first practice fixed steps movements to train the balancing of the body, keeping opposite power and coordination of the body with stepping.

a. Up and Down Pressing

Press the foot downward continuously with opposite power. When the foot presses down, your head and body rise in the opposite direction in order to enhance your leg power.

b. Four Directions Sliding

Place both hands sideways and move one leg to slide sideways, frontward, and backward. Train the standing power of one leg and the flat movement of the feet.

c. Cheng Bao Zhuang (Prop Hug)

Hold Cheng Bao Zhuang to practice the above foot movements. These will pass from keeping the hands sideways to a combat guarding posture.

2. Don Bu (Moving Steps)

a. Mo Ca Bu (Friction Steps—Rubbing and Sliding Step) 摩擦步

The following patterns of movement of footwork are practiced in different hand postures. The requirements are the same:

1. Apply intention of Test Strength, moving with resistant power.
2. The legs are tied by rope so that they move heavily.
3. The stepping of legs forward and backward should be light and flat; the foot should not rise more than an inch above the ground.
4. Do not "flutter and float" when stepping (太飄). You must move heavily like a mountain yet light and fast like the wind.

Patterns

1.	Cheng Bao Zhuang Step	撐抱樁走步
2.	Hands at Sideways Step	分撐手上下按走
3.	Hands at Split Water Step	提趟扒縮步 – 分水
4.	Hands at Skim Water Step	提趟扒縮步 – 點水

Stepping carefully

Footwork must be very careful and light; the movement of raising the front leg is described as "like stepping on the ice of a frozen lake" (如履薄冰).

b. Driving Boat Step 陸地行舟

I. Gou Gua (Push Drag and Hook Hang) 推拉勾掛手, 雙點步走

Hold a Gou Gua Zhuang hand shape to move forward and backward. The stepping involves stopping over at the side of each foot when moving—the "double stop pace."

II. Forward and Backward Free Stepping 進退活步走

These are free movements of footwork. Move forwards and then backwards or sideways.

3. Footwork together with Shi Li 走步試力

Coordinate the footwork with Shi Li. Apply Shi Li with moving steps in the following types of movements:

Up and Down	上下
Pull In	內撥
Split Water	分水
Rotate Hands	旋手
Flying Bird	飛鳥
Big Eagle Spreads Wings	大鵬展翅

The footwork of Yiquan is derived from Bagua Zhang's mud walking steps and Xing Yi Quan's triangle steps. The following intentions can be applied:

1.	Move Like a Bulldozer	推土機
2.	Cow Farming with Plough	牛犁田
3.	Horse Drawn Carriage	馬拉車
4.	Pull Cart in Supermarket	推超市車

MO CA BU ILLUSTRATED BY MASTERS

Master Li Jiang Yu

Master Wang Yu Fang

Master Yao Zong Xun

FOOTWORK PRACTICE PROGRAM FOR A 60-MINUTE CLASS

Footwork can be integrated into system training as part of specific practice. It can be inserted after Static Stance. It is a training progress topic, which requires step-by-step training.

	Duration	Movements
1.	2 min	Warm up
2.	2 min	Dun Yao

Total: 4 min

Static Stance

	Duration	Movements
3.	5 min	Fu Bao Zhuang
4.	5 min	Fu An Zhuang
5.	5 min	Cheng Bao Zhuang
6.	5 min	Tui Tuo Zhuang

Total: 20 min

Test Strength

	Duration	Movements
7.	15 min	Test Strength practice

Total: 15 min

Footwork

	Duration	Movements
8.	20 min	• First week: Single leg push down (left and right) • Second week: Four directions leg slides • Third week: Moving steps forward with intention, triangle pace • Fourth week: Driving Boat Step, parallel and double stop paces

Total: 20 min

	Duration	Movements
9.	1 min	Cool down

Total: 1 min

Chapter 18

FALI

EMIT STRENGTH

PRINCIPLES OF FALI

Fali is an extension of Shi Li. It is the "acceleration" and "sudden stop" of Shi Li movement. During the movement, maintain and fix the structure without collapsing.

Maintain spherical force 形不破體，力不出尖

When emitting strength, your structure must be fixed and must not collapse your unity. The force must be global, spherical, thick, and strong, and must not be out-of-bounds.

Emergency brake force 剎車力

All Fali training, including fixed steps, moving steps, and free steps, must apply a force called "braking force." It is so called because the Fali movement should simulate the sudden stop of a car by pressing on the brakes. When the car hits a person, the car stops suddenly, and the person is struck and thrown far, far away.

We also simulate this when the line of a kite suddenly snaps and the kite is blown away (斷線風箏).

The effect of the opponent being thrown backwards and sticking to the wall is called "Hanging a Painting on the Wall" (牆上掛畫).

Fali is usually trained solo, but should be tested with partners.

TYPES OF YIQUAN FORCE

- Brake force 剎車力
- Opposite force 爭力
- Explosive force 爆發力
- Shock force 驚力

OVERVIEW OF FALI (EMIT STRENGTH) 發力

1. Fixed Steps Fali 定步
    a. Structural Fali 間架發力 – 正側撐抱, 定樁被按發力
    b. Forward Fali 前發力
    c. Upward Fali 上發力
    d. Downward Fali 下挫發力
    e. Slant Fali 斜砍發力
    f. Down Chop Fali 下劈發力 (鬼斬手)
    g. Rooting Strength Fali 落地生根接發力
    h. Crash Fali 對撞發力
2. Moving Steps Fali 動步發力
3. Free Steps Combination Fali 活步自由組合發力

Preparation posture of Upward Fali

THE STEPS IN DETAIL

1. Fixed Steps Fali 定步發力

a. Structural Fali 間架發力 – 正側撐抱, 定樁被按發力

Using Cheng Bao Zhuang and rolling arms, boost the waist and Dantian to emit strength.

Training: Opponent presses down on your structure and uses ground force to emit strength forward. This is a test of Fali.

b. Forward Fali 前發力

Emit strength forward to strike. Opponent jumps backward.

c. Upward Fali 上發力

Emit strength upward to throw opponent up against the wall.

d. Downward Fali 下挫發力

Raise up arms and then emit strength downward, so that opponent loses balance and falls towards you.

e. Slant Fali 斜砍發力

Hand chops at a slant.

f. Down Chop Fali 下劈發力 (鬼斬手)

Raise the body and one hand, then chop downward.

g. Rooting Strength Fali 落地生根接發力

This is training between two persons when one rushes and pushes the opponent, and the opponent must sink his weight and receive his force.

The opponent must be stable and resist the coming force without losing balance. The opponent then makes use of ground force to emit strength, and throws the other up and away.

h. Crash Fali 對撞發力

This is training between two persons when one rushes and pushes the opponent; the opponent will not avoid the coming force, but will crash into him. This will train the intercepting power and build up your rush power and confidence.

Fali

With strong structure, move forward like a tank! Nothing can stop you.

形意拳 訣：硬打硬進無遮攔

The secret of combat of Xing Yi Quan: "Stiff fight and stiff entry, meet no blocking."

2. Moving Steps Fali 動步發力

After training for different methods of Fixed Steps Fali, practitioners can practice the second level of Fali by coordinating Fali with advancing steps so as to increase the intensity of strength.

Repeat all the methods of Fixed Steps Fali with advancing steps:

1. Structural Fali
2. Forward Fali
3. Upward Fali
4. Downward Fali
5. Slant Fali
6. Down Chop Fali
7. Rooting Strength Fali
8. Crash Fali

3. Free Steps Combination Fali 活步自由組合發力

This is the third level of Fali training, in which the practitioner will move randomly in different directions, say forward and suddenly turn left and then right, to apply the following methods of Fali:

1. Forward Fali
2. Upward Fali
3. Downward Fali
4. Slant Fali
5. Down Chop Fali

SUMMARY: THE WAY TO PRACTICE FALI

First week

Start practice daily with Fixed Steps Fali:

- Structural Fali
    - left front stance 40 times
    - right front stance 40 times
- Forward Fali
    - left front stance 40 times
    - right front stance 40 times

Second week

Repeat:

- Structural Fali
  - left front stance 20 times
  - right front stance 20 times
- Forward Fali
  - left front stance 20 times
  - right front stance 20 times

Add:

- Upward Fali
  - left front stance 20 times
  - right front stance 20 times

Add:

- Rooting Strength Fali—with partners 20 times

Third week

Repeat the above and add the following:

- Downward Fali left and right stance 20 times each
- Slant Fali left and right stance 20 times each
- Down Chop Fali left and right stance 20 times each
- Crash Fali with partners

Fourth week

Repeat all the above methods 10 times each and then add the following moving steps training 10 times each:

- Moving Steps Fali

Fifth week

- Free Steps Combination Fali

Keep moving freely as if you are surrounded by enemies; emit strength to all random directions. Each Fali should be real and conscientious. This will train your force, flexibility, response, and endurance.

FALI ILLUSTRATED

"Hanging a Painting on the Wall" by C S Tang and Allen Lui.

DRAWINGS FROM C S TANG, 1970

These drawings describe the process and the power of Fali.

1. The process and types of effect of Fali

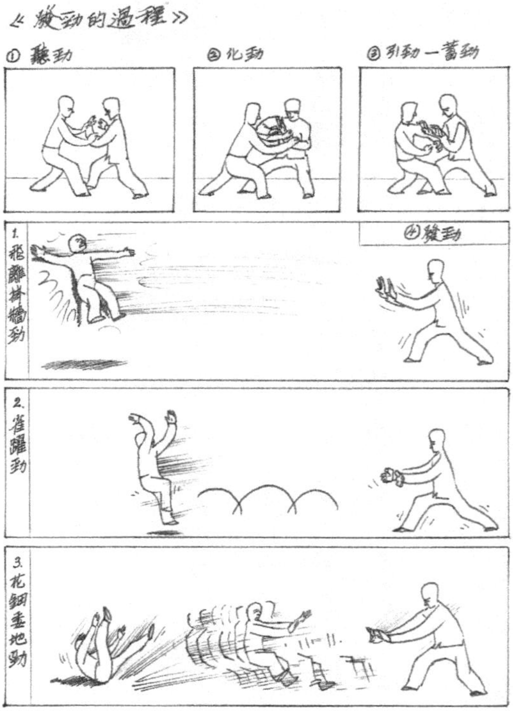

2. The power of Fali

Chapter 19

FA SHENG
EMIT SOUND

C S Tang at Shaolin Monastery, China, 2007

The four sounds of Fa Sheng are:

1. Fixed Steps Emit Sound 定步發聲
2. Tiger Roars Sound 虎嘯
3. Dragon Roars Sound 蒼海龍吟 (神龜出水+發聲)
4. Moving Steps Emit Sound 動步發聲

SHAOLIN XIN YI BA

Here, C S Tang illustrates the Thunder Sound of Xin Yi Ba in Shaolin Monastery.

COMPRESS BODY METHOD

縮身法

TIGER SMASH RISE GESTURE

虎撲把起勢

...**YEE!** (依!)

FALLING GESTURE

落勢發聲

...**WAH!** (嘩!)

ORIGIN OF FA SHENG

The Fa Sheng training of Yiquan is mainly derived from Xing Yi Quan's Thunder Sound (雷聲). Xing Yi Quan's techniques can be traced back to its origin, the old Xin Yi Liu He Quan (心意六合拳). Xin Yi Liu He Quan places emphasis on Liu He—that is, six harmonies.

The six harmonies consist of chicken leg, dragon body, bear shoulders, ape arms, tiger head, and thunder sound. Their sounds will emit after strong use of power such as the Eagle Grasping movement.

However, according to their history, they are also related back to the Shaolin Xin Yi Ba (少林心意把), a very old traditional form of Shaolin martial art, which is still practiced in Shaolin. The harmonies are practiced as individual movements. It is claimed to be the style from which Xin Yi Liu He Quan is derived. In the past, Yiquan masters have visited Shaolin Monastery to find this rare form.

FIVE SOUNDS OF THUNDER

Xin Yi Liu He Quan has five sounds, called the Five Sounds of Thunder. They are:

噫	吆	嗳	呵	哈
yi	**yao**	**ai**	**o**	**ha**

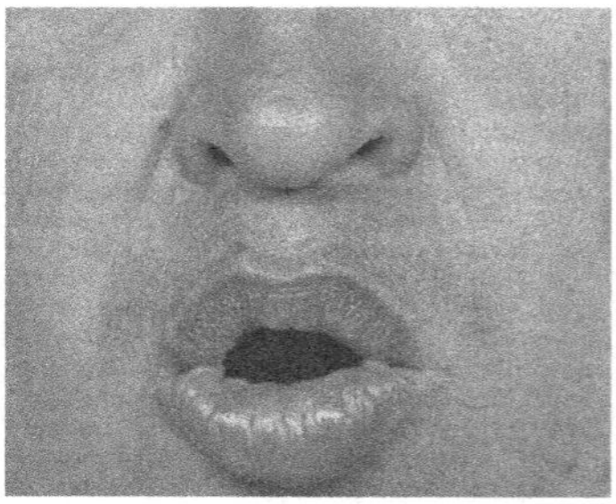

The five sounds correspond to the five organs, and echo with five different Fali. Yiquan has adopted the main sound, "Yi," for the upward or downward emission of strength.

Fa Sheng uses pressure at the Dantian area to burst Thunder Sound, and is done without thinking. A sound done without purpose is loose, but the sound done from the Dantian is focused, short, urgent, and deep-mouthed. The sound starts from the abdomen, vibrates at the lungs, trembles at the throat, emits from the mouth, and shocks your opponent.

ADVANTAGE OF FA SHENG

Practicing Fa Sheng frequently will improve blood circulation because of the expansion of your body when you emit sound, and also prevents internal damage from exerting too much pressure in your chest and abdomen when you practice Fali. Your sound will become louder and stronger after daily practice. If you meet your opponent, the emission of sound will shock him, and the power of your attack is also enhanced when you strike with sound.

Master Wang Xiang Zhai performed this Fa Sheng with Fali in a martial arts gala and all the audience were surprised.

心意六合拳經云:『五行一發響雷聲，拳去雷動響山林。

Once the five elements of strength are initiated, the thunder emitted.
Punches struck with thunder shakes the forest.

(From *Treatise of Six Harmony Xing Yi Quan*)

THE SOUND OF THUNDER

The stages to practice

- At the beginning stage, start in a combat stance and then use your Dantian to emit a small sound, "Ng." The Master said that it sounds like a child urinating.
- At the second stage, try to prolong the sound of "Ng," adding "Yuk."
- At the third stage, the sound combines into "Yau."
- Another version of the practice of sound burst is Tiger Roars, combining "Yee" and "Yuk" into "Yit."

Types of sound

1. *Tiger Roars.* Sound emits from the Dantian through the throat and mouth, like "Wah."
2. *Dragon Roars.* Sound emits from the Dantian through the spine and back of the brain, like thunder roaring "Yi."

YI!

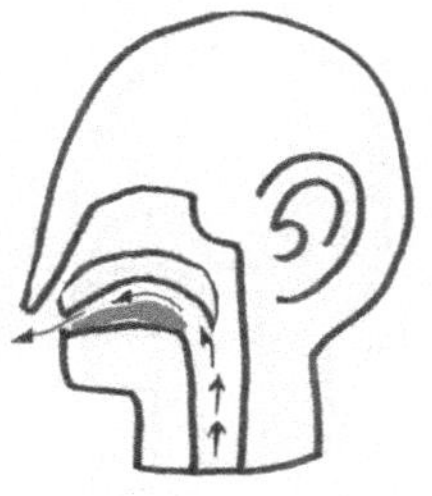

THE WAY TO PRACTICE EMIT SOUND

To practice, train in the following sequence:

1. Fixed Steps Emit Sound 定步發聲
2. Tiger Roars Sound 虎嘯
3. Dragon Roars Sound 蒼海龍吟 (神龜出水+發聲)
4. Moving Steps Emit Sound 動步發聲

1. Fixed Steps Emit Sound

Hold a combat stance; try to emit sound slowly and be patient. Progress from the basic stage through to the third stage.

Class training:

1. Hold a combat stance, Gou Gua Zhuang, for 5 minutes.
2. Perform a Combat Test Strength of up and down, or forward and backward. Breathe in strongly to pump air into your body.
3. Perform an Up Fali lightly three times.
4. Perform an Up Fali, gradually increasing its strength. Perform Fa Sheng with Fali movements.
5. Repeat Fali with Fa Sheng continuously three times.

2. Tiger Roars Sound

Hold a Gou Gua Zhuang, pull both hands inward as a Shi Li, breathe in deeply to the Dantian, store the Qi in the abdomen, and make a sudden burst of Qi and Fali. Qi passes from the Dantian to the chest, to the throat along the Ren channel (Conception Vessel) in the front part of the body, and emits through the mouth. The sound spreads widely and shocks people. The sound is a combination of “Yee” and “Yuk” into “Yit.” The ultimate sound burst is “Yi.”

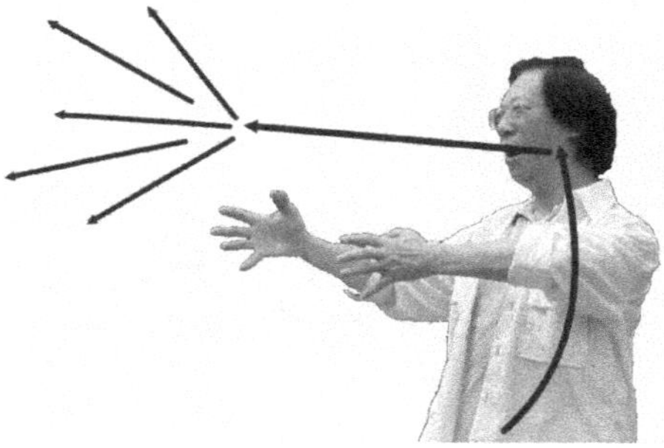

Fa Sheng illustration at
Guangzhou Museum, 2007

Tiger Roars

3. Dragon Roars Sound

Hold a Fu An Zhuang and perform a Shen Gui Chu Shui (Holy Turtle Comes from Water) Shi Li with a higher stance such as Fu An Shi Li. Press both hands downward and inward, breathe in deeply to the Dantian, gather Qi, and store it. Hold your breath, swallow the Qi, press it down, and pass through the Du channel (Governor Vessel) of the spine at the back. Push the Qi through the back of the brain, go through to the top of the head, and then down to the throat. When you emit power downward or outward, emit the third stage sound, a short burst with a low voice like thunder crossing the sky. The Dragon Roars sound is a combination of "Ng" and "Yuk" into "Yau."

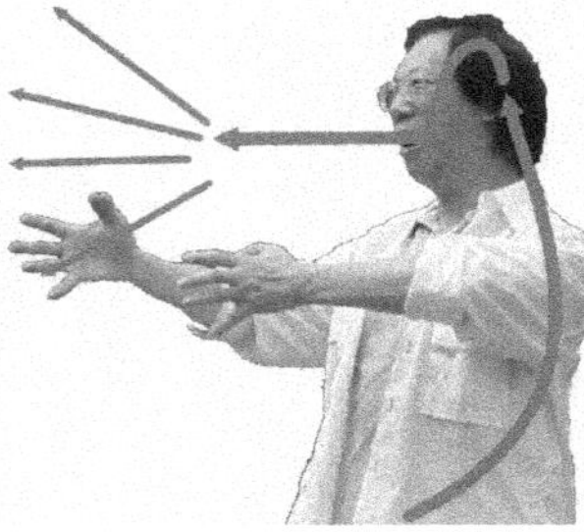

DRAGON ROARS FROM THE SPINE COMBINED WITH FALI

4. Moving Steps Emit Sound

Practice Moving Steps Fali, and when emitting strength, emit the sound at the same time.

1. Hold a Fu An Shi Li movement.
2. Perform an Upward Fali, Fa Sheng "Yi," and move steps forward.

Finally, this practice will be combined with Fist Dance in a performance. Normally we will end the Fist Dance with a strong and short emission of sound.

EFFECT OF EMITTING SOUND

- Promotes blood circulation to the whole body and to the tips of the limbs.
- Increases the pressure of your body to practice Fali.
- Gives you courage to face a strong opponent.
- Shocks your opponent to a sudden stop and lowers his defenses.

Chapter 20

TUI SHOU
PUSH HAND

C S Tang pushing hands with Master Wang Yu Fang

TWO MEN DRILL

Practical martial arts are confrontational sports. Solo practice will build up your body condition and your skeleton, and strengthen your muscles, tendons, and bones. Basic exercises can improve your flexibility and endurance. However, if you want to take your training approach to a further stage and become more practical, you need to train with partners.

Think of Chinese chopsticks; they are a pair. One stick alone would not perform its function. Losing one stick will make the other stick meaningless. Training with a partner will improve your sensitivity, speed, endurance, loading, resistance, and power. The most important thing is to make your previous training become relevant, useful, and applicable.

CHINESE CHOPSTICKS

My Bagua Zhang teacher, Ho Ke Cai, always said, "You cannot take away my kung fu, except you come with two persons [a partner]."

So our training is a daily two men drill, so that what you have learnt can be applied and used immediately by experience with your classmate. Through this interchange, you will learn by your mistakes and, through trial and error, how to use strength correctly and how to avoid the coming power and attack.

Master Wang Xiang Zhai also said, "If you find something wrong, go back and check it yourself." That is to say, during push hand or non-contact fighting, if you have some questions on attack or defense, go back to check whether the position or requirement of your stance is wrong and needs to be improved.

The practice of Yiquan push hand places emphasis on:

1. Control
2. Emit
3. Strike.

意拳之推手技巧在 (控, 發, 打)

A. CIRCLING

1. Dan Tui Shou (Single Push Hand) 單推手
2. Shuang Tui Shou (Double Push Hand) 雙推手
    a. Both up
    b. Both down
    c. Up and down
3. Moving Steps Push 2 and 2 活步雙推 (進2退2)
4. Moving Steps Push 3 and 3 活步雙推 (進3退3)

1. *Dan Tui Shou (Single Push Hand)* 單推手

2. *Shuang Tui Shou (Double Push Hand)* 雙推手

3. Moving Steps Push 2 and 2 活步雙推 *(*進*2*退*2)*

4. Moving Steps Push 3 and 3 活步雙推 *(*進*3*退*3)*

B. TECHNIQUES FOR ATTACK AND DEFENSE

1. Dan Tui Shou (Single Push Hand) 單推手

a. Cheng Bao—Fu An Fali 撐抱 – 扶按發力
b. Gou Gua—Ping Tui Fali 勾掛 – 平推發力
c. Bo Lang Fali (Wave Shock Emit) 波浪剎車發力
d. Jie Fa Training (Hand-out Push) 接發力

2. Shuang Tui Shou (Double Push Hand) 雙推手

a. Si Fang Fali (Practice Emit) 練習發力 (前撞, 上發, 下發, 側發)
b. Fu An Fali (Floating Press Emit) 扶按發力 (下按上推)
c. Xuan Fali (Rotate Emit) 橫旋發力(偏掛/旋法轉圈)
d. Gou Gua Fali (Hook Hang Emit) 勾掛發力 (勾掛前撞)
e. Fen Gua Fali (Open Hook Emit) 分掛發力 (左右分掛前打)
f. Xia Gou Fali (Down Hook Emit) 下勾發力 (槓桿)
g. Xia Cuo Fali (Down File Emit) 下挫發力 (滑車)
h. Pian Gua Fali (Spin Side Hang Emit)(偏掛返中 – 左鑽右橫旋打)
i. Xia Cuo Fali (Side Slant Plant Emit) (左右斜栽發力)
j. Hung Fali (Chest Emit) 胸接力/胸發力

a. Si Fang Fali (Practice Emit) 試發力

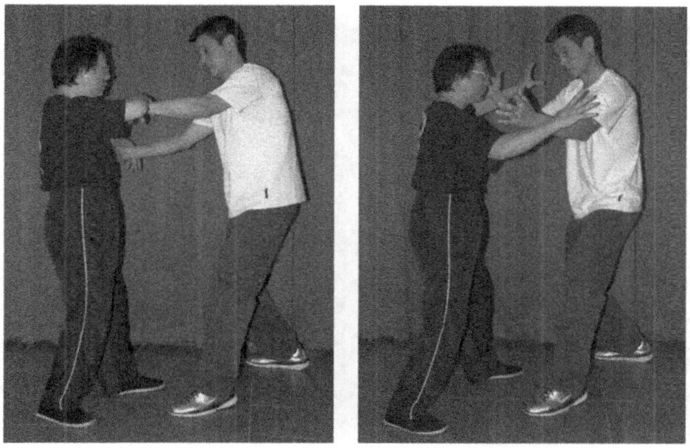

b. Fu An Fali (Floating Press Emit) 扶按發力 (下按上推)

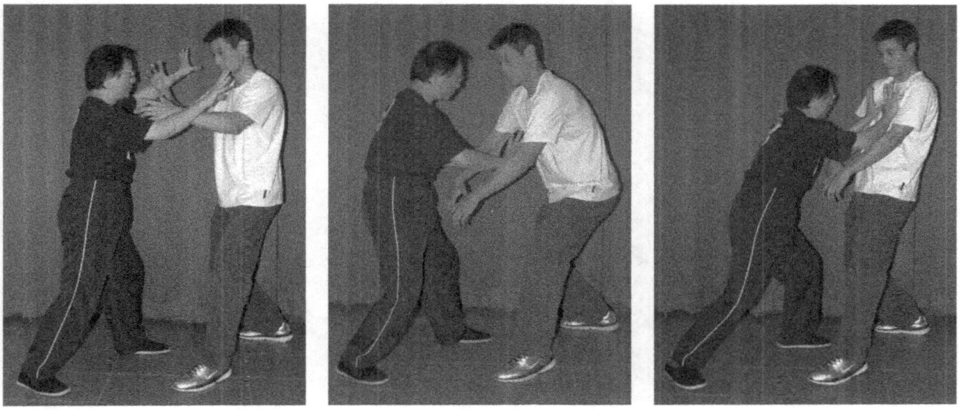

c. Xuan Fali (Rotate Emit) 橫旋發力 (偏掛/旋法轉圈)

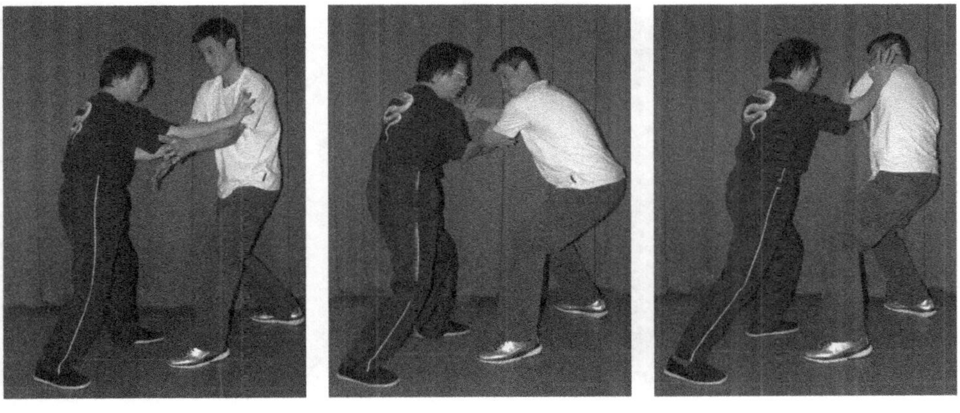

d. Gou Gua Fali (Hook Hang Emit) 勾掛發力 (勾掛前撞)

e. Fen Gua Fali (Open Hook Emit) 分掛發力 (左右分掛前打)

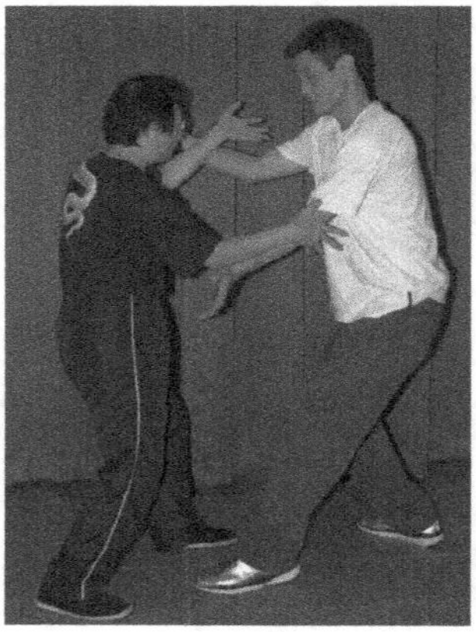

f. Xia Gou Fali (Down Hook Emit) 下勾發力 (槓桿力)

g. Xia Cuo Fali (Down File Emit) 下挫發力 (滑車力)

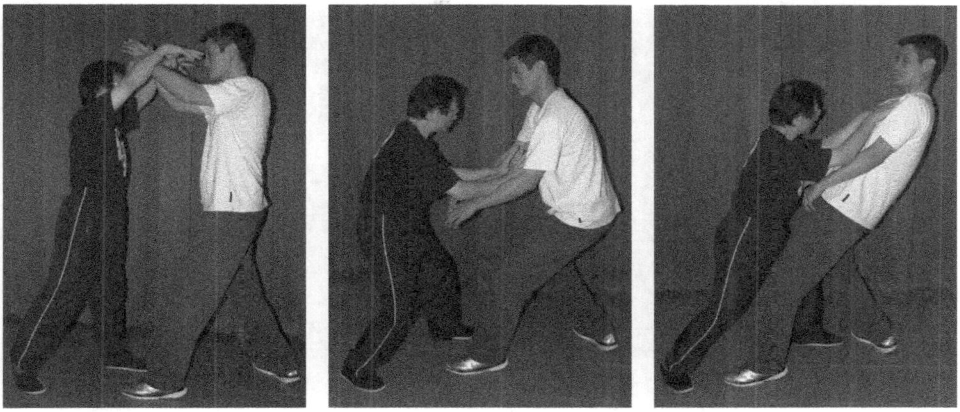

There are other Fali techniques that can be used in push hand entry and attack:

h. Pian Gua Fali (Spin Side Hang Emit)
(偏掛返中 – 左鑽右橫旋打)

i. Xia Cuo Fali (Side Slant Plant Emit) (左右斜栽發力)

j. Hung Fali (Chest Emit) 胸接力/胸發力

PUSH HAND TECHNIQUES IN MORE DETAIL

1. Dan Tui Shou (Single Push Hand)

Training techniques

I. CONTACT POINT MUST BE TIGHT, AND SURFACE RELAXED

II. Turn, lead, and circling

III. Rotate and point to center

IV. Penetrate to center line, then attack

Application

I. Turn in and push

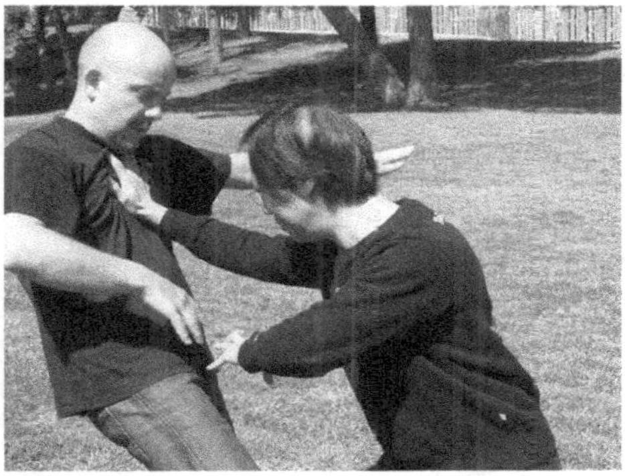

II. Point to center

Horse punch

Collapse palm

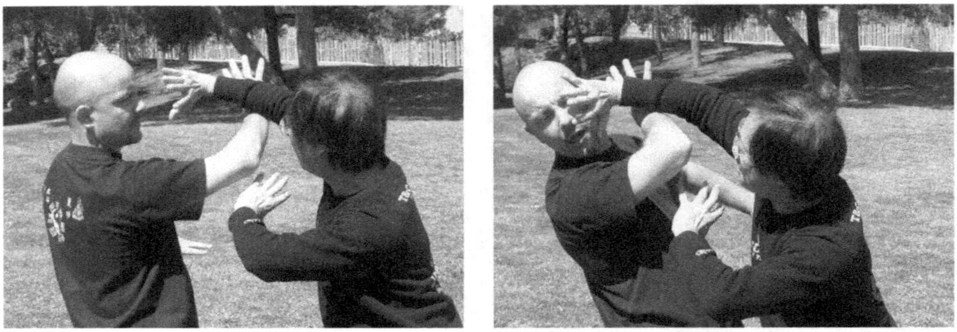

Plant punch

III. Upper drill

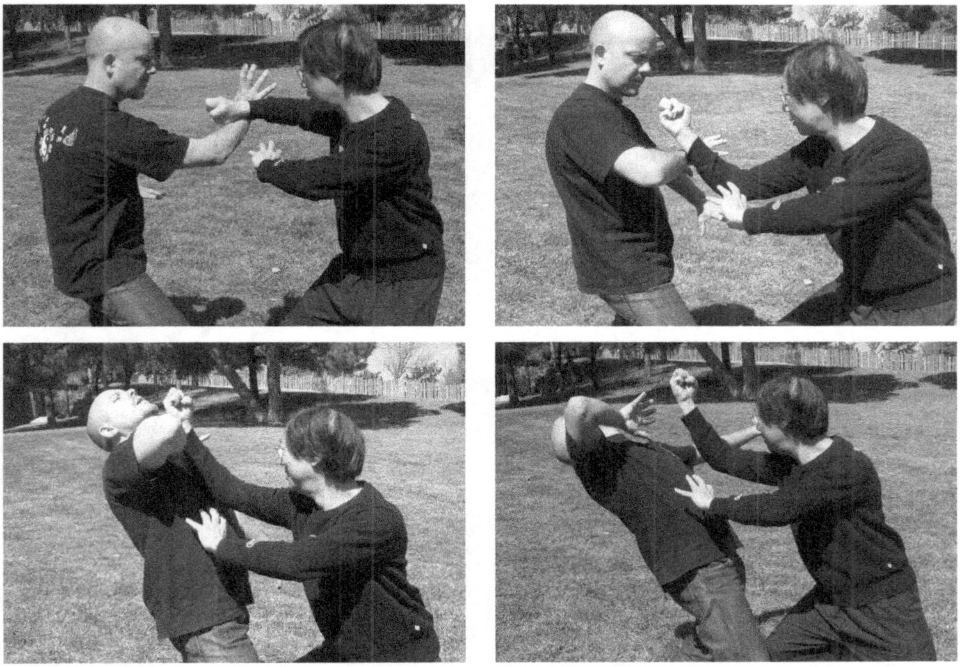

IV. Press down and cross punch

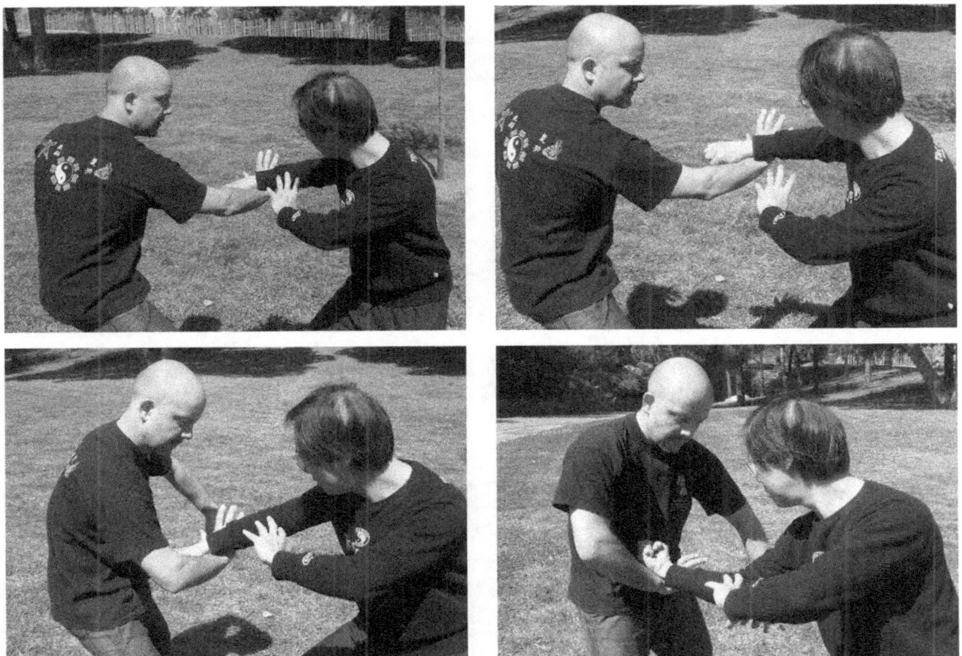

v. Press down and rub upwards

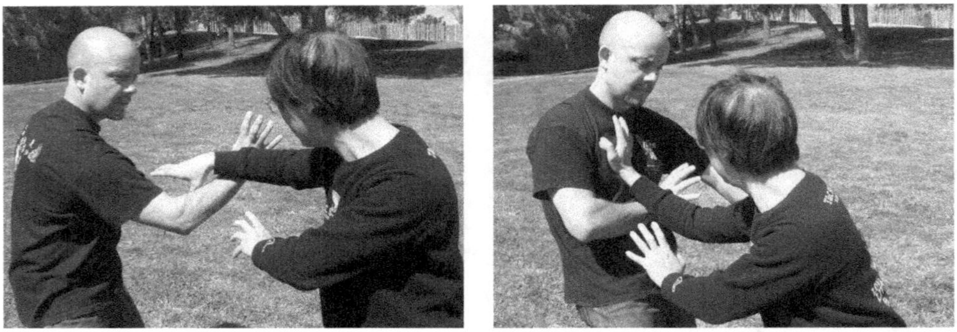

vi. Low hang and up chop

2. *Shuang Tui Shou (Double Push Hand)*

We have selected several push hand techniques here to illustrate how to break the guarding posture and strong structure of your opponent. These involve entering techniques, breaking techniques, and off-balance techniques.

a. Si Fang Fali (Practice Emit) 試發力

When your hands are beneath your opponent's hands, use Wave Fali: raise your wrists to release and destroy his structure, then emit strength towards his chest.

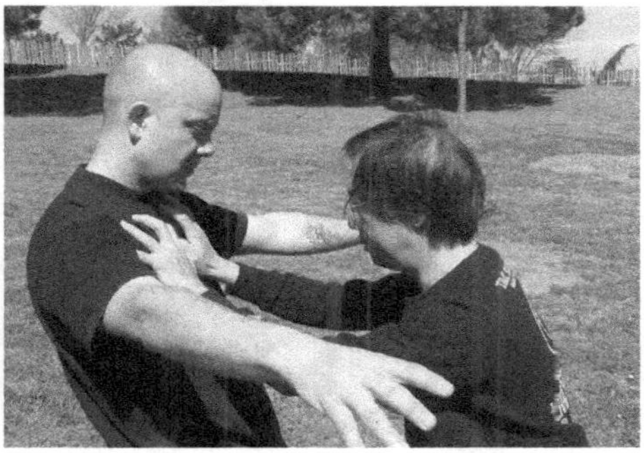

b. Fu An Fali (Floating Press Emit) 扶按發力 (下按上推)

When your hands are placed above your opponent's hands, use Fu An Fali: press with shock power, create a gap at his center line, and then emit strength towards his chest, rubbing upwards so that his root is destroyed and he has to float upwards and fall backwards.

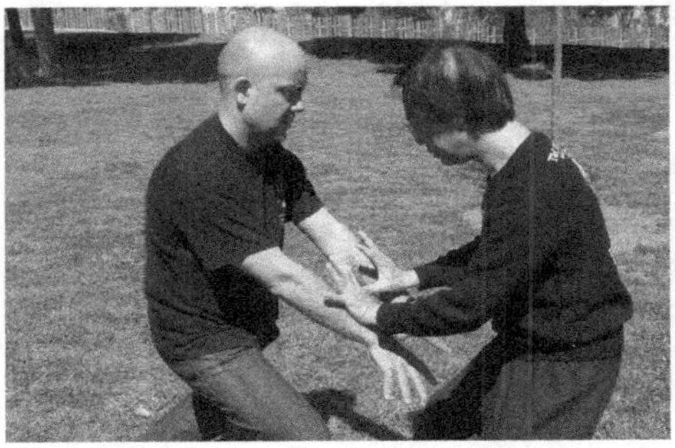

c. Xuan Fali (Rotate Emit) 横旋發力 (偏掛/旋法轉圈)

Apply the Li Yao Test Strength: vertically turn and lead your opponent's hand sideways, cross his center line, and then grasp his arm with your other hand and push his shoulder so that he will twist and fall backwards. The movement must be done quickly and suddenly.

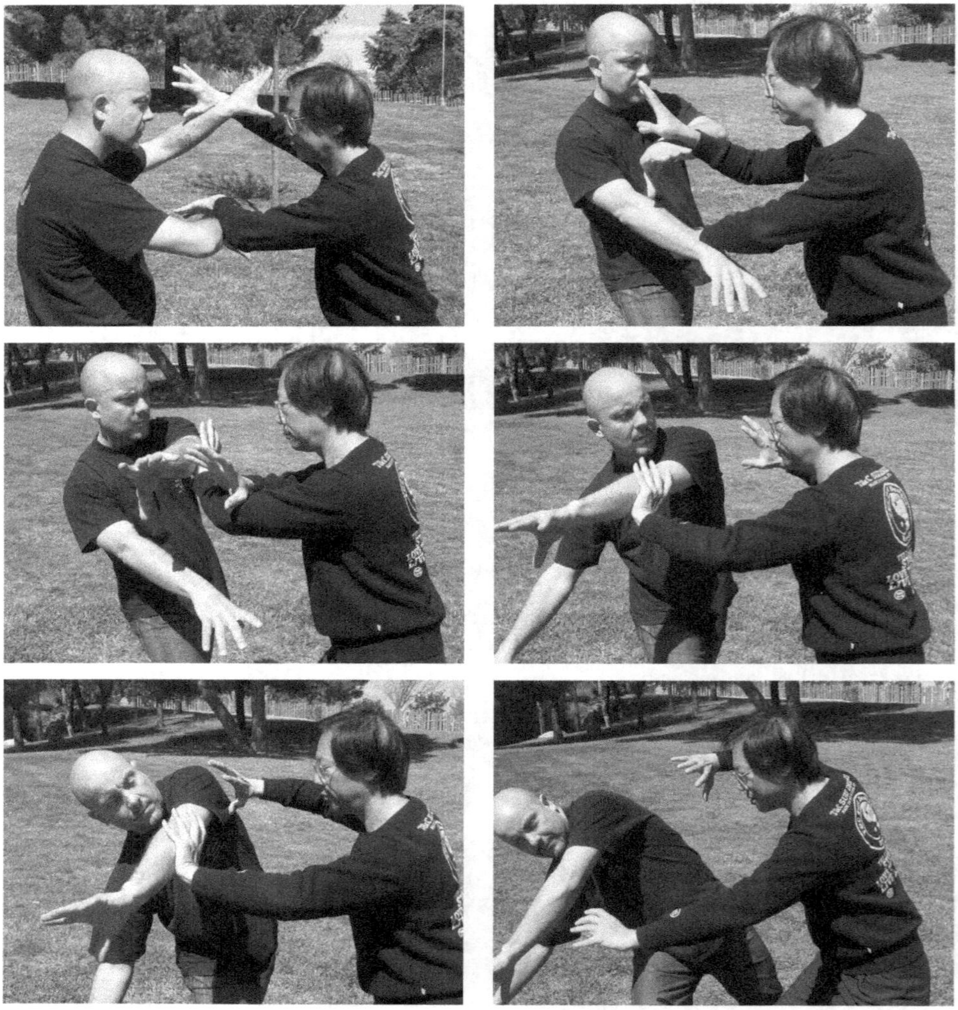

d. Gou Cuo Fali (Hook and File Emit) 勾挫發力 (勾挫前撞)

When your hands turn upwards, use the hook shape hand to separate your opponent's hands. Apply Hook and File Shi Li: hook the opponent's hands apart to open his guarding posture and apply file power to rub downwards, so that he loses balance and falls towards you. Then apply Tiger Smash to throw him away.

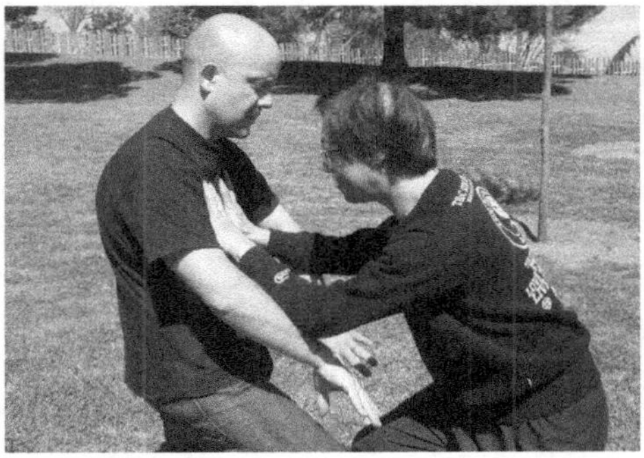

e. Fen Gua Fali (Open Hook Emit) 分掛發力 (左右分掛前打)

Split your hands sideways, applying Open Hook Shi Li to tear his hands apart, and then attack his chest.

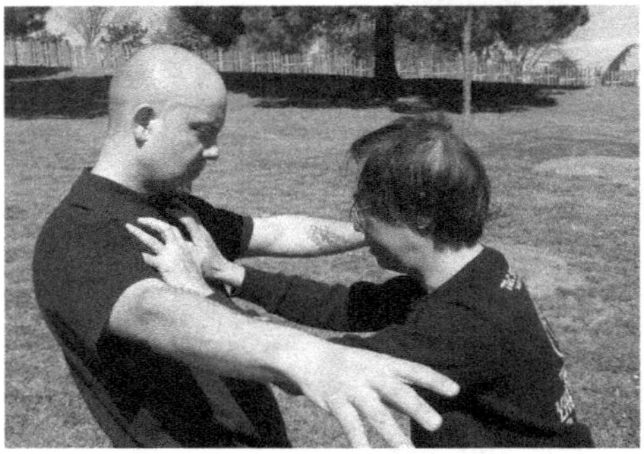

f. Pian Gua Fali (Spin Side Hang Emit) 偏掛返中 – 左鑽右横旋打

Try to use left drill fist to entice him to resist, and then turn your palm to push his elbow. Grasp his right elbow with your other hand and turn him to fall sideways.

g. Xia Cuo Fali (Side Slant Plant Emit) 左右斜栽發力

Roll your hands left and right to destroy his skeleton. Then apply a plant punch. Your hands should move like the pincers of a crab; expand and support strongly, and coordinate with opposite power.

h. Drill punches 左右鑽拳

Yiquan push hand is a free fighting form, so you can apply punches during your circular rolling movements. With your left upper hand, drill and press his arm; make use of his resistance. Your right lower hand attacks his lower jaw with the drill fist.

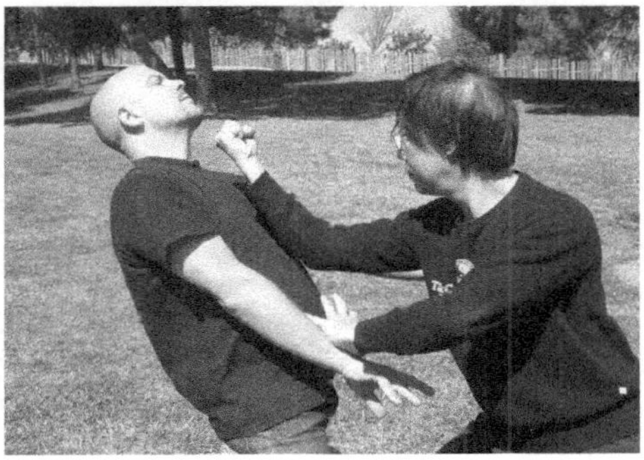

i. Horse punches 馬形拳。左右勾擊

Make use of the circular movements to attack your opponent with a right horse punch from the top, and then use your inner left hand to make use of this gap and attack with another horse punch.

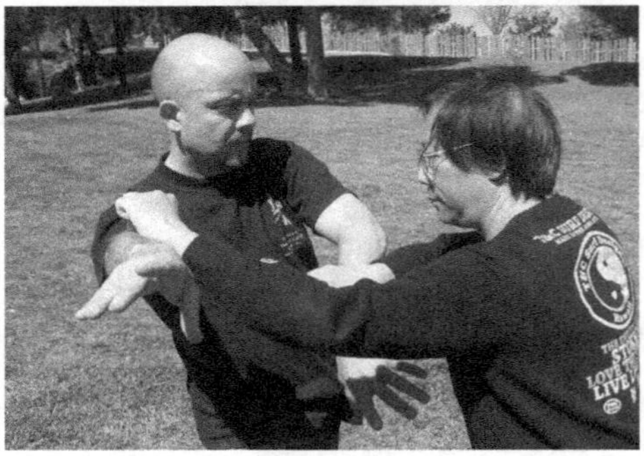

PUSH HAND ILLUSTRATED

Ian Fok, Chairman of the Hong Kong Yiquan Association, illustrating push hand with Yang Shao Geng

Ian Fok illustrating push hand with Chen Zheng Zhong, 2007

YIQUAN PUSH HAND COMPETITION RULES

1. Rules of engagement of Yiquan

1.1 The size of the sparring area shall be a circular competition area of 6 meters in diameter with a marked circle in the center of 1.5 meters in diameter.

1.2 The sparring area should be clean, flat, and matted to protect the athletes from injuries in the match.

1.3 Matches will have several rounds of push hand; each round comprises a maximum of three bouts where individuals are paired against each other. The one who first wins two rounds will be the winner.

1.4 Each bout will have 70 seconds of continuous sparring time or more under the discretion of the Tournament Director.

1.5 Show respect by bowing to your opponent, referee, officers, and audience when entering the ring.

1.6 At the beginning, participants should be in the small circle in the center of the sparring area, in contact with each other's forearm with one above and one underneath. Once the referee calls "Start circling," participants should start push hand in circling only. The participants should not move out of the small circle in the center before "Start" is announced.

1.7 When the referee announces "Start," participants can use push-hand techniques to push each other.

1.8 The one who pushes his opponent out of the sparring area (6 meters in diameter) or pushes down his opponent (to the ground) will earn some scores. (Stepping on the edge of the circle is counted as out of the area.)

1.9 The individual who gets the highest score in each bout will be the winner.

2. Scoring and penalties

2.1 During push hand, participants must keep contact with each other; never strike your opponent without controlling his arm. The referee should call "Stop" to interrupt the bout when participants have lost contact with each other's arm. If a participant is found to intentionally avoid contact with his opponent more than three times, 3 penalty marks will be awarded to his opponent.

2.2 Never use punches, elbows, knees, kicks, and head-butts on your opponent. Attacks on the eyes, face, nose, throat, groin, and the head are not allowed. When any of the above actions happen and have not yet caused any injury to the opponent, the referee should call "Stop" and 2 penalty marks shall apply. If serious injury is caused, the referee shall hold up a red card and stop the bout, while the offenders are liable to compensate for the injuries made.

2.3 Never push the throat and mandible; 2 penalty marks apply.

2.4 Grappling or wrestling techniques extending more than two seconds are worth no marks even with a successful take-down.

2.5 Holding and pulling your opponent's arms or legs for more than two seconds will incur 2 penalty marks. If it occurs more than three times, the individual will lose the bout.

2.6 Grabbing your opponent's clothes for more than two seconds will incur 2 penalty marks. If it occurs more than three times, the individual will lose the bout

2.7 During the bout, 1 mark will be deducted if both of the participants do not follow the referee's instructions and begin to attack without having officially been told to. A participant who intends to hurt his opponent will be disqualified from the match.

2.8 During the match, the one who falls on the ground will lose 2 marks. If one leg is launching on the ground or one hand is supporting on the ground, 1 mark will be deducted. No score is awarded if both sides fall to the ground.

2.9 Passive defenses are not allowed in the match. The first time will incur a warning, the second time 1 penalty mark, and the third time 2 penalty marks. If it happens a fourth time the participant will lose the bout.

2.10 Bonus marks will be awarded for the following:

1. Initiating proper attacking methods and remaining active in the bout; 2 marks are awarded for that bout.
2. Carrying out the techniques in a reasonable manner and with correct timing; 2 marks are awarded for that bout.
3. Applying push hand techniques effectively; 3 marks are awarded for that bout. (Push hand techniques include power testing, power release, and stepping. Grappling or wrestling techniques are not push hand techniques.)

Chapter 21

DAN CAO

PUNCH FIGHT

Master Wang Yu Fang demonstrating Yiquan punches

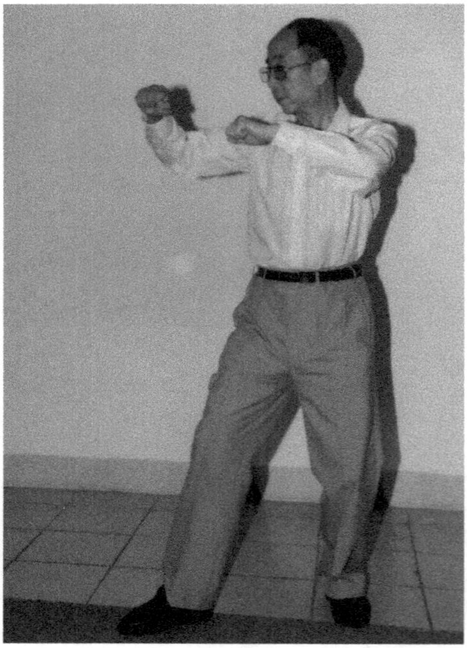

Master Han Si Huang holding a Shan Cao stance

1. Chong Quan (Straight Punch) 沖拳 (豹拳)
2. Zuan Quan (Drilling Punch) 連環勾鑽拳
3. Beng Quan (Breaking Punch) 連環崩拳
4. Pao Quan (Cannon Punch) 鑽炮拳
5. Heng Quan (Cross Punch) 扯橫拳
6. Zai Quan (Planting Punch) 下栽拳

7. Guan Quan (Hook Punch) 貫拳 (馬形拳)

   Single Hand Contact Attack 單搭手打法

   a. Direct Punch 横旋指中沖拳
   b. Upper Cut 上鑽拳下膀
   c. Press and Attack Heart 下壓直崩心
   d. Hook Back and Attack the Face with Palm 勾旋塌面
   e. Press and Attack Rips 下壓横崩肋
   f. Upper Turn and Downward Punch 上旋下栽胸

YIQUAN PUNCHES

The essence of Yiquan combat is "Opposite Power." Without this power, the punches would be the same as in boxing and long fist punches. "Opposite Power" means pulling the rear hand backwards when the front hand punches.

Yiquan punches are part of the training of Duan Shou. In order to make punches effective, you must have the following:

- Opposite power
- A structure like a steel frame.

You must also have experience of the following:

- Defense:
    - Resisting strong attack
    - Knowing your protective techniques
- Training in shadow boxing and long cross and short upper cuts
- Training in combination punches
- Actual combat:
    - Punching sand bags
    - Punching an opponent who is just guarding
    - Punching an opponent with protective hand guards
    - Punching an opponent who counter-attacks
- Undergoing professional massage after intensive punch training.

A fighter must be flexible with jumping and have fast footwork, be able to resist an attack with strong punches, know how to protect himself from injuries, have endurance, punch strongly for every hit, have focus and full concentration, be keen and alert, and know when to change strategies.

1. Chong Quan (Straight Punch) 沖拳 (豹拳)

2. Zuan Quan (Drilling Punch) 連環勾鑽拳

3. Beng Quan (Breaking Punch) 連環崩拳

4. *Pao Quan (Cannon Punch)* 鑽炮拳

5. *Heng Quan (Cross Punch)* 扯横拳

6. *Zai Quan (Planting Punch)* 下栽拳

7. Guan Quan (Hook Punch) 貫拳 (馬形拳)

MASTERS' DEMONSTRATIONS

Master Han Si Huang performing Zai Quan in Hong Kong

Master Wang An Ping performing Yiquan punches in Hong Kong

Master Han Xing Yuan demonstrating Yiquan-style Pei Quan

Yao Cheng Guang and Yao Cheng Rong demonstrating Yiquan punches

DEMONSTRATION BY C S TANG

PUNCHES PRACTICE PROGRAM FOR A 60-MINUTE CLASS

	Duration	Movements
1.	2 min	Warm up—Five relaxation exercises

Total: 2 min

Punches

	Duration	Movements
2.	5 min	Chong Quan (Straight Punch) 沖拳 (豹拳)
3.	5 min	Zuan Quan (Drilling Punch) 連環勾鑽拳
4.	5 min	Beng Quan (Breaking Punch) 連環崩拳
5.	5 min	Pao Quan (Cannon Punch) 鑽炮拳
6.	5 min	Heng Quan (Cross Punch) 扯横拳
7.	5 min	Zai Quan (Planting Punch) 下栽拳
8.	5 min	Guan Quan (Hook Punch) 貫拳 (馬形拳)

Total: 35 min

Combinations Set 1: Left stance

	Duration	**Movements**
9.	5 min	Chong Quan—Left right, left right+ Zuan Quan—Left right, left right+ Guan Quan—Left right, left right+ Repeat 10 times and change to right left, right left+
10.	1 min	Quick and non-stop shadow punching of Set 1

Total: 6 min

Combinations Set 2: Right stance

	Duration	**Movements**
11.	5 min	Beng Quan—Left right, left right+ Pao Quan—Left right, left right+ Heng Quan—Left right, left right+ Zai Quan—Left right, left right+ Repeat 10 times and change to right left, right left+
12.	1 min	Quick and non-stop shadow punching of Set 2

Total: 6 min

	Duration	**Movements**
13.	5 min	Target punching—All seven punches: Left right, left right
14.	5 min	Free shadow punching
15.	1 min	Cool down

Total: 11 min

ACTUAL APPLICATION

C S Tang illustrating Zuan Quan in a seminar in Barcelona, Spain, June 2008

His student, James Carss, applying a good Zuan Quan in a boxing fight in Hong Kong, October 2008

The fight of James Carss

Applying Yiquan punches

The knock-out and the winner

Chapter 22

DUAN SHOU

COMBAT FREE SPARRING

斷手，即斷開不連，離開手打之謂也。
Duan Shou means fighting apart, separately with non-contact.

致勝之道，其訣曰：

1. 兵貴神速
2. 長守必輸
3. 最好的防守就是進攻

The way to win:

1. Troops must move fast.
2. Defense will always lose.
3. The best defense is attack.

In March 1992, I asked Madam Wang Yu Fang about the secret of fighting of Yiquan. Wang said that her father, in his later years, decided on six words and passed them on to her:

1. Persistence
2. Endurance
3. Ruthless
4. Cautious
5. Stable
6. Accurate

王玉芳老師謂王老晚年總結技擊為六字：長 忍 狠 謹 穩 準

PRINCIPLES OF DUAN SHOU

Duan Shou (斷手) literally means "severed fighting." This is full-contact sparring which is performed without contacting hands before the fight. Training the Static Stance is to practice isometric power, to increase a steel-shape body, the elasticity of muscle, and the flexibility and extendable length of limbs. Training Shi Li and Fali are ways to develop strong explosive power. Footwork will enable quick and stable movement. Punches and kicks are techniques ready to be used in Duan Shou. Duan Shou is the ultimate objective of practicing the Static Stance or Yiquan.

Duan Shou is a kind of free fighting. It could be street fighting or fighting in the ring. The strategies between these two kinds of fighting are different. In street fighting, you need to be quick and strong to finish the fight as soon as possible, so therefore explosive power is more important than all other factors. There may be more than one opponent around you. While in the ring, however, you have gloves or protection. Your opponents are always well prepared and in good condition and you may have a long fight. You need good endurance and body fitness. You just focus on one opponent.

Factors in combat may include the following:

1. Body fitness and conditioning: speed, intensity, power, entry, movement, a stiff structure, and a quick response.
2. Beating resistance training: the capacity to take blows.
3. Enemy distance and scope: timing and distance.
4. Strategy before fighting and tactics during the bout.

1. Body fitness and conditioning

a. Ten key elements of body fitness

1. *Strength*—the extent to which muscles can exert force by contracting against resistance (holding or restraining an object or person).
2. *Power*—the ability to exert maximum muscular contraction instantly in an explosive burst of movements (e.g., jumping or sprint starting).
3. *Agility*—the ability to perform a series of explosive power movements in rapid succession in opposing directions (e.g., zigzag running or cutting movements).
4. *Balance*—the ability to control the body's position, either stationary (e.g., a handstand) or while moving (e.g., a gymnastics routine).
5. *Flexibility*—the ability to achieve an extended range of motion without being impeded by excess tissue—that is, fat or tight muscle—and the ability to move joints and use muscles through their full range of motion. The sit-and-reach test is a good measure of flexibility of the lower back and the backs of the upper legs.

6. *Muscular endurance*—the ability of a muscle, or a group of muscles, to sustain repeated contractions or to continue applying force against a fixed object (e.g., rowing or cycling). Push-ups are often used to test the endurance of arm and shoulder muscles.
7. *Cardiovascular endurance*—the heart's ability to deliver blood to working muscles and their ability to use it (e.g., running long distances).
8. *Cardio-respiratory endurance*—the ability to deliver oxygen and nutrients to tissues, and to remove waste, over sustained periods of time (e.g., long runs and swims).
9. *Strength endurance*—a muscle's ability to perform a maximum contraction time after time (e.g., continuous explosive rebounding through an entire basketball game).
10. *Coordination*—the ability to integrate the above-listed components so that effective movements are achieved.

b. A workout schedule

How often, how long, and how hard you exercise, and what kinds of exercises you do, should be determined by what you are trying to accomplish. Your goals, present fitness level, age, health, skills, interest, and suitability are among the factors you should consider. For example, an athlete training for high-level competition fighting would follow a different program than a person with an office white-collar job whose goals are good health and the ability to meet work and recreational needs.

Your exercise program should include something from each of the ten basic fitness components described above. Each workout should begin with a warm-up and end with a cool-down. As a general rule, space your workouts throughout the week and avoid consecutive days of hard exercise.

Below are the amounts of activity necessary for the average healthy person to maintain a minimum level of overall fitness. Included are some of the popular exercises for each category:

- *Warm-up*—5–10 minutes of exercise such as walking, slow jogging, knee lifts, arm circles, or trunk rotations. Low-intensity movements that simulate movements to be used in the activity can also be included in the warm-up.
- *Muscular strength*—a minimum of two 20-minute sessions per week that include exercises for all major muscle groups. Lifting weights is the most effective way to increase strength. But stretches are also important for relaxing the muscles after weight-lifting.
- *Muscular endurance*—at least three 30-minute sessions each week that include exercises such as calisthenics, push-ups, sit-ups, pull-ups, and weight training for all the major muscle groups.

- *Cardio-respiratory endurance*—at least three 20-minute bouts of continuous aerobic (activity requiring oxygen) rhythmic exercise each week. Popular aerobic conditioning activities include brisk walking, jogging, swimming, cycling, rope-jumping, rowing, cross-country skiing, and some continuous action games such as racquetball and handball.
- *Flexibility*—10–12 minutes of daily stretching exercises performed slowly, without a bouncing motion. This can be included after a warm-up or during a cool-down.
- *Cool-down*—a minimum of 5–10 minutes of slow walking and low-level exercise, combined with stretching.

c. Principles

The keys to selecting the right kinds of exercises for developing and maintaining each of the basic components of fitness are found in these principles:

- *Specificity*—pick the right kind of activities to affect each component. Strength training results in specific strength changes. Also, train for the specific activity you're interested in. For example, optimal swimming performance is best achieved when the muscles involved in swimming are trained for the movements required. It does not necessarily follow that a good *runner* is a good swimmer.
- *Overload*—work hard enough, at levels that are vigorous and long enough to overload your body above its resting level, to bring about improvement.
- *Regularity*—you cannot "hoard" physical fitness. At least three balanced workouts a week are necessary to maintain a desirable level of fitness.
- *Progression*—increase the intensity, frequency, and/or duration of activity over periods of time in order to improve.

Some activities can be used to fulfill more than one of your basic exercise requirements. For example, in addition to increasing cardio-respiratory endurance, running builds muscular endurance in the legs, and swimming develops the arm, shoulder, and chest muscles. If you select the proper activities, it is possible to fit parts of your muscular endurance workout into your cardio-respiratory workout and save time.

d. Readiness

Prepare yourself enough for speed, intensity, power, entry, movement, a stiff structure, and quick response training before any fight:

- *Speed*—punch fast and move fast in all directions.
- *Intensity*—never one punch but continuous punches.

- *Power*—every punch is full power.
- *Entry*—seek a good chance to enter; enter actively.
- *Movement*—always moving; do not stand still.
- *A stiff structure*—your structure is like steel.
- *Quick response*—attain good timing and a quick defense.

意拳致勝之道: 體能 抗打 入位 走位 拳重 架硬 快密 閃搖

2. Beating resistance training

Overview of the training methods:

- Static Stance to build up isometric power
- Shi Li with intention
- Resist punches training
- Two men blocking exercises.

The training methods in detail:

Static Stance to build up isometric power

Select a stance, such as Mao Dun Zhuang, Fu Yun Zhuang, Gou Gua Zhuang, or Dun Bao Bei Zhuang. Imagine that there are enemies attacking your body using bare hands and weapons from the front, back, and both sides. You tighten parts of your body to resist and bear the attack.

Shi Li with intention

Select a Shi Li posture, such as Up and Down Shi Li, Forward and Backward Shi Li, and Split Shi Li.

- Imagine you are surrounded by a net with weapons placed on it. You have to apply stretches and contractions to bring up whole body resistance.
- Imagine you are captured in a cell and are surrounded by walls. You have to strike and break these walls into pieces.

Resist punches training

Hold a Mao Dun Zhuang. The coach will strike the trainee and proceed step by step using light-to-heavy punches. The position and parts of the body to be punched:

- Both arms held as frame
- Chest
- Abdomen

- Hips
- Thighs and legs
- Back
- Face and jaw
- Neck.

Two men blocking exercises

- Two men practicing traditional Blocking Three Stars
- Punch and block combinations.

3. Enemy distance and scope

- *Timing*—control the most effective opportunity when the opponent retrieves his attack. Observe his regular patterns and rhythm.
- *Distance*—apply footwork to adjust distance and combat scope between you and your opponent; always be on the initiative.

4. Strategies before fighting and tactics during the bout

In the old Chinese martial arts manuscripts and masters' proverbs there are several very important phrases concerning combat:

- "Advancing with each step, unrivaled under heaven."

  From the *Bible of Sword* (步步前進 天下無敵).

  My Taiji Quan teacher, Master Pan Yan Li (潘炎流), always said, "Move forward, move forward, but do not retrieve."
- "View the impossible as possible, keeping your distance, but do not engage the enemy if you are not well prepared."

  This phrase means that, when in combat, neither party knows how the opponent will attack and react. So you must train yourself to fight and respond by reflection (by Huang Han Xun, master of Northern Seven Stars Praying Mantis).
- "讓得人, 輸了。.林耀桂說"

  This means that once you come into the combat, you must win. Do not think about giving way to your opponent, because if you are humble, eventually you lose your reputation (by Lin Yao Gui, master of Southern Dragon Form).

  The same old phrase also said, "If you give way, you feel fantastic but actually you lose your reputation."

- "Non-movable mind" (不動心)

  One of the purposes of training Static Stance is to develop a non-movable heart (mind). A Chinese proverb said, "泰山崩於前而色不變，麋鹿興於左而目不瞬." That is to say, even if the mountain collapses, you do not show any surprise. Even if there are deer dancing at your left, you are not eager to look at them.

- "Do not fear your enemy, calm down, and do not fear death. Try to train more meditation; develop a state of mind of no motion."
- "Train with your instructor; when you perform a static stance, he tries to push you and you must stand like a rock. When he pulls you, you move like a whole substance, without collapsing any certain part. The instructor has to induce your hand or chest, so that you may fall on him and lose your balance."
- "In your guarding posture, do not show any attempt to attack (不露形), but you are alert and well prepared to attack. When you keep your stance, try to sense his desire to attack (殺氣): when it is strong and when it is weak. His skin pores will release Qi. If his desire to attack becomes strong, he is trying to attack."

ACTUAL PRACTICE

1. Palm strikes

a. Gui Zhan Shou (Ghost Chop) 鬼斬手

APPLICATION: STRIKING FROM TOP TO BOTTOM

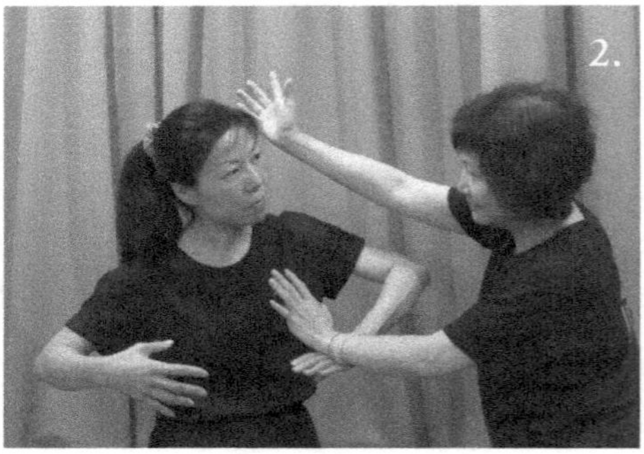

b. Xue Zhang (Cutting Palm) 削掌

APPLICATION: BACK HAND STRIKE

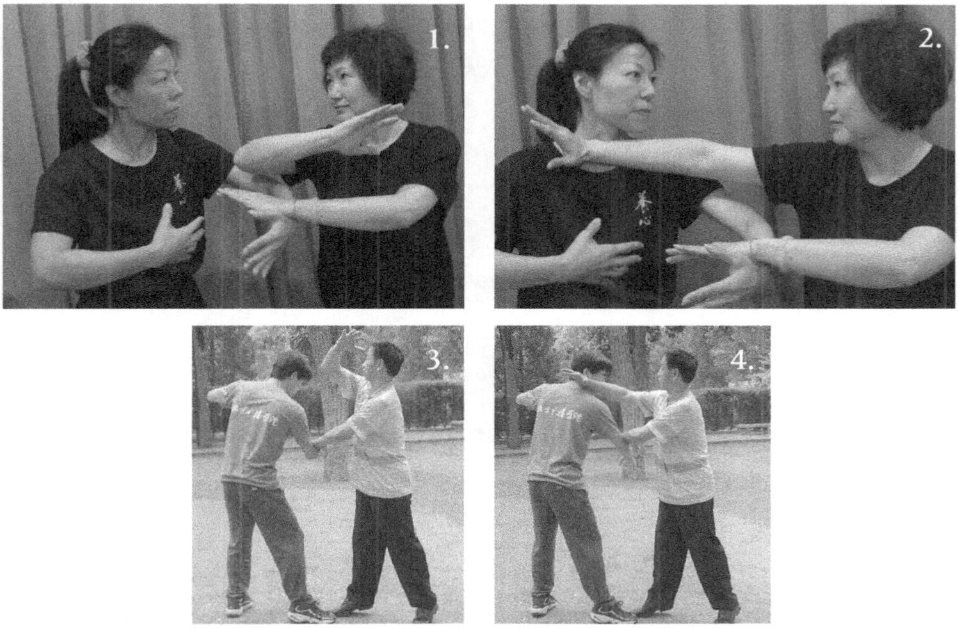

c. Ta Zhang (Collapse Palm) 塌掌

APPLICATION

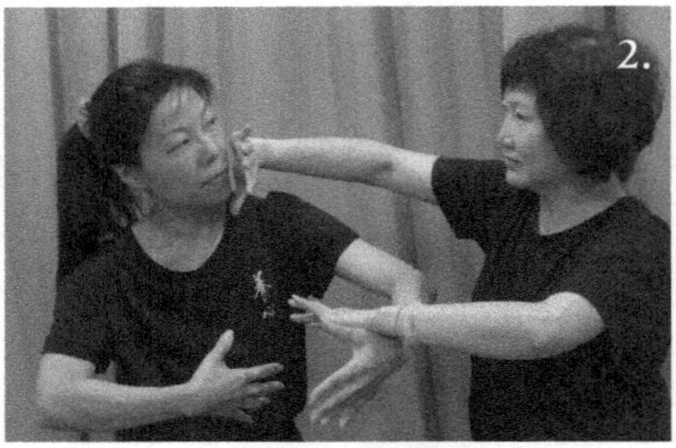

2. *Kicks*

Master Wang Xiang Zhai performing the Kick Stance.

Basic exercises—Press legs 壓腿

a. Bow Step Press Leg 弓步壓腿
b. Empty Step Press Leg 虛步壓腿
c. Crouch Press Leg 仆步壓腿
d. Front Press Leg 正壓腿
e. Side Press Leg 側壓腿
f. Front Split Leg 正劈腿
g. Side Split Leg 側劈腿

In order to kick with power and flexibility, you have to do basic exercises frequently. Here are some of the usual practices performed in my class. The performer is Miss Annabel Cheng.

A. Bow Step Press Leg 弓步壓腿

B. Empty Step Press Leg 虛步壓腿

C. Crouch Press Leg 仆步壓腿

D. Front Press Leg 正壓腿

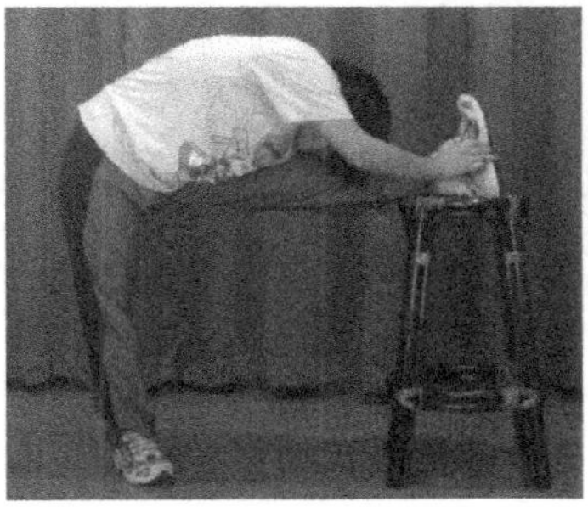

E. Side Press Leg 側壓腿

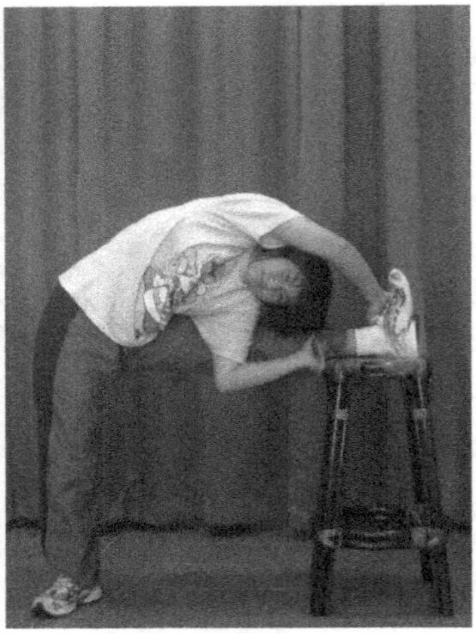

F. Front Split Leg 正劈腿

G. Side Split Leg 側劈腿

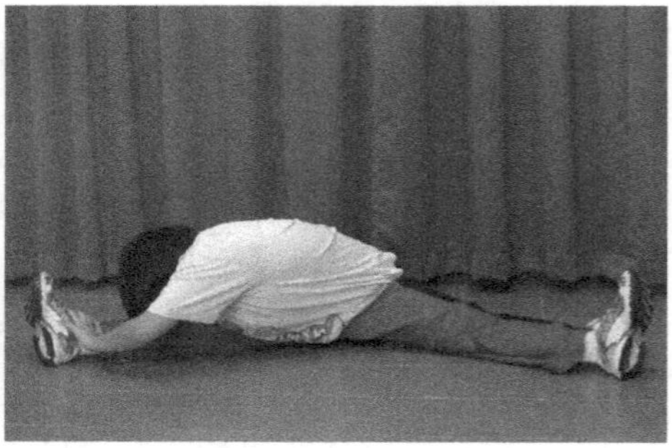

Types of kick

a. Cai Tui (Step/Straight Kick) 踩腿
b. Ding/Dian Tui (Nail/Straight Kick) 釘腿/點腿
c. Heng Duo Tui (Slant Stamp Kick) 橫跺腿/截腿 (攔門腿)
d. Ce Chuai (Side Kick) 側踹腿
e. Deng Tui (Stomping Kick) 蹬腿 (穿襠腿及撩陰腿)
f. Po Ma Tui (Breaking Steps) 破馬腿

Special stance for kicks: Cheng Tui Zhuang (Stretch Leg Stance), also called Dragon Came Out from the Sea 撐腿樁 (蛟龍出海)

A. Cai Tui (Step/Straight Kick) 踩腿

b. Ding/Dian Tui (Nail/Straight Kick) 釘腿/點腿

This kick is derived from Xing Yi Quan, called Juan Di Feng (捲地風), meaning Sweeping Ground Wind.

In Bagua Zhang, this is the first kick technique, called Qu (趨).

c. Heng Duo Tui (Slant Stamp Kick) 横跺腿/截腿 (攔門腿)

d. Ce Chuai (Side Kick) 側踹腿

E. Deng Tui (Stomping Kick) 蹬腿 (穿襠腿及撩陰腿)

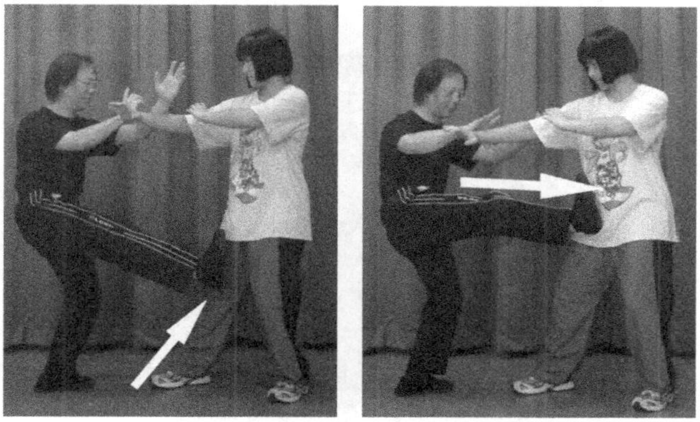

Linking kicks

Right Cai Tui, left Heng Duo Tui, and right Deng Tui 連環腿

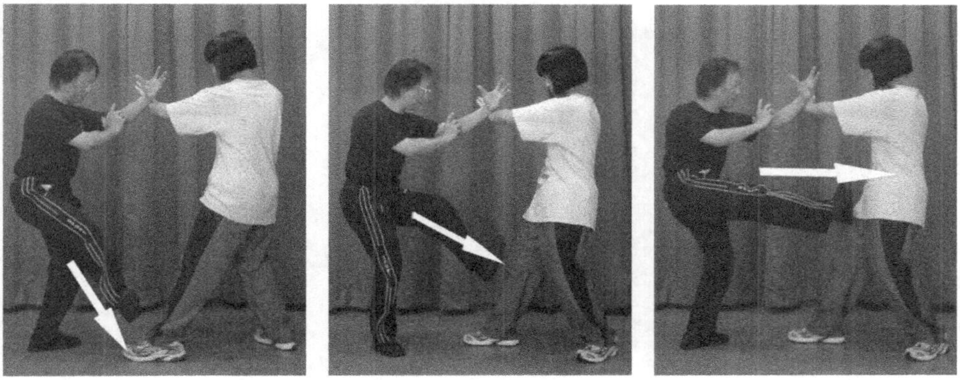

F. Po Ma Tui (Breaking Steps) 破馬腿

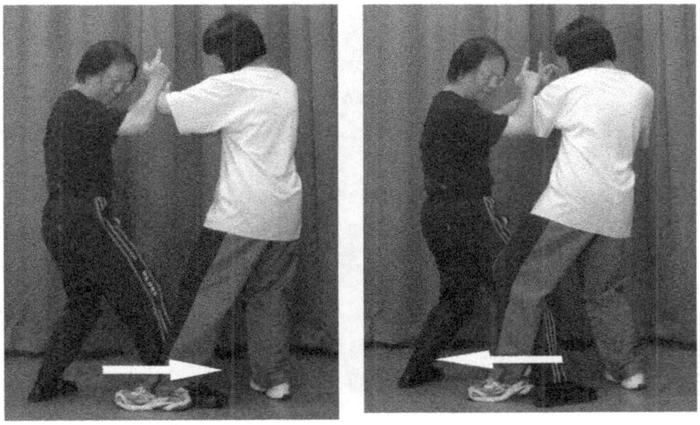

Stances that can improve the power of kicks

Deng Tui (Stomping Kick)

Stomp Crotch Kick 穿襠腿

Bottom Kick 撩陰腿

Kick Stance illustrated by Master Yao Zong Xun

Chapter 23

YIQUAN TACTICS AND STRATEGIES

INTRODUCTION

Han Si Huang's (韓嗣煌) aspiration was to apply Sunzi's war tactics to Yiquan. He always mentioned that Master Wang Xiang Zhai discussed Sunzi's theories with him. He was deeply impressed with the knowledge of Master Wang and liked to express Yiquan tactics following the theories of Sunzi in a systematic way in his lifetime. When Han came to Hong Kong to teach, he discussed these theories several times with us. He bought many different editions of *The Art of War* and wrote down his notes. He knew that I had graduated from a Sports Management Program and possessed some modern knowledge of sports training and field tactics, so he shared most of his knowledge with me.

This chapter is based on Han's speech and notes and our experience in organizing many push hand competitions.

I have been a judge in traditional martial arts and Wushu-form competition and San Shou ring fighting for a long time. I have organized several push hand competitions among Yiquan practitioners in Hong Kong. We have gathered information and rules for the combats and developed a series of tactics for the participants. We hope the participants will follow the way of training and consider all factors before entering the combat.

Sunzi (544–496 BC) was the author of *The Art of War*, an immensely influential ancient Chinese book on military strategy. He was also one of the earliest advocates of international relations theory.

The name Sunzi ("Master Sun") is an honorific title bestowed upon **Sun Wu** (孫武), the author's name. He also has a courtesy name, **Chang Qing** (長卿).

TACTICAL TRAINING AND TACTICS CONSCIOUSNESS

No matter whether in push hand, free sparring, or street fighting, tactics are important factors in Yiquan combat. Nowadays, people work and live in safe places; their awareness of being attacked is lacking. Even when they enter the ring, they still retain passive gestures and a lack of consciousness.

Tactics consciousness is the key to tactical ability, and the cultivation and strengthening of tactics consciousness are important ways to improve a fighter's capabilities.

Tactics consciousness is a kind of consciousness that fighters have, which guides their actions and their use of appropriate tactics, in response to situations arising in the course of the game. This ability is also a way by which athletes can demonstrate their maturity and experience in the fight. This tactics consciousness is practiced by showing the combat stances in a spirit of high alert. The Yiquan manuscripts always describe this spirit as the Chicken Upright Stance posture and the Hedgehog (刺蝟) Preparing for War. This is to use all one's power against the opponent no matter whether they are stronger or weaker than you. This is the theory of when the lion attacks, he will treat his enemy as having the same destructive power whether it is an elephant or a rabbit.

The level of a fighter's ability demonstrated in competition depends mainly on the degree to which the fighter is able to put his ability to use in the actual fight. Sports ability depends upon many factors, including form, movement, coordination, technique, tactics, psychology, and intelligence.

The structure of competitive ability

Physical	Sports ability	Strength, speed, endurance	Shape, function
Skill	Sports technique	Quality and consistency of performance	Cooperation
Competitive ability	Tactics	Perform well, distract rival, affect judgment	Intelligence, knowledge
Mental	Emotion	Mobilization, control	Motivation
	Psychology	Conscientious, indomitable	Character

VALUE OF *THE ART OF WAR* BY SUNZI

The Art of War by Sunzi is an ancient masterpiece on military theory, which was written by Sun Wu of Qi in the Chun Qiu period. Sun Wu, who is also called Chang Qing, lived during 544–496 BC. It is the earliest, most intact, and most famous work of military theory from ancient times in China. There are 13 chapters in the manual.

Contents of *The Art of War*

Chapter	Title	Contents
1.	Planning	Five factors, seven counsels, deception, planning
2.	Waging War	Victory, not prolonged warfare
3.	Strategy of Offense	Block the enemy's strategy, know the enemy well
4.	Dispositions	Fight when victory is assumed
5.	Forces	Normal force to engage and extraordinary will to win
6.	Weaknesses and Strengths	Avoid strong points, attack weak points, use the enemy's own tactics to produce victories
7.	Maneuvering	Avoid enemy when his spirit is keen, attack when he is sluggish and his soldiers are homesick
8.	Nine Variations of Tactics	A wise general considers both favorable and unfavorable factors
9.	Army on the March	Observe the land and the enemy's situation
10.	Terrain	Conforming to conditions of the ground is the greatest advantage in battle
11.	Nine Varieties of Ground	Place them into perilous situations, then they will survive; place them on desperate ground, then they will live
12.	Attack by Fire	No sovereign should launch a war out of rage; no general should fight a battle out of resentment
13.	Use of Spies	The five classes of spies

In keeping with the progressive dialectical materialism at that time, *The Art of War* is an intelligent crystallization of ancient military thought in China. It served to establish China's classical military theoretical system and provides the basic framework of the system. It also establishes extensive general principles of warfare and provides the outstanding concepts, propositions, methods, and principles which may be used to guide warfare, develop strategies and tactics, train armies, and hold sports competitions. It melds military science, philosophy, and literature into an organic whole and represents the highest attainments in philosophy and literature.

COMBAT TACTICS AND STRATEGY

Strategy can be defined as leadership ability and the actions taken to realize short- and long-term goals. Strategic goals may be long term, such as for an entire season of competition, or applicable to a specific match. Strategy can include many factors, such as the intensity and methods of training before competition, team spirit and cooperation, understanding the significance of the match, tactical planning for the match, scheduling factors, and meals. These all can affect a team's performance. Strategic planning has to take into consideration all factors—external conditions, organization, training conditions, rest and relaxation, and the order and rules of the competitions and tactics.

Tactics can be defined as pertaining to preparations for a match and their stages of implementation. These include the plan for the whole competition season for the purpose of maximizing one's own team's competitive advantage and exploiting a rival's weaknesses, and they also include step-by-step measures to achieve the goal. The study of tactics encompasses not only the views and decisions of team leaders and coaches governing game plans, plays, and ways to ensure the highest performance, but also analysis of individual performance and finding ways to balance individual performance with external game conditions.

The word "strategy" is believed to have originated in China, as evidenced by Sima Biao's *First Volume on Strategy*. Sima was a historian in the Jin dynasty who lived around AD 238/246–306 (the date of birth is uncertain).

Clausewitz, a famous military theoretician, historian, and Prussian general, defined in his *Theory of Warfare* that tactics concerns the wisdom of the use of troops in the battle, and strategy is the application of planning knowledge in fighting for the purpose of war.

Basic principles

Yiquan combat can be classified as follows:

1. Push hand—restricted
2. Push hand—limited for no striking; can apply locking and wrestling
3. Duan Shou—free sparring
4. Attack and defense
5. Street fighting.

Tactics is about the principles and methods of combat and includes the theory of tactics and the execution of tactics. There are rules and regulations or standards which govern our action and speech in the field of competition. There are different tactics for real fights, street fights, and fights for life or death. The training programs also differ according to the different aspects. However, for all circumstances we train mentally and physically by pre-arranged sets of entry methods and defense techniques. The instructor will arrange numerous repetitions to refine and correct mistakes and train reaction by reflection with thinking. Then he will arrange internal competition among classmates and lead the team when meeting outside competitors.

Basic tactical principles

- Principle of full protection
- Principle of fast reaction
- Principle of being fully involved and following through
- Principle of focusing troops
- Principle of total unity offensive
- Principle of taking advantage of battlefield
- Principle of surprise attacks
- Principle of close combat
- Principle of fast, decisive engagement and attack segments.

Basic tactical techniques

- Know yourself and know your enemy well. Use different tactics with different enemies.
- Eliminate the enemy and protect yourself and survive.
- Focus your force and eliminate your enemies one by one.
- Prepare well and gain opportunities.
- Unite your forces.
- Aim for initiative and vary flexibility.
- Apply a sudden and surprise attack.
- Be brave and diligent; maintain continuous fight.
- Protect your combat by comprehensive planning and control.
- Get a chance to rest and recover during breaks in combat.

APPLICATION OF SUNZI'S TACTICS

There are close similarities between military warfare and competitive fights, and the principles for achieving victory found in Sunzi's book are particularly relevant to competitive sports. We can apply Sunzi's principles as follows:

1. The principle of knowing yourself and your enemy well
2. The principle of being confident of winning before engaging
3. The principle of initiative
4. The principle of using regular methods to engage and special methods to win
5. The principle of psychological attack.

In Chinese:

- 知已知彼
- 先勝後戰
- 以我為主
- 正合奇勝
- 攻心為上

1. The principle of knowing yourself and your enemy well

In the chapter "Strategy of Offense," it says, "If you know your enemy and yourself well, you win hundreds of battles. If you know yourself but not your enemy, you win once and lose once. If you do not understand yourself and your enemy, then you will be defeated in every battle."

To know yourself means that you know all your factors, including the political situation, weather, terrain, and the field commander, and also your own power and situation. Knowing your enemy is difficult, because the enemy will often resort to duplicity, feigning weakness when actually strong, and posing as being inactive when he is actually on the move.

Before the combat, conducting effective research and investigation are important steps and the prerequisites of developing tactics for the contest and for success.

2. The principle of being confident of winning before engaging

Sunzi said, "The skillful fighter places himself into a position which makes defeat impossible and does not miss the opportunity for defeating the enemy. Thus the victorious strategist only seeks battle in which he assesses the victory has been assured. The loser will always fight first and look toward winning."

In another chapter, "Nine Variations of Tactics," he said, "The art of war teaches us to rely, not on the likelihood of whether the enemy is not coming, but on our own readiness against them; not on the chance of whether he will attack, but rather on the fact that we have made our position unassailable."

First, there must be a sense of confidence in victory, and this is a crucial factor in combat. In the process of achieving various goals and expectation of success, one will accumulate experiences of success, which lead to having confidence regarding future outcomes, and this becomes part of one's personality.

If one lacks confidence, one tends to suffer from anxiety before and during competition. Anxiety hinders concentration and coordination, and can cause mistakes. Athletes who lack confidence often focus on their weaknesses, and this frustrates their ability to concentrate on their techniques, causing them to lose confidence in the contest. Because they think they will fail, they defeat themselves before the contest.

Confidence is a kind of auto-suggestion, or self-hints. When faced with new challenges, if one is aware of his own power and has the courage to undertake new tasks from the beginning, the possibilities of success are much greater. So lack of self-confidence is surely failure.

Having confidence in one's own competitive ability, one will not collapse when suffering one or two defeats. In the long run, these are just common occurrences. Good fighters use their performance index from every competition as a measurement of their progress in the pursuit of long-term goals. Winning a contest is not the most important goal, but attaining improvement is a vital purpose.

3. The principle of initiative

In the chapter "Weaknesses and Strengths," Sunzi said, "Thus, the good fighter controls his enemy and is not controlled" (故善戰者, 致人而不致於人).

The tactic is to take the initiative and force the enemy to deploy according to your strategy, as opposed to being in a passive position and reacting against the enemy's moves. This is the most important tactic against all tactics.

In a contest, the principle of taking the initiative and controlling the opponent's action is equally important. Strive for control so that one can succeed with one's tactics, control the direction of the contest, prevent the opponent's use of tactical skills, and impose a psychological advantage over the opposing side. The result of this is that opponents lose their psychological advantage, are unable to use their tactics effectively, and, ultimately, are defeated. The vital point is never to give control of the contest to your opponent.

4. The principle of using regular methods to engage and special methods to win

Direct attack is the normal way; side attack, surprise, or secret attack is a unique way. Using regular methods of warfare to engage the enemy and using special methods to win in battle affords opportunities for gaining the initiative in warfare.

The aspect of a fighter's abilities which is at the highest level is called his "specialty." The techniques and tactics which he uses consistently with the highest success rate to overcome his rivals is called his unique skill (絕招). The ability to use these specialties and unique skills can have an important effect on the results of contests. Therefore, in addition to overall, all-round training, the best fighters must also establish their own style and develop their own set of specialties and unique skills. It is only then in the preparation of combat that one can achieve "I have, you do not have" and "If you have, I have better than you."

5. The principle of psychological attack

In addition to the influence of factors such as timing, weather, geography, weapons, and so on, Sunzi also emphasized the importance of psychological factors in warfare, such as the spirit of the teams, their emotional condition, and their mental readiness for fighting. Sunzi had a good understanding of combat team psychology, group psychology, and leadership psychology.

In the chapter "Maneuvering," Sunzi says, "A whole army may be robbed of its spirit; a commander in chief may be robbed of his presence of mind. Know that the soldier's spirit is keenest in the morning; by noon it will begin to flag; and in the evening, his mind is bent only on returning to camp. A clever general will avoid any army when its spirit is keen and attack it when they are sluggish and inclined to return."

Affecting the spirit of the contending sides has two aspects. One is to raise the morale of one's own forces, and the other is to psychologically weaken the morale of your opponent. The main purpose is to place the enemy in a psychologically negative position. Turning favorable conditions to unfavorable, making the enemy feel pressed and weak of heart, will create negativism among them and ultimately lead to their defeat.

Although psychological factors such as morale, willpower, and courage in battle are not material resources, nevertheless they affect the use of team power. Team morale will directly affect the outcome of battles. Thus, military leaders and strategists all want to destroy the enemy's morale, while at the same time encouraging the morale of their own side.

APPLYING SUNZI'S THOUGHT TO COMBAT TACTICS

In *The Art of War*, Sunzi employs pairs of opposites, Chinese Yin and Yang theory, such as:

> Enemy versus us, active and passive, many against few, strong against weak, offense versus defense, advance and retreat, direct and indirect, weak points and strong points, movement versus stationary, brave against timid, long duration versus short, agitation versus calm, work versus rest, and so on.

He used these opposites to demonstrate how to prevail against one's opponent. These provide useful references in designing combat tactics nowadays.

1. Factor of time

Timing is the main and most essential factor in fighting. Sunzi insisted, "The battle should be quick to fight and quick to finish."

Of course, high speed does not mean that you just aim for fast action; you have to take advantage of opportunities and rhythms.

In the chapter on maneuvering, Sunzi suggested the following:

> Swiftness like wind, compactness like forest, raid like fire, and immobility like a mountain. Let your plans be covered in darkness and be impenetrable as night, and you move like a thunder-bolt.

Therefore in combat, tactics which enable a team to get a head start disrupt the rival team's timing and their ability to effect a strong defense. These tactics also give the team a psychological advantage over the other.

Sometimes, to save energy and reserve power, or to confuse opponents, fighters will change tack at a key time, using the tactics of "Control your opponent by moving even later than him."

Control the pace of the contest by changing the rhythm and break the opponent's normal action routine (動作結構) and force pattern (動力定型)—these are the normal application of effective tactical techniques.

2. Factor of space

First, consideration must be given to the whole and subsequently to its individual parts. Sometimes the price of victory of the whole is gained from sacrifice of its parts. In the essay "The Thirty-Six Stratagems," "If you want to arrest the thieves, capture the leader first" is a typical example which reflects the idea of solving the conflict between right and wrong.

3. Factor of quantity

In the chapter "Strategy of Offense," Sunzi proposed the following guidelines: "In the rule of war, if our forces are ten times the enemy's, surround him; if five times, attack him; if twice, separate them. If equally matched, offer battle; if slightly inferior, avoid the enemy; if quite unequal, flee from him."

4. Factor of dynamic force

Competition is hostility. Actually it is a competition of one power over another. It is a comparison of manpower, resources, and spirit and strength.

It is important to note that, in addition to tangible elements which make up the strength of the team, there are also psychological factors which have to do with the way field commanders think and the morale of their team. Battle effectiveness is the sum of good training, high morale, teamwork, and confidence.

Strictly speaking, the strong will prevail over the weak and the greater will overcome the lesser. However, in competition, the weak have their chances to defeat the strong. The weak defeating the strong is not just by a single action—it is the result of a series of developments. They must develop their particular strengths and act with initiative to overpower the opponents' particular weak points. Knock them down at once, and take care of the rest individually. The whole situation then changes to superiority and initiative.

Strong and weak are opposites. Their meanings include competent or incompetent, many or few, and separate or united.

With regard to the team, the meanings include hard fighting or weak, hungry or well fed, alert or lax, well deployed or scattered, efficient or bungling, high morale or low morale, brave or cowardly, and obedient or disobedient. With regard to battle situations, the meanings include safe or dangerous, high risk or low risk, and advantage or disadvantage.

5. Factor of conditioning

There are both external conditions and internal conditions. There are also two kinds of appearances, the true and the false.

Sunzi said, "All warfare is based on deception," and "In war, if you practice dissimulation, you will succeed." He considered trickery and dissimulation as good ways to defeat the enemy and as methods by which commanders could grasp the initiative in warfare. He liked to use "show your shape" to imply illusion. Illusion causes confusion in how people see and hear, disrupting the intellectual process and the entire process of knowing what is reality.

In many cases, when one is weak, show your shape of illusion as strong. Threatening your opponent with false strength is a technique of deception. Then when one is very strong, show your shape of illusion as weak; conceal the truth, thus deceiving the enemy.

CONCLUSION

Sunzi's theories and tactics are very useful and must be carefully studied and applied to the combat situation. Coaches and fighters should design relevant training programs by understanding the strengths and weaknesses of upcoming opponents.

Part III

ADVANCED TECHNIQUES

Chapter 24

DAI BU ZHANG

BIG STEP STANCES

INTRODUCTION

At the beginning, Zhan Zhuang is the entry to Yiquan. We need to practice different postures of stance to develop Hun Yuan strength and a stiff structure. For the next stage, we practice Shi Li, Fali, footwork, and push hand to perfect our strength and techniques.

However, do we need to continue to practice Zhan Zhuang after we have reached a higher level?

The answer is yes, for two purposes. One is to cherish our internal organs and Qi for health and a longer life. The second is to maintain our structure. But we do not need to practice all the postures of stance. After our broad learning, it is time for us to focus our training (由博歸約).

Chang Zhi Lang (常志朗) has been teaching two stances to experienced practitioners. These stances include most of the requirements of Yiquan training.

The stances are Wen Zhuang (文樁) and Wu Zhuang (武樁) or, in technical terms, we say Bao Zhuang and Cheng Zhuang. Bao Zhuang is a front stance with arms pulling inwards. Cheng Zhuang is a side stance with arms pushing outwards. Both have big, wide steps and a low stance. Big stances require a lower stance, twisted waist, extended elbows, and rounded back. These stances are more difficult but will enhance our endurance and strength. Due to their higher level, the time required for each stance is two hours.

THE STANCES IN DETAIL

1. Wen Zhuang 文樁 *(Bao Zhuang* 抱樁*)*

The requirements of this stance are the same as with normal Cheng Bao Zhuang. The difference is that this Zhuang has a low stance. The thigh is flat and horizontal to the ground.

Practicing this big stance will enhance the strength of your punches and maintain the pulling-inwards strength of the upper body. The fingers of both hands face each other. The gripping strength of both legs and the elastic force of the whole body, coordination, and the ability to tense and relax will be trained effectively.

2. Wu Zhuang 武樁 *(Cheng Zhuang* 撐樁*)*

1. Palms holding back

2. Palms pushing out

3. Second finger linking back against your eyebrow

3. Santi Stance

This is still a very important stance which generates much power and Qi. Below is the stance at different angles. Spend half an hour on each side.

4. One Leg Stance

This stance will enhance the power of the legs and the balance of the structure.

5. Iron Shirt 鐵布衫 (Stomach resistance posture)

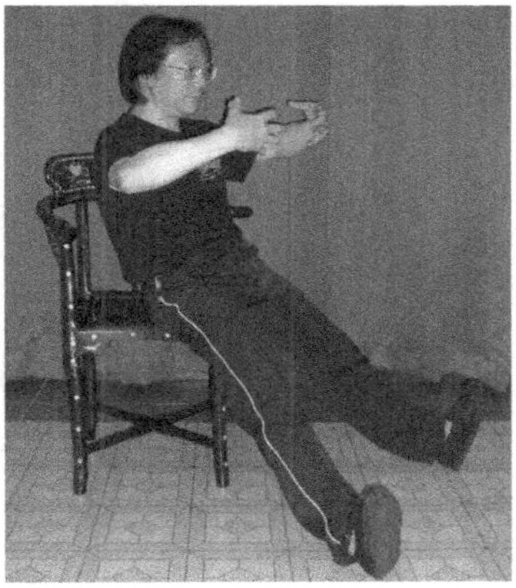

This method was taught by Li Ying An. He said it was a secret method of Zhan Zhuang to achieve an "Iron Shirt" body.

Leung Zhi Peng also taught students that the secret of Iron Shirt was just to inhale about 80 percent and hold your breath. Proper Zhan Zhuang can bring about an Iron Shirt. This Qigong method relies heavily on the contraction of the urogenital diaphragm in the direction of the area to be protected—that is, the solar plexus, kidneys, and armpits. Proper twisting of the torso, correct breathing, and Static Stance theory are the core principles of the practice.

Sunzi always taught students to hold a Cheng Bao Zhuang and then to punch their hips, back, and chest to enhance their protective force.

Iron Shirt should come about from proper practice and should not be emphasized. It should be viewed as the equivalent of a gunfighter training himself to dodge bullets instead of focusing on how to hit the other shooter. This iron body nei gong has a reputation for building great strength and robust health.

The way to practice Iron Shirt

- Sit on the edge of the chair.
- Hold a Cheng Bao Zhuang.
- Raise up your leg from the ground and lean your back forward.
- Keep this posture for 10 to 30 minutes.
- Keeping the abdomen tensed, use your fists to hit your abdomen gently for 5 to 10 minutes, adding strength to the punches gradually.
- After practice, rub and pat your abdomen lightly with your palm.
- Repeat three times a day for three months.

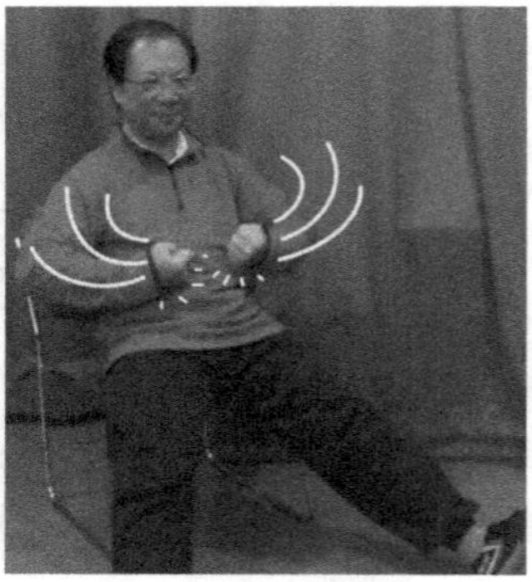

Yiquan meditation

The practice of Iron Shirt should be accompanied by *sitting meditation* and *Zazen meditation.* You can practice this in your office or home, at any time convenient to you. During practice, you should use your thumb to press on the upper side of your middle finger, so that you can feel the pumping of the blood and help you concentrate. The skeleton of your body keeps to the same requirement.

Sitting meditation

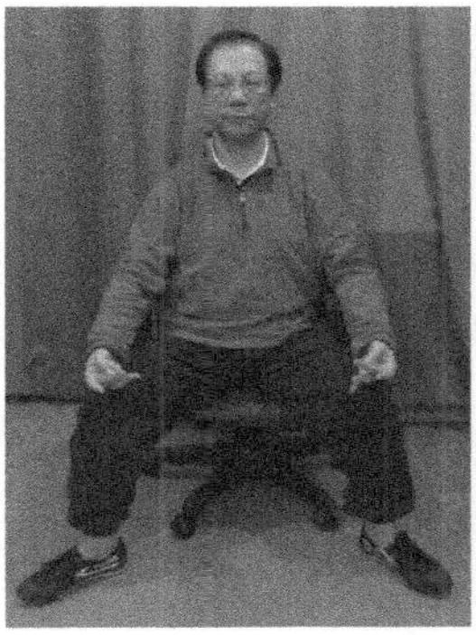

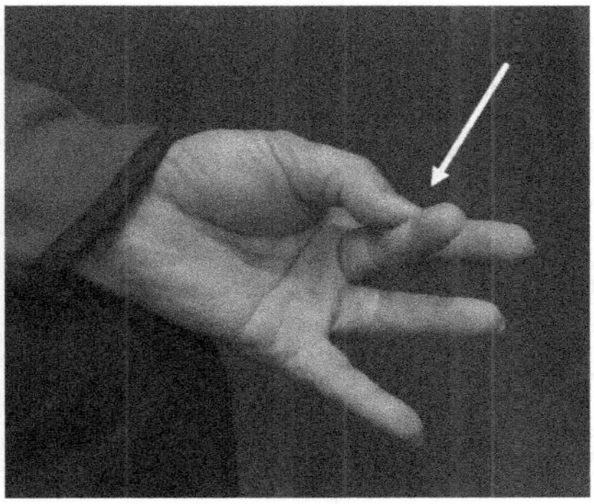

Zazen meditation

Make it a routine practice to do Zazen meditation at 11pm every night. This is the time when your body generates Qi and blood.

Chapter 25

QUAN ZHANG
FIST STANCES

Classical teachers like to keep back something to protect their own interests. Fist Stances are secret stances that are taught to students only after they are accepted as disciples. There are several postures of Fist Stances and each has their own effects.

Master Li Jiang Yu's Fist Stance posture

There are ten fist stance postures; here is one demonstrated by Master C S Tang. The fists twist and bend inwards, so that the arms and wrists become very strong and powerful.

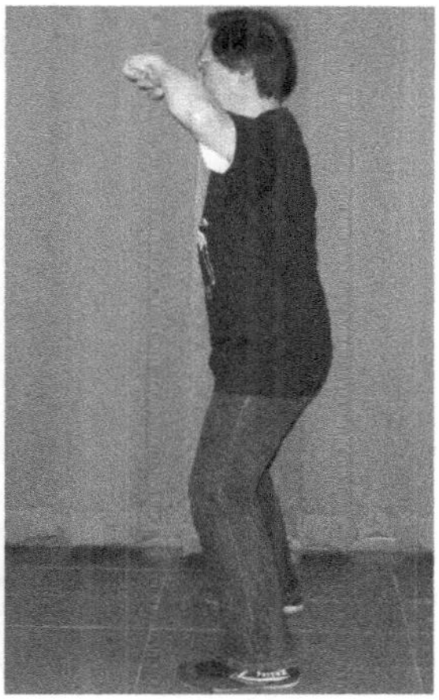

Stories of Mian Zhai (Exert Workshop) 勉齋物語

Tension and relaxation

I taught a group of overseas students from the USA in 1990. They were led by a so-called Yiquan teacher. During the first night, before the lesson, the teacher talked with me and said he had brought his students to learn from me, but needed my promises. First, never teach their students privately—even if they come to Hong Kong by themselves and want to learn from me, refuse them. Second, tell him or teach him first, before I teach anything to them. Third, when they practice Static Stance, do not ask them to tense—tell them that relaxation is the priority.

I asked why. He said:

1. He does not want to lose his students. They are his students, so I must not take away his students.
2. He was supposed to know many things. If I teach them things he does not know, they will query him or will ask him how to do it after they return to their country. So I must teach him first before I teach his students.
3. They are tall and strong. If I teach them to tense and resist, he can never push and control them. That is why he teaches them to do all exercises in a relaxed manner. Once they start to be hard and resisting, he will stop them and say they have used the wrong power and it is wrong.

I said, "This is cheating, I will not do that. I have to tell the truth."

So my teaching project vanished later. But I feel I am happy with my attitude, because I never teach false martial arts. I can stand upright and face my conscience.

Chapter 26

JIAN WU
FIST DANCE

Jian Wu is a freestyle movement of Yiquan techniques used to express the coordination of different kinds of Shi Li and Fali. Jian Wu means Health Dance, and is also called Quan Wu, the Fist Dance. The origin relates back to the Zhan Wu, the War Dance of ancient China.

The performance still retains the spirit of a war dance, though nowadays it is performed with the bare hands and so is called Fist Dance. The movements can also be done in a more rhythmic way that is suitable for practitioners of all ages and even for those not aiming for fighting. In this instance it is called Health Dance. In summary:

Jian Wu—Health Dance	健舞
Quan Wu—Fist Dance	拳舞
Zhan Wu—War Dance	戰舞

War Dance was a traditional dance in ancient times. It was performed mainly for warriors before they entered battle. They would drink a lot of achohol for amusement, and with high spirits and courage would proclaim their strength and prowess. Various actions are employed in the course of a performance, including bare-handed fighting and holding short weapons or long weapons. They would dance solo or as a pair drilling with each other, or perform a group dance. Normally they would sing warrior songs or recite poems vigorously.

War dances can also be found in Fukien White Crane Fist, Thai boxing, and the Haka native dance of New Zealand.

Before a Thai boxing fight, the boxers will perform ceremonies at the ringside, including the worship of teacher Wai Kru (拜師舞), the War Dance (戰舞), and the Ceremony Dance Ram Muay (儀式舞). The War Dance will include three arm movements followed by three stepping and holding up the knees repeatedly. The dance is accompanied with by Thai music that stimulates the emotions of the boxer and makes him fully prepared for the fight.

In China, before the Han dynasty, the general Liu Bang (劉邦) was invited to go to a dangerous banquet set by his enemy, Xiang Yu (項羽). Liu drank a lot and then performed the War Dance in front of those enemies to show his strength and courage. This is the famous warrior story called the Hong Men Yan (鴻門宴).

PERFORMANCE BOXING

Origin

Performance boxing or Quan Wu, also called the Health Dance or Martial Dance, was already well established by the Sui (AD 581–618) and Tang (AD 618–907) dynasties and was performed by martial artists and literati alike.

Martial Dance is an ancient form of Chinese dance which involves the use of weapons, and can be traced back to exercises used to train soldiers to fight during wartime. The philosopher Han Fei Tzu (280–233 BC) said, "In the time of the Emperor Shun (2255–2205 BC), the Miao [a minority tribe] rebelled… Thus he trained his troops for three years, and using the Dance of Shield and Ax, pacified the Miao." From the fact that the Shield and Ax Dance led the Miao peoples to accept the authority of the Emperor Shun, we can understand that this was probably a euphemism for a victory through combat. This Shield and Ax Dance was a form of martial dance. In the *Classic of the Mountains and Seas*, a geographical and cultural account of pre-Qin dynasty China as well as a collection of mythology that is at least 2000 years old, it is recorded that Duke Xia danced the Dance of the Nine Cuts with the barbarians of the Great Eastern wilderness. The Duke of Xia is also known as Xia Qi, the son of mythological Emperor Yao (2357–2255 BC), and he founded the Xia dynasty (2205–1806 BC).

What are the Nine Cuts? The *Book of Rites* explains that "one attack, one thrust is called one Cut," so the Nine Cuts are nine exchanges of attack. From this one can probably infer that the "Nine Cuts" were probably also a form of martial dance. It is also recorded that King Wu of the Western Zhou dynasty (1134–256 BC) used Martial Dance when on a military expedition to raise the morale of his troops. This style of attack, when paired with music, was called Wu Xiang or Symbolic Dance.

Thus it can be seen that the Dance of Shield and Ax, Nine Cuts, and Wu Xiang were all dances that took place during a time of war and helped cultivate one's attack and defense capabilities. During each attack, if there was partnered training and an exhibition and an exchange of martial techniques, this naturally led to the development of stronger and more effective techniques and the birth of martial arts.

The founder of the Han dynasty (206 AD–220 BC), Liu Bang, when present at Hongmen Banquet, drank three rounds of wine, stood up, and, while singing and drinking, ran through a round of boxing to demonstrate his strength and courage. This was also a type of performance boxing.

Wang Xiang Zhai, the founder of Yiquan, also called this Quan Wu. In 1925, during the time of the Northern Expedition, when visiting Huainan in Anhui province, he studied Health Dance or Jian Wu from Huang Mu Zhao. Huang was inspired by the Dunhuang cave paintings and the dancing postures from ancient Terracotta figurines. Wang combined this with Yiquan and, casting off bounded forms, moved as his mind wished.

Yiquan performance consists of Moving Waves, Swimming Dragon, Attacking Snake, and White Crane, which use Shi Li (slow moving exercises), Fali (exercises which include the use of explosive force), and San Shou (free-form fighting) and combine them with dance movement, retaining a set style but no set method of execution.

Development

The ancients listed rites, music, archery, riding, calligraphy, and mathematics as the foundation of cultivation; however, all this was destroyed at the beginning of the Qing dynasty (1644–1911). In the past one did not talk of scholars and warriors, for they studied both arts diligently. Scholars were able to fight, and for the most part warriors were also literate. However, since the Qing dynasty, the Art of Fighting has been extinguished and the Way of Dance has been lost.

Actually Quan Wu is a teaching that is able to bring out Man's natural ability for movement, and is an art form of the highest order that is able to calm the emotions and steady one's concentration. It can also dispel illness and promote health, heal psychological illness, and extend the lifespan.

Performance boxing is divided into four types: Bailing Waves, Swimming Dragon, Crane Plays, and Startling Snake. When one begins to learn this art, the muscles of the whole body are extended, the ligaments are stretched, the head is straight, the eyes are bright, the spirit is concentrated, and the intention is calm. The fingers are lightly curved and have the power to hook, embrace, twist, thrust, wrap around, prop up, sweep, and roll the opponent. The feet move as though they seek purchase on mud or ice, the knees are lifted up and out, and the energy is like reeling silk. The eyes look towards the distance and the palms have a natural indentation. After one has grasped these basic movements, then one is able to move on to more complex routines.

THE ART OF PERFORMANCE 表演藝術

Yiquan is martial arts without fixed routine forms, such as Jeet Kune Do. However, arranging a sequence of movements can train one's response, flexibility, and coordination.

When masters of Yiquan are asked to demonstrate, they will usually perform the Fist Dance. There are no fixed sequences; however, in order to let students have an example to follow, sampling sequence patterns have been listed and practiced.

"我之為我，自有我在."

"I will do it in my own way." A seal artwork engraved by Feng Kang Hou, describing the attitude towards arts that every artist should have their own style and not to follow the others.

THE PERFORMANCE OF FIST DANCE

The performance of Fist Dance mainly consists of four forms. However, all Yiquan techniques can be applied and shown here. Normally we will start the performance with wave-like Shi Li movements as a warm-up exercise and then we will move our steps forward and backward with the wave form, modify them into fist or palm Fali striking, and then turn to Crane Shi Li stretches, Shock Snake Shi Li with up and down movements, and shaking of our waist. Finally we will turn around in circles or an "S" shape in the form of a dragon swimming and then end with vigorous Fa Sheng (sound) and Fali.

The guiding form examples and procedures are shown as follows.

The patterns of Jian Wu

Jian Wu is combinations of sets of Test Strength:

1. *Bailing Waves* 揮浪: Up and down erect stretching movements; trains heavy power; represented by Shen Gui Chu Shui Holy (Turtle Comes from Water) 神龜出水.
2. *Swimming Dragon* 游龍: Front and side movements; raise, press, open, and close; trains length and breadth power; represented by Dragon Sound 蒼海龍吟 (神龜出水+發聲).
3. *Crane Plays* 鶴戲: Arms crossed with outward to inward circle movements; trains leg power and stamping power; represented by Qing Ting Dian Shui (Dragonfly Skims Water) 蜻蜓點水.
4. *Startling Snake* 驚蛇: Upper left hand draws inward to outward circle movements, and lower right hand draws outward to inward circle movements.

FIST DANCE ILLUSTRATION AND TRAINING

Fist Dance is placed in the last part of training in Yiquan, and represents a conclusion to the whole system. Fist Dance can be a self-entertaining routine of combination movements of what you have learnt, or a martial arts performance which can be presented to an audience.

1. Bailing Waves 揮浪

Bailing Waves can be practiced in the following formats:

1. Ba Shui Shi Li (Pushing Water)—both hands, single hand, and punch fists.
2. Shen Gui Chu Shui (Holy Turtle Comes from Water)—both hands: (backwards and forwards) and single hand.

These represent the up and down wave Fu An Shi Li and side Shi Li. At the same time, one can use the straight punch, Zhi Quan, upper cut, and horse punch.

2. Swimming Dragon 游龍

The formats include forward and backward Ping Tui Shi Li and Hook and File Shi Li. Others include Dragon Sound Shi Li and Dragon Turns Arms Shi Li. Normally we apply swimming dragon side low stretches—Shen Long Bai Wei (Dragon Swings Tail)—for turning towards the back.

3. *Crane Plays* 鶴戲

The formats include Qing Ting Dian Shui (Dragonfly Skims Water) and Tuo Yao movements.

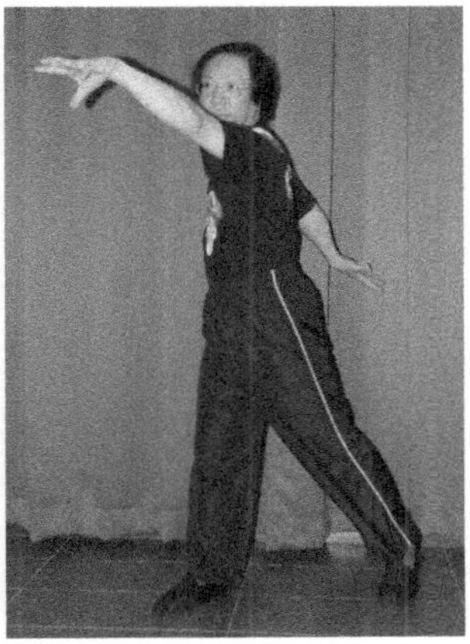

4. *Startling Snake* 驚蛇

The formats include Tuo Yao and Fu An Shi Li movements; sometimes we combine these with emit sound.

Below is the Tuo Yao movement with startling simulation. Move fast backward and then forward. The key point is to maintain the body at the same height while the hands swing horizontally.

a. Horizontal Stroll

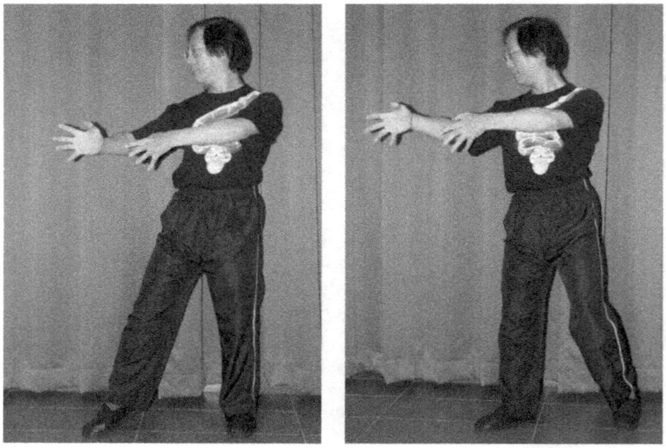

b. Vertical Stroll

THE WAY TO PRACTICE THE LEARNING STAGES OF JIAN WU

1. First stage, beginners: Fixed steps

Carry out each movement six times and then approach the next movement.

Format	**Shi Li**
1. Bailing Waves 揮浪	1. Ba Shui Shi Li 2. Shen Gui Chu Shui
2. Swimming Dragon 游龍	Shen Long Bai Wei

3. Crane Plays 鶴戲	Qing Ting Dian Shui
4. Startling Snake 驚蛇	Tuo Yao

2. *Second stage, intermediate: Moving steps*

For each movement, 3 steps forward and 3 steps backward, and then approach the next movement.

Format	**Shi Li**
1. Bailing Waves 揮浪	1. Ba Shui Shi Li 2. Shen Gui Chu Shui
2. Swimming Dragon 游龍	Shen Long Bai Wei
3. Crane Plays 鶴戲	Qing Ting Dian Shui
4. Startling Snake 驚蛇	Tuo Yao

3. *Third stage, advanced: Free steps and movements*

At the beginning, follow the above sequences of movements and steps. Then start moving at random and add all Yiquan punches during the performance.

Format	**Shi Li**
1. Bailing Waves 揮浪	1. Ba Shui Shi Li 2. Shen Gui Chu Shui
2. Swimming Dragon 游龍	Shen Long Bai Wei
3. Crane Plays 鶴戲	Qing Ting Dian Shui
4. Startling Snake 驚蛇	Tuo Yao
5. Punch Fight	
a. Chong Quan (Straight Punch)	沖拳 (豹拳)
b. Zuan Quan (Drilling Punch)	連環勾鑽拳
c. Beng Quan (Breaking Punch)	連環崩拳
d. Pao Quan (Cannon Punch)	鑽炮拳
e. Heng Quan (Cross Punch)	扯橫拳
f. Zai Quan (Planting Punch)	下栽拳
g. Guan Quan (Hook Punch)	貫拳 (馬形拳)

Notes for advanced stage

- Use both hands for Shi Li; use single hand movements for Fali.
- Apply punches during Bailing Waves.
- During Startling Snake, practice step forward and backward, applying the following Shi Li and Fali:
    - The body is low when stepping forward; the body will be high when retrieving backwards.
    - With single-hand stepping, the hands perform in-and-out circle movements.
    - Apply Ping Tui Shi Li and Hook and File Shi Li.
    - Apply Dragon Turns Arms Shi Li.
    - Apply single-hand Snake Winding Shi Li (蛇纏手).
    - Apply Shen Long Bai Wei Shi Li.
- First, do the practice slowly. Try and test, and feel the force. Second, enter into the condition, and then move fast and emit strength.

JIAN WU PERFORMANCE SET 1: DRAGON HEALTH LINKING STYLE

1. Start

Stand straight and bow.

2. Bailing Waves 揮浪

Ba Shui Shi Li (Pushing Water) 分水

1. same place, do 3 times
2. left steps forward 1 time
3. right steps forward 1 time
4. left steps forward 1 time
5. left steps backward 1 time
6. right steps backward 1 time
7. left steps backward 1 time

3. Swimming Dragon 游龍

Shen Long Bai Wei (Dragon Swings Tail) 神龍擺尾

1. left steps forward 1 time
2. right steps forward 1 time

3. left turn
4. right steps forward 1 time

4. Crane Plays 鶴戲

Qing Ting Dian Shui (Dragonfly Skims Water) 蜻蜓點水

1. left steps forward 1 time
2. right steps forward 1 time
3. left steps forward 1 time
4. left steps backward 1 time
5. right steps backward 1 time
6. left steps backward 1 time

5. Startling Snake 驚蛇

Tuo Yao (Drag Waist) 拖腰

Both hands

1. same place, do 3 times
2. left steps forward 1 time
3. right steps forward 1 time
4. left steps forward 1 time
5. left steps backward 1 time
6. right steps backward 1 time
7. left steps backward 1 time

Single hand, horizontal

1. left steps forward 1 time
2. right steps forward 1 time
3. left steps forward 1 time

Single hand, vertical

1. left steps backward, raise body 1 time
2. right steps backward, raise body 1 time
3. left steps backward, raise body 1 time
4. same place, move and then emit sound

6. Ending

1. Ling He Tong Tian (Clever Crane Reaches Sky) 靈鶴通天—stretch one hand up and one hand down
2. Dragon Sound 蒼海龍吟—emit sound
3. Stand straight and bow.

JIAN WU PERFORMANCE SET 2: TIGER SPARRING LINKING STYLE

1. Start

Stand straight and bow.

2. Bailing Waves 揮浪

Ba Shui Shi Li (Pushing Water) 分水

Forward and backward 3 times and move hands 3 times each

1. same place, do 3 times
2. left steps backward 3 times
3. right steps backward 3 times
4. left steps backward 3 times
5. left steps forward 3 times
6. right steps forward 3 times
7. left steps forward 3 times

3. Swimming Dragon 游龍

Shen Long Bai Wei (Dragon Swings Tail) 神龍擺尾

Left turn, right steps forward 1 time

4. Crane Plays 鶴戲

Qing Ting Dian Shui (Dragonfly Skims Water) 蜻蜓點水

Forward and backward 3 times and move hands 1 time each

1. left steps backward, sticky step 1 time
2. right steps backward, sticky step 1 time
3. left steps backward, sticky step 1 time
4. left steps forward, sticky step 1 time

5. right steps forward, sticky step 1 time
6. left steps forward, sticky step 1 time

5. Startling Snake 驚蛇

1. Single hand Tuo Yao—horizontal wave, backward 6 steps
2. Single hand—Snake Winding Shi Li (蛇纏手), forward 6 steps
3. Single hand—Fu An (包椿), backward 6 steps

6. Bailing Waves 揮浪

Shen Gui Chu Shui (Holy Turtle Comes from Water) 出水

Forward and backward 2 times and move hands 2 times each.

7. Fali

Perform all, or selectively and randomly, at moving steps

1.	Structure Fali	間架發力
2.	Forward Fali	前發力
3.	Upward Fali	上發力
4.	Downward Fali	下挫發力
5.	Slant Fali	斜砍發力
6.	Down Chop Fali	下劈發力 (鬼斬手)

Single hand and both hands at intervals.

8. Ending

1. Ling He Tong Tian (Clever Crane Reaches Sky) 靈鶴通天—stretch one hand up and one hand down
2. Dragon Sound 蒼海龍吟—emit sound
3. Stand straight and bow

JIAN WU PERFORMANCE SET 3: EAGLE COMBAT LINKING STYLE

1. Start

Stand straight and bow.

2. Bailing Waves 揮浪

Ba Shui Shi Li (Pushing Water) 分水

1. Fixed steps, move both hands 3 times each
2. Open and close, body shifts forward and hands backward

Shen Gui Chu Shui 出水

1. Fixed steps, move both hands backward 3 times each
2. Stretch and lengthen hands up and down; enter opponent's range

3. Swimming Dragon 游龍

Basic Shi Li

1.	Li Yao Test	立搖, 神龍布雨
2.	Fu An	包樁
3.	Ping Xuan Test	平旋, 烏龍攪海
4.	Shen Long Bai Wei	神龍擺尾
5.	Big Eagle Spreads Wings	大鵬展翅—spread hands sideways

4. Crane Plays 鶴戲

Tuo Yao 拖腰

Arms crossed with outward to inward circle movements

1. Fixed steps, both hands
2. Move steps forward, single hands alternately
3. Move steps backward, blocking arms
4. 3 fists, 1 kick
   a. Chong Quan
   b. Guan Quan
   c. Zai Quan
   d. Ding Tui 釘腿捲地風

Qing Ting Dian Shui (Dragonfly Skims Water) 蜻蜓點水

1. Forward and backward 3 times, and move hands up and down at sides
2. Forward and backward 3 times, and move hands forward+up and backward+down at sides

5. Startling Snake 驚蛇

1. Both hands move in outward circles (穿雲掌)
2. Single hand—Snake Winding Shi Li (蛇纏手), forward 6 steps
3. Single hand—Fu An (包樁), backward 6 steps
4. 3 fists
    a. Zuan Quan
    b. Beng Quan
    c. Back strike Beng Quan

6. Ending

1. Shen Long Bai Wei 神龍擺尾—left turn
2. Big Eagle Spreads Wings 大鵬展翅—spread hands sideways
3. Dragon Sound 蒼海龍吟—emit sound
4. Stand straight and bow

Chapter 27

YIQUAN WEAPONS

ANCIENT CHINESE WISDOM SAID, "SWORD MEANS INSPECTING." ALWAYS INSPECT THE CONDUCT OF ONESELF, FOR WHETHER YOU DO ANYTHING WRONG

古者，劍通檢，常檢查自己之為人，有否犯錯，代表其人格。

劈劍。
意拳器械，首重實用，無招無套，樸素無華。而其氣勢雄渾，名之曰劈劍。
王師爺嘗謂；「器械乃手之延長. 手能仆人，器械亦能仆人也。」實為至理。
意拳劈劍，最重整體力。初練時雙手持劍，由項上向下直劈，全身完整一氣，混元一體，一劍直落，劍刃能側用，偏左斜右皆可，氣勢果敢，用勁渾然。尤要豎項凝神，挺腰坐馬，鬆胯提膝，立意直劈，人劍合一。身法絕不能前俯後仰。
直劈練熟，則練左右斜劈，左右橫劈。再練左右斜上劈，熟至身手劍氣勢合一，即須習單手劈劍。單手雙手，其理唯一。
明其變，則一劍之出，有上中下三路可運使，那時千變萬化，不可方物，聚精會神，劍劍取人，以心役劍，總之不離樁法, 爭力, 試力之理。至此化境，上下, 左右, 前後, 皆可揮劍如意。

INTRODUCTION

The weapons of Yiquan have no fixed forms. The priority is practical use, avoiding fancy movements.

The founder of Yiquan, Master Wang, said, "Weapons are the extension of the hands. If you can throw your enemy with your bare hands, you can defeat your enemy with weapons."

THE WEAPONS IN DETAIL

1. Pi Jian 劈劍

The way to practice sword

Prepare a broad and thick straight sword or a broadsword to practice. Heavy weapons can improve the power of strikes:

1. Hold the sword with both hands. Raise above the head and chop straight downwards. The movement must be coordinated into unity.
2. The next stage is to hold the sword with one hand to strike.
3. Your momentum must be resolute and courageous.
4. Your posture must be strong, with the back upright and the neck straight, and you must have full concentration. Avoid bending forwards and backwards.

Types of movement

1. Fixed Step Downward Pi
2. Fixed Step Reverse Pi
3. Forward Step Pi
4. Backward Step Pi
5. Pad Step Pi
6. Left Cross Pi
7. Right Cross Pi
8. Left Slant Pi
9. Right Slant Pi
10. Left Upward Pi
11. Right Upward Pi
12. Turn Back Pi

Variations

Apply the above 12 techniques towards the upper, middle, and lower sections of your opponent. Then you can use your sword in six directions without fear.

Requirements

1. Concentration and focus.
2. Each strike must be effective.
3. Use your "heart" to control your sword.
4. Apply the foundation power of the stance, opposite power, and Shi Li that you have practiced.
5. The emphasis is on body power.

2. *Pi Gun* 劈棍

The way to practice pole

1. Hold the pole with both hands. Stretch the index finger and stick to the pole. The rest of the fingers grasp the pole. The hold should be flexible; avoid holding too tight.
2. Use the waist to shake. The strength of shaking is the same as Fali.
3. The force has to reach the tip of the pole.
4. Your posture must be strong with the back upright and the neck straight, and you must have full concentration.

Types of movement

1. Pierce and Downward Shake Pole
2. Cross Shake Pole
3. Upper Shake Pole
4. Slant Shake Pole
5. Chop Pole
6. Rub Pole (rub against the body of the tree; push forward and pull backward)

Pierce and Downward Shake Pole

Rub Pole

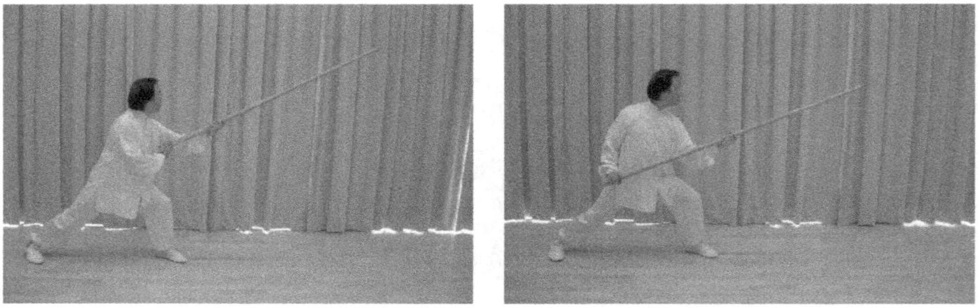

Practice rubbing against standing pole

HISTORICAL PHOTOS

Han Xing Yuan illustrating Shake Pole

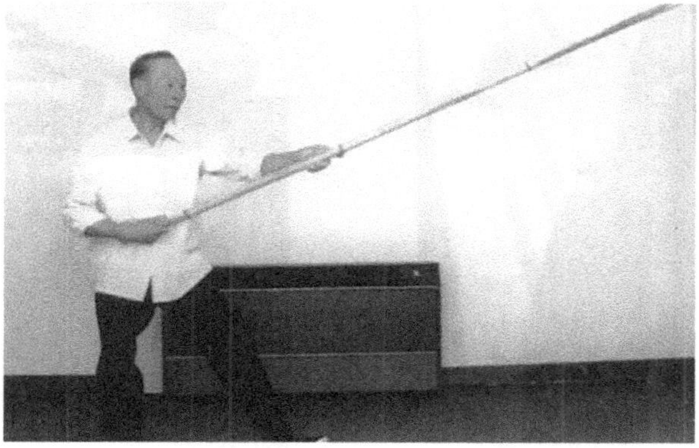

Master Yao Zong Xun illustrating Yiquan Pole

Old photo of Pi Jian

Part IV

SPECIAL FEATURES

Chapter 28

HEALTH ASPECTS

HEALTH BENEFITS OF YIQUAN

In our classes, there are often people who do little activity in their normal lives and who suffer from insomnia, constipation, and neurasthenia. They may have been practicing Taiji Quan and Qigong but they find that Zhan Zhuang is easy to practice and that the effect is very great. They often say that, after standing for half an hour a day at a fixed posture, these illnesses are all gone.

On the other hand, there are people whose lives are full of activity and stress, and they need to learn how to slow down and reduce stress.

So whatever your lifestyle, start now to improve your health dramatically and change your life. Obtain relief from grief, despair, and illness and gain health, happiness, and wealth.

THE HEART OF THE METHOD OF ZHAN ZHUANG—HUN YUAN ZHUANG

There are many postures of Yiquan stances, including Hun Yuan Stance, Descending Dragon Stance, Taming Tiger Stance, and Three Talent Stance. Yiquan Hun Yuan consists of seven postures that can be combined into one and is also called Hun Yuan Zhuang. These seven postures are simple and suitable for people seeking to improve their health. The postures are:

1. Cheng Bao Zhuang
2. Fu Yun Zhuang
3. Tui Tuo Zhuang
4. Fu Bao Zhuang
5. Fu An Zhuang
6. Ti Cha Zhuang
7. Xiu Xi Zhuang

Hun Yuan refers to the homogeneous, formless, and indivisible, before matter is differentiated into Yin and Yang. Hun Yuan Zhuang is beneficial for generating internal power or Jing and is useful for actual fighting. This practice is suitable for any age or gender. It can be practiced at any time and any place, does not require deep mental or muscular exertion, and generates power through a relaxed and comfortable stance. Through it, one can achieve improved health, deeper theoretical understanding and interest, and the practical application of fighting techniques.

FUNDAMENTAL PRINCIPLES

When you are practicing the following are important:

- The left hand should not cross to the right side of your nose; the right hand should not cross to the left side of your nose.
- When the hands are held up they should not pass above the eyebrows, and downward motion should not pass the navel.
- When the hands are close, they should not touch the body; and when they are far apart, they should not be further than one foot.

These are the fundamental principles of the standing exercises and are unchangeable.

GENERAL PRINCIPLES

The practice of Zhan Zhuang does not require dogged adherence to set forms that exhaust your body, but consists of emptying the mind of external influences.

When practicing Zhan Zhuang the following are important:

- The two legs are separated at the width of the shoulders.
- Both hands are raised slowly without using any muscular strength.
- The head is lifted like a taut rope, but the spirit should be soft.
- The tongue is lightly curled and touching the top part of the mouth.
- The teeth are lightly clenched.
- The shoulders are sinking.
- The elbows hang down.
- The armpits are half open, as though one could cradle an egg.
- Both arms are spread in a circle with the fingers spread.
- The fingertips lead the energy.
- The palms are soft and empty.
- The chest is slightly concave but the spine is erect.
- The Qi returns to the Dantian and the stomach is round.
- The inner thighs are rounded.

- The knees are lifted with the weight evenly balanced between both feet.
- The whole body is relaxed but not collapsed.
- The joints are lightly bent but not collapsed.
- The muscles and tendons are extended and the pores are open.
- The four limbs are connected, sending the internal energy outwards.
- The mind is empty.
- Breathing is kept light to the point of almost ceasing.
- The ears are listening lightly but everything is in a state of deep stillness.

Without forcing or hoping for a particular result, one should stand in silence and stillness, forgetting the self and that others exist. Zhan Zhuang is an exercise in self-renewal, like a large tree lengthening its roots and sprouting buds, unnoticed and yet growing daily.

If one practices like this, one's endurance will become greater, internal heat will be generated, the lungs' capacity to pass out carbon dioxide and take in oxygen will be strengthened, and the metabolic activity of the body's cells will increase. Without straining, the heart will not be burdened, and the muscles and tendons will be stretched. Without the need for external massage, circulation and Qi flow will increase and asthma or arrhythmia will disappear. By practicing when the spirit is resting, one is in accordance with the principles of the human body and the processes of nature.

THE WAY TO PRACTICE ZHAN ZHUANG FOR HEALTH

1. Use a teacher

Strictly speaking, it is necessary for an instructor to guide you during the practice so that you will learn well. If you want to reach a peaceful state of mind, the teacher may use different ways to guide you to reach that state. Otherwise, if you have too many thoughts during your practice and your posture is incorrect, then you will not be able to reap the benefits of the practice. Furthermore, the practice needs to be developed step by step. The teacher will guide you, according to the Qi that you experience. Not only an impatient student will not be able to improve his health, but he may also damage his Qi.

2. Time to practice

You can practice at any time. If there is enough time, you can practice the whole set. If there is not enough time, it is possible to practice two stances in the morning and then practice the static and then the moving stance. The best times to practice are: 11pm to 1am, 11am to 1pm, 5am to 7am, and 5pm to 7pm. Although the Qi will come with practice, it is not advisable to look for certain kinds of sensations. You can also increase the practice time, though each practice should be around one hour. Do not over-exert yourself during the practice, and leave some energy and on-time after the practice.

Han Si Huang's (韓嗣煌) recommendation is to practice for at least 45 minutes. The first 15 minutes is used to gain concentration and for relaxing the muscles. Wang An Ping (王安平) used the practice to treat cancer and other diseases and achieved good results. His method is relaxation, and his patients have to practice for six hours in three sessions (morning, afternoon, evening) every day. During winter, the practice time can be longer; during the summer, it can be shorter; and there is a normal duration for spring and fall. By means of this intensive standing, most of Wang's patients recovered.

3. Place to practice

Choose a quiet place with fresh air to practice, such as the seaside, park, or forest. If you are feeling weak you can practice at home, but remember to open the window to let the air circulate. Try to avoid using an air-conditioner, because the cold air may enter the body through your pores.

4. Important notes

- Do not practice after extreme happiness or sorrow.
- Do not practice if you are too tired.
- Do not practice immediately after a meal. Wait for half an hour.
- Go to the bathroom before practicing.
- Avoid being frightened during the practice.
- Do not practice outdoors in the rain or during a storm.

5. Key points of the practice

A correct posture, mindful concentration, and natural breathing are the three most important points for taking care of your body, spirit, and breathing while standing.

6. Key points for successfully recovering from illness

- Keep to one specific posture; do not change posture.
- Stand in that posture for half an hour at least, without changing.
- You can change posture after an interval, but always keep to your favorite posture.

- Sink your body as if sitting on a high chair; do not just stand. This is so that your body weight can sink downward and your Kau will open.
- Keep the back and head upright.
- Keep long and slow breathing; do not use reverse breathing.
- Clear your mind and concentrate on imagery.
- Listen and feel the blood flowing in your body.
- Do not try to force Qi sensations from your body; these sensations will arise naturally when you practice and should be cherished continuously.

THE SEVEN HEALTH POSTURES ILLUSTRATED

The postures are demonstrated by Erica Liu.

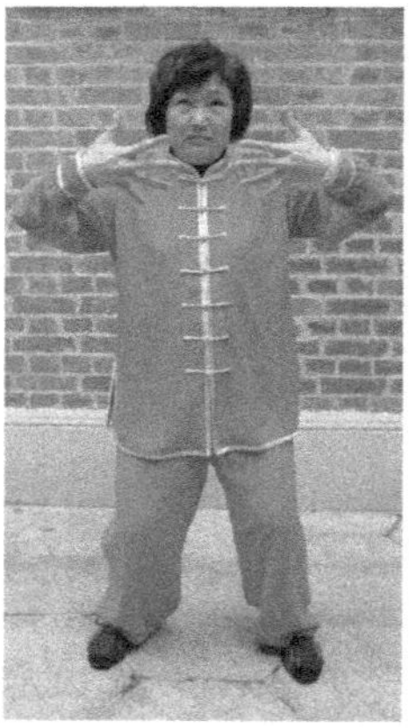

1. Cheng Bao Zhuang

2. Fu Yun Zhuang

3. Tui Tuo Zhuang

4. Fu Bao Zhuang

5. Fu An Zhuang

6. Ti Cha Zhuang

7. Xiu Xi Zhuang

PRACTICE YIQUAN ZHAN ZHUANG AT ANY TIME

Yiquan can be practiced at any time and anywhere. Whenever you get the urge, try to stand in a posture of Zhan Zhuang. Concentrate and think how you can relax your body further. How can you sink your body weight? How can you generate your energy internally? If you can maintain a serious practice, for every moment you have practiced your internal kung fu will improve a little. Kung fu is the result of accumulation, and there is no short cut. Nowadays though, life is full of pressure and spare time is limited for most people, so it is very common to squeeze 30 minutes for practice. However, practicing in such a way will mean that improvement is very slow.

The ancient wisdom said, "Walking, stopping, sitting, and lying, do not leave this." "This" means practicing internally. We have to incorporate the practice into our daily life in order to gain more time.

When you take a metro or subway train, do not find a seat; simply make use of the time to practice Zhan Zhuang. Hold a newspaper in front of you to practice Cheng Bao Zhuang. Build up your body structure, seek opposite power, and make yourself like a balloon to push back the press from overcrowded passengers. Use intention to relax all your joints and let your body weight shift from one leg to the other. Follow the vibration of the train to move and try to feel how you can keep your balance. If you take the train for 20 minutes, you will have trained for 20 minutes.

When you walk back to your office or to your home, apply Mo Ca Bu to walk on the street. Try to maintain a very straight and upright back and waist; walk with friction and rubbing between the legs.

When you get inside an elevator, stand close to the wall; hold either a Cheng Bao Zhuang, Fu An Zhuang, or Yang Shen Zhuang until the elevator reaches your floor.

Now go to your office desk, glance at your pile of documents, and forget them for a while. Sit on your chair, hold a Cheng Bao Zhuang, and tense and relax the arms to seek strength. Practice for a while, then return to your busy work.

Note: I saw Ian Fok, the chairman of the Hong Kong Yiquan Association, practicing Zhan Zhuang in the elevator and in the office in these ways. He is a very busy man and he knows how to make use of his time to practice.

When working with a computer, do not sit on a chair. Start with a horse stance and sink downward. Pass on your endurance to your thighs and legs to build up your lower strength.

Note: One of my students told me that in London he saw Chen Xiao Wang, Chen-style Taiji master, sitting in a horse stance to check his email.

If you feel tired after typing at the keyboard for a long time, apply intention to shift your weight from shoulder to elbow and then pass to wrist and finger.

Repeat ten times and you will feel the stiff part of your shoulder released. These exercises will improve your kung fu and also keep you healthy.

Whenever you have to push a door, place your palm on the door with the wrist relaxed and back straightened; do not use excess power but use the weight of your body to push it open.

If you are sitting for too long in your office, you can try to sink your abdomen downward, and raise the part of the body above the abdomen upward towards your head. At the same time, practice raising your head and sinking the Dantian. These exercises will relax the muscles of the waist.

Actually, if you pay attention to your daily life, you can create many chances to practice Yiquan. Even the people around you will not be aware that you are practicing. How fun is that!

DAILY PROGRAM

Try to incorporate training into your daily life. What should you do?

Waking up

- Brushing teeth—stand on one leg
- Warm up with Shi Li, Fali, and Fa Sheng
- Pushing doors—Shi Li

The working day

- Walking to station—Mo Cha Bu
- On public transport—stand in Yan Xin Stance, Ti Cha Zhuang
- In the elevator—Fu An Stance, Ti Cha Zhuang, Xiu Xi Zhuang
- Beyond your desk—hold Big Steps Low Cheng Fu Stance
- Break from computer—perform some Shi Li to relax
- Going to the toilet—perform Cheng Bao Stance
- Make use of office equipment to practice—Shi Li
- Light lunch to refresh your mind
- Walking back home—Mo Cha Bu

After dinner

- Watch TV—selective stance while watching
- Ready to sleep—lying stance
- Deep sleep
- If you have insomnia, get up at night to stand

James Carss practicing Fu An Zhuang and Ti Cha Zhuang in an elevator

In the office you can practice some stances to relax from busy work

Chapter 29

SUPERNATURAL POWER

Supernatural power refers to the special phenomena that may appear after reaching a certain stage of Zhan Zhuang. These include the following:

- Empty force
- Moving objects
- Hearing from long distance
- Out of body experience
- Supernatural power
- Special strength
- Iron Shirt
- Emitting external Qi for healing.

THE WAY TO PRACTICE SUPERNATURAL POWER

Timing

You must keep a constant and regular timing for your stance. Maintain three sessions a day, with two hours for each session:

1. First session: six to eight o'clock in the morning
2. Second session: three to four o'clock in the afternoon
3. Third session: eleven to one o'clock at night.

All stances must face the East direction.

The third session is the most important session—it is the time that the Qi rises from your body and the environment is quiet. When you practice the stance, you can feel the internal Qi movements.

Duration

Keep to the stance duration and practice this over a period of three years. Each year, check your performance and measure your progress. Set your targets to the four phenomena of stance. These phenomena appear as feelings on the hands: hot, numb, swollen, and heavy. Each year you will feel differently.

Postures

In the first month, within the three sessions, change postures every 15 minutes. The purpose is to test which posture feels comfortable and generates the most feeling for you. Each person feels differently.

In the second month, select the posture that generates the most feelings. Stand in this posture for half an hour.

Starting from the third month, minimize your posture and stand in the re-selected posture for at least one hour. The target is to stand in each posture for two hours.

Cheng Bao Zhuang is the most essential posture, so you must select this one as your night stance.

Concentration

You have to stand in posture for a long time, so at the beginning of each session open your eyes and concentrate. After half an hour, your muscles and tendons will relax automatically. Now you can enter into a really relaxed state. Close your eyes, maintain your structure, feel the internal movements, control your breathing, and search for your balance and your strength. Enjoy the stance.

Correctness of your postures

If your posture is placed correctly, the longer you stand the more difficult it is to correct. There will be no way for you to succeed; instead more pain will occur after your long hours of standing.

Guidance

At the beginning, a good teacher's guidance is very important. Because during the stance you cannot see your own posture, you may be bending backward or keeping all your balance at one side, the elbows are not stretching enough, you are dropping your head, you are bending your spine, you have weak legs, your stance is too low and is hurting your knees, the buttocks and chest are thrust out, and so on.

A good teacher can observe your wrong posture and also your internal feeling through his experience. Do not let your wrong postures persist.

Test of your features

After a year, you should know what you have felt during your stance. Apply the feeling and close your eyes. Try to feel how you can make use of the Qi to circulate through the internal parts of your body.

Check whether the Qi can come to your hands and finger tips and eventually be released from the tips of your fingers.

Achievement of supernatural powers is not a must, and cannot be rushed through practice. When the time comes, the powers will appear. Do not be distressed and do not be hurried; be patient—you will be excited when they come. You have to grasp how they manifest, when they will come, and how to control them. You will then enjoy these special features.

Emit external Qi

When you practice absorbing Qi, face a tree to absorb the fresh Qi. Do not absorb cold Qi or you will be sick. Try to absorb hot Qi.

When you try to emit external Qi to treat diseases, you must be very careful. Feng Zhi Qiang mentioned that one should always practice a stance to save Qi; try not to release Qi. If you have saved Qi for one week, when you treat a patient using released Qi, then in only ten minutes you will lose all your saved Qi. If you emit more Qi, you will be very weak.

Master Li Li Gun, of Wu-style Taiji Quan, also mentioned that when you try to treat people by emitting Qi, be careful, because some patients will absorb your energy and release to you their illness energy. If they are weak and belong to Yin body, they will absorb your energy. If they are strong and belong to Yang body, they will reject your energy and transfer their bad energy to your body and make you sick. Therefore, unless necessary, try not to show that you are capable of curing people.

Chapter 30

GRADING OF YIQUAN

BEGINNER'S LEVEL

Entry requirement

3 to 6 months of training time by student.

Health postures

Eight postures: 2 low, 2 high, 3 middle sideways, 1 back.

Time requirement

Beginners stand in each posture for a minimum of 5 minutes (pass or fail)

- 5–10 minutes (good pass)
- > 10 minutes (strong pass).

Requirements for pass

- Must achieve "pass" in 4 postures.
- If failure in any ONE posture, the overall section is "fail."
- If there is a "good pass" in at least 5 postures, overall it is a "good pass."
- If there is a "strong pass" in at least 5 postures, overall it is a "strong pass."

Postures must demonstrate the correct placement of arms, wrists, elbows, shoulders, and legs. The instructor will randomly raise the arms, wrists, or legs to test if the student is "grounded":

- Such a test is to be applied lightly, with no "power."
- The test is only in ONE direction.

Total test time

- ~ 40+ minutes to achieve a minimum "pass"

- ~ 90 minutes for a "strong pass."

Shi Li

Six types: 1 Dun Yao, 2 front, 3 basic Shi Li.

- Beginners to demonstrate Shi Li, each for a minimum of 5 minutes (pass or fail section).
- Shi Li must demonstrate strong intention. The instructor can hold the student's hands lightly, and feel if PUSH/PULL or UP/DOWN comes from the legs, and whether he has total body power.

Requirements for pass

Finish 10 movements of each within a specific time:

1. Dun Yao—back straight, thigh flat; 10 movements in 3 minutes.
2. 2 front Shi Li—10 movements each in 3 minutes.
3. 3 basic Shi Li—10 movements each in 2 minutes.

The results:

- If failure in any ONE Shi Li, the overall section is "fail."
- Must pass all 3 Shi Li groups to pass the section.

INTERMEDIATE LEVEL

Degree of intensity

There are more requirements than for Beginner's level. Each requirement is tougher.

Entry requirement

From Beginner to Intermediate will take a minimum of 6 months to 1 year, as it adds Combat Postures, Shi Li, and Fali.

Health postures

Three postures: Cheng Bao Zhuang, Tui Tuo Zhuang, Ti Bao Zhuang.

Time requirement

The student stands in each posture for a minimum of 10 minutes (pass or fail)

- 10–15 minutes (good pass)
- > 15 minutes (strong pass).

Requirements for pass

- Must achieve "pass" in all 3 postures.
- If failure in any ONE posture, the overall section is "fail."
- If all are only a minimum pass, then "fail"—still a beginner, not an intermediate-stage student.
- If there is a "good pass" in at least 2 postures, overall it is a "good pass."
- If there is a "strong pass" in all 3 postures, overall it is a "strong pass."

Postures must demonstrate the correct placement of the arms, wrists, elbows, shoulders, and legs. The instructor will randomly raise the arms, wrists, or legs to test if the student is "grounded."

- Such a test is to be applied with some light power.
- To test resistance in FOUR DIRECTIONS, the instructor can raise UP, DOWN, LEFT, or RIGHT. The instructor will punch on the hips, chest, back, and abdomen to test resistance.

Combat postures

Select 4 out of 7 postures.

Time requirement

The student stands in each posture for a minimum of 5 minutes (pass or fail)

- 10–15 minutes (good pass)
- > 15 minutes (strong pass).

Requirements for pass

- Must achieve "pass" in 2 postures.
- If failure in any ONE posture, the overall section is "fail."
- If all are only a minimum pass, then "fail"—still a beginner, not an intermediate-stage student.
- If there is a "good pass" in at least 3 postures, overall it is a "good pass."
- If there is a "strong pass" in at least 3 postures, overall it is a "strong pass."

Shi Li

Seven types of side Shi Li.

- Students to demonstrate Shi Li, each for a minimum of 5 minutes (pass or fail section).

- Shi Li must demonstrate strong intention. The instructor can hold the student's hands lightly, and feel if PUSH/PULL or UP/DOWN comes from the legs, and whether he has total body power.

Requirement for pass

- Must do all Shi Li to pass section.

Footwork (Mo Ca Bu)

- Up and Down Pressing, one leg 3 minutes each
- Four Directions Sliding, one leg 3 minutes each.

Passing the above will obtain a "pass." If not, "fail."

Tuo Yao (Drag Waist)

- Fixed Step—Both Hands Drag, one leg 3 minutes each
- Moving Step—Both Hands Drag, forward and backward 3 minutes.

Passing the above will obtain a "pass." If not, "fail."

Fali sections

Three types: Forward, Upward, and Downward Fali. The student must demonstrate "Fali" on another student or teacher at least 10 times for each type.

Requirements for pass

At least 5 times successful "Fali" on the student/teacher, otherwise "fail."

- 7 times: Good pass
- 8 times: Strong pass.

The student must "pass" all sections. Pass status is the best result of the 3 types of Fali.

ADVANCED LEVEL

Entry requirement

From intermediate to advanced will take a minimum of 1 year's training, as it adds all combat training.

Health postures

Not necessary at this level.

Combat postures

Seven postures: Gong Li Zhuang 5, Dai Bu Zhuang 2.

Time requirement

Student to select 5 postures; stand in each posture for 15 minutes (pass or fail)

- 10–15 minutes (good pass)
- > 15 minutes (strong pass).

Requirements for pass

- Must achieve a "good pass" in 3 out of 5 postures.
- If failure in any ONE posture, the overall section is "fail."
- If all are only a minimum pass, then "fail"—still an intermediate-stage student, not an advanced-stage student.
- If there is a "good pass" in at least 5 postures, overall it is a "good pass."
- If there is a "strong pass" in at least 7 postures, overall it is a "strong pass."

Challenging: Stand in 2 postures of Dai Bu Zhuang for 1 hour each; this will be marked as "excellent."

Shi Li

Ten combat Shi Li.

- Students to demonstrate Shi Li for 5 out of 10 stances, each for a minimum of 5 minutes (pass or fail section).
- Shi Li must demonstrate strong intention. The instructor can hold the student's hands strongly, and feel if PUSH/PULL or UP/DOWN comes from the legs, and whether he has total body power.

Requirement for pass

- Must do all 5 stances selected to pass section.

Fali

Eight types: The student must remember and handle all 8 patterns of Fali. He has to demonstrate 5 patterns of "Fali" on an opponent at least 10 times.

Requirements for pass

At least 7 times successful "Fali" on the student/teacher, otherwise "fail."

- 7 times: Good pass
- 8 times: Strong pass.

The student must "pass" all sections. Pass status is the best result of the 8 types of Fali.

Tui Shou (Push Hand) 揉手

Shuang Tui Shou

- Sequentially, the instructor uses 5 out of 10 entry techniques mentioned in the course; the student can use the listed defense techniques to get away from the attack.
- Free sparring.

Requirement for pass

The student must show that he has a strong structure, can keep out the techniques of the opponent, and can control and use Fali with the right timing.

Punches

- Sequentially, the student will shadow box for the 7 punches—10 minutes.
- The student will create his own combinations of 7 punches—5 minutes.

Requirement for pass

The student must demonstrate that his combination punches are non-stop with power and speed.

Duan Shou

- Sequentially, the student will demonstrate palm and kick techniques.
- Free sparring:
    - The student attacks the instructor (with protection uniform)—2 minutes
    - The instructor attacks the student—3 minutes
    - Free sparring—2 minutes a round, for 3 rounds.

Requirements for pass

- In his demonstration, the student must punch or kick effectively and explicitly 5 times.
- In free sparring, the student will "fail" if beaten more than 5 times.
- If the student is exhausted and hands drop down all the time then it is a "fail."

Note: Weapons and Fist Dance are not included in the test syllabus. They are practiced only for the student's own benefit.

Chapter 31

TEACHING AND SEMINARS

THE WAY OF TEACHING

Teaching according to different kinds of students 因材施教

The way of teaching martial arts in ancient China was mainly in a one-to-one private class. Now, of course, we have group teaching techniques.

In the old days, the same syllabus was taught to everyone, but it would look deeply into the special characteristics of each student and check his strengths and weaknesses, develop his strengths, and concentrate more on correcting and improving his weaknesses.

Body shape of the five elements 五行身形

If a person has Wood style, his back and waist are always very straight and his arms are extended like the branches of a tree. He cannot relax freely. So the teacher should always remind him to relax and turn into water and mud. If he has Soil style, he is loose and soft like wet mud, so the teacher has to prop up his leg and support his body to be strong enough to resist the body—to stand like a tree. If he is flexible and can twist his body, but without strong power, then he must pass through a process of Test Power to develop whole body power. That is, changing from Water style to Fire style. If the student is tense and nervous and he cannot relax, then he has Fire style and you must ask him to stand with the intention of standing under a shower, letting the cool water sprinkle from the head, the shoulders, and the body to the legs. Relax and change from Fire style into Water style.

WHY CAN'T I PROGRESS?

You have to ask yourself:

- How much effort have I made?
- How much belief and confidence do I have?
- How many hours of training have I done?

- How much intensive training have I done?
- How much focus and concentration have I put in during practice?

Yiquan performance can be tested and measured. However, progress will only be made if you find a good teacher and follow his instructions. Attend class often and have private talks and consultations with your instructor. Only if you keep up the discipline of practice, and perform as instructed, with intensity and correctness, will you reach a higher level of Yiquan, in body health and strength and in spiritual mind.

Chapter 32

CONCLUSION

This book has listed and summarized most of the techniques of Yiquan. It has provided programs for students to carry out in each chapter for each section of the system. However, in order to be successful in training, there are two things you have to bear in mind. The first is dedication; and, second, you have to find a good teacher.

FOUR FACTORS THAT LEAD TO SUCCESS IN YIQUAN

In MBA studies, students learn that four factors lead to success, and the same is true for Yiquan:

1. Planning
2. Organization
3. Implementation
4. Control.

Control means discipline.

If you decide to practice Yiquan, you have to know your aim and what you want to achieve: for health, for fun, for combat, for self-defense, or for building up more power and strength?

Your objective must be very clear, or else it will be a waste of time, except perhaps if you just want to relax and have fun. But even if that is so, why not put some time and effort into real practice so that you gain good results at the same time as you are having fun?

Discipline means that you keep to a fixed schedule to do pre-scheduled activities and a set number of exercises. In this way your path to success will be straightforward and your achievement will be only a matter of time. Hence, discipline can only be enhanced by a clear objective of purpose.

The key to success in training is to know what stage you want to achieve. Therefore, you should strive towards your goal, you must have a definite degree of control, and you must understand that the exertion and difficulty of today will definitely achieve success in the future.

If you have discipline and dedication but without direction and objective, you behave like a robot—you practice day after day, night after night, but it will be the same as an ox. If you have high ambition and a clear objective (胸懷大志), and execute it with discipline accordingly, you can succeed in anything. The best way is to seek a mentor in your training life in order to guide you to maturity. He will know how to explore the resources of your surroundings, making use of your limited resources to expand into a whole new horizon. Such learning will have a snowball effect so that you can accumulate your knowledge and strengthen yourself and become an outstanding martial artist.

THE PURPOSE OF LEARNING MARTIAL ARTS

以仁為本，忌凶殘。
以溫養為本。
不要霸道，不做流氓。
Be merciful, do not be cruel.
Be cherishing; do not be violent and fierce.
When facing a challenge, think first, and be calm.
Don't be arbitrary, be civilized;
Don't become a gangster, be an artist.

The characters of the seal:

"沈默不是懦弱，忍耐不是麻木."
Silence does not mean you are weak, endurance does not mean you are insensitive.

—On the right, the seal artwork engraved by C S Tang

THE WAY OF LEARNING

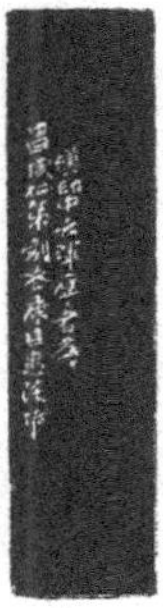

欲速不達，忌揠苗助長
學習是有過程的。
There is a process for learning. You cannot short-cut the process.
Do not intentionally show you are outstanding, just be natural.
My teacher of seal engraving, Master Feng Kang Hou (馮康侯), carved a seal for me and said, "The best art is natural and powerful, 渾厚平實. There is no affectation."

This has become the maxim of my whole life.

—On the right, the seal image

REVIEW

Finally, let us briefly review below most of the stances taught.

Please start straight away to practice and work consistently, with a longer duration, harder, and with a well-planned and organized schedule. I wish you every success in self-training.

1.

2.

3.

4.

5.

6.

7.

8.

9.

10.

11.

12.

13.

14.

15.

16.

17.

18.

19.